Object-Oriented Database Design Clearly Explained

Object-Oriented Database Design Clearly Explained

Jan L. Harrington

Morgan Kaufmann

AN IMPRINT OF ACADEMIC PRESS

A Harcourt Science and Technology Company

San Diego   San Francisco   New York   Boston
London   Sydney   Tokyo

 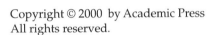
ACADEMIC PRESS
A Harcourt Science and Technology Company
525 B Street, Suite 1900, San Diego, CA 92101-4495, USA
http://www.academicpress.com

Academic Press
24–28 Oval Road, London NW1 7DX, United Kingdom
http://www.hbuk.co.uk/ap/

Morgan Kaufmann Publishers
340 Pine Street, Sixth Floor, San Francisco, CA 94104-3205, USA
http://www.mkp.com

Library of Congress Catalog Card Number: 99-65380
International Standard Book Number: 0-12-326428-6

Printed in the United States of America
99 00 01 02 03 IP 9 8 7 6 5 4 3 2 1

Contents

Chapter 2: Introducing the Object-Oriented Paradigm   17

Chapter 3: The Object-Oriented Data Model   39

Chapter 4: The Proposed Object Database Standard   65

Preface

Although the theory of logical database design is one of the slowest changing areas in computing today, it does change. Right now database designers are dealing with the emergence of a new logical data model—the object-oriented data model—and the integration of object-oriented elements into the relational data model.

It is still too soon to know which of these two approaches to using objects in data management will survive. Nonetheless, there are several database management systems based on the object-oriented data model that are robust enough to use in large corporations, while at the same time the well-established relational databases are adding support for objects.

This book looks at both ways of integrating objects into a database. You will first read about the concepts behind the object-oriented paradigm and then see how those concepts translate into the data model for pure object-oriented database management systems.

Then the book will look at the way in which the hybrid object–relational products handle objects. As you will discover, the two approaches are fundamentally different and have a major impact on what can be done with a database.

> *Note: The controversy between the pure object theorists and the object–relational theorists seems to have taken on a bit of a religious fervor. As you read about the topic beyond this book, you will discover that people have very strong feelings about which approach is best. This author has no strong preferences either way and believes that there are specific applications for which each approach is best suited.*

Unlike that for relational databases, there is no official standard for object-oriented databases. The Object Database Management Group (ODMG), which does publish a standard, is working outside the normal standardization channels. You will read about elements of their proposed standard in this book, but you will also see examples of specific product implementations, something that is not necessary for relational database software because there is tacit agreement among theorists as to what constitutes a relational database and the SQL standard for a relational data manipulation language is relatively universally accepted.

This book is a companion to *Relational Database Design Clearly Explained* (published by AP Professional) and therefore it is no accident that the database design case studies in Chapters 6, 7, and 8 are the same scenarios as those used in the earlier book. The intent is to allow you to easily compare and contrast the pure relational designs for these databases with the pure object and hybrid object–relational designs. You will then be better equipped to make a good choice of a data model for your organization's needs.

What You Need to Know

To get the most out of this book, you should be thoroughly familiar with the relational database model. You should understand the full implications of terms such as relation, domain, candidate key, primary key, foreign key, entity integrity, and referential integrity. You should also know SQL and the basic constructs used in entity–relationship diagrams.

On the other hand, you do not need a background in the object-oriented paradigm; that will be explained in full within this book. You also do not necessarily need to know how to write a computer program, but today's pure object-oriented DBMSs are closely tied to programming languages and the syntax used define database structure is based on programming concepts. Therefore, it will help a great deal if you are familiar with C++ or Java. In particular, Chapters 9 and 10, which deal with specific object database implementations, will be more useful if you can program.

Acknowledgments

Writing a book for the folks at Morgan Kaufmann is always a joy. I would therefore like to thank the following individuals who helped make this one possible:

- ◆ Ken Morton, Editor, who, as always, is an immense pleasure to work with.
- ◆ Gabrielle Billeter, Editorial Assistant, who looks after all the details.
- ◆ Julie Champagne and Shawn Girsberger, Production Editors.
- ◆ Mary Prescott, the copy editor, who has a great eye and a light hand.
- ◆ Carole McClendon, my agent, who hooked me up with Morgan Kaufmann in the first place (back when they were still AP Professional).

JLH

http://www.blackgryphonltd.com

Part One

Theory

The first part of this book considers the theoretical aspects of the object-oriented paradigm and how that paradigm has been extended to represent database entities and the relationships between them. You will read about the proposed standard for object-oriented databases and see how object-oriented databases can be modeled using entity–relationship diagramming techniques.

Note: Although the purpose of object-oriented ER diagrams is the same as that for relational databases, the diagramming models themselves are somewhat different.

1

Introduction

As far as a database professional is concerned, *data modeling* is the art of identifying the entities that must be represented in a database and the relationships among those entities. The object-oriented data model is the latest in a sequence of data models that has been evolving since the early 1960s.

In this chapter, you will find an overview of the history of data modeling so that you will understand why the object-oriented data model is both a step forward and a step backward. You will also be introduced to the two ways in which objects have been integrated into the data model and read an overview of current uses for object-oriented databases.

A Short History of Data Modeling

Prior to the development of the first database management system
(DBMS), access to data was provided by application programs that
accessed flat files. The data integrity problems and the inability of
such file processing systems to represent logical data relationships
easily led to the first data model—the hierarchical data model.

The Hierarchical Data Model

The *hierarchical data model*, which was implemented primarily by
IBM's Information Management System (IMS), allows only one-to-
one or one-to-many relationships between entities. Any entity at the
"many" end of a relationship can be related to only one entity at the
"one" end.

As an example, take a look at Figure 1-1. This ER diagram represents two relationships between Product and Vendor entities. The
first is a many-to-many relationship indicating which vendor can
supply which product. The second is orders placed for products
with specific vendors.

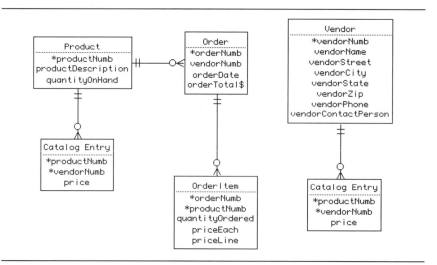

Figure 1-1:   Two database hierarchies

The many-to-many relationship that represents the products sold by a vendor requires a composite entity to contain the price charged by the vendor for that specific product. Logically, this entity— Catalog Entry in Figure 1-1—is related to both the Product and Vendor entities. However, the hierarchical data model forbids this type of *multiple parentage*.

> *Note: To be strictly correct, IMS does allow multiple parentage in some limited instances, in particular when the parent entity types are in different hierarchies. There are, however, significant restrictions on exactly where this can be used.*

One solution is to duplicate the entity, as was done in Figure 1-1. Alternatively, you could relate an entity to only one of its two parents, the solution used to handle the Product to Order to OrderItem relationships in Figure 1-1.

Neither solution is optimal. The duplicated Catalog Entry entities introduce possible problems with data consistency. The single Order and OrderItem entities cut down on the type of access provided by the database.

Hierarchical databases are *navigational*. That means that data access is only through the predefined relationships. In addition, access to a hierarchy is typically through the entity at the top of the hierarchy (the *root*) and must proceed in hierarchical order. For example, to reach an instance of the Order Line entity, an application program must first find the appropriate instance of the Product entity and then traverse all Order instances related to that Product until the correct product is found. Then the program can access the OrderItem instances related to that Order. In a hierarchy, direct access to data is very limited, if available at all.

Using the two hierarchies in Figure 1-1, there is no reasonable way to answer the question "From which vendor did we order that specific product?" The only way to complete that query would be to search from the Product to the Order to the OrderItem to find all instances in which the product was ordered. Then an application would need to search the Catalog Entry instances in the second hierarchy to find the vendor.

The benefit of a hierarchical database is that its navigational nature makes access very fast when you are following the predefined relationships. However, the rigidity of the data model—in particular, the inability to give an entity multiple parents and the absence of direct data access—makes it unsuitable for environments where ad hoc queries are important.

IMS is still in use today in some legacy mainframe systems. However, IBM no longer sells the product and encourages its customers whenever possible to migrate to a relational DBMS.

The Network Data Models

Long before computer networks came to the forefront of our consciousness, database designers created two data models that represented networks of data relationships: the *simple network data model* and the *complex network data model*. The intent of these data models was to eliminate the restrictions placed on databases by the hierarchical data model.

The Simple Network Data Model

In a simple network database, all relationships are one-to-one or one-to-many—direct many-to-many relationships are not allowed—but multiple parentage is permitted. As you can see in Figure 1-2, allowing multiple parentage eliminates the problems with unnecessary duplicated data and access restrictions.

Simple network databases are nonetheless navigational: Most access is through the predefined relationships. Some direct access to instances of entities is supported through hashing, but because hashing affects the physical placement of data in a data file, in a practical sense only one entity in a hierarchy of entities can be given a hashed fast access path. For example, in the Product and Vendor database that we have been using as an example, the Product and Vendor

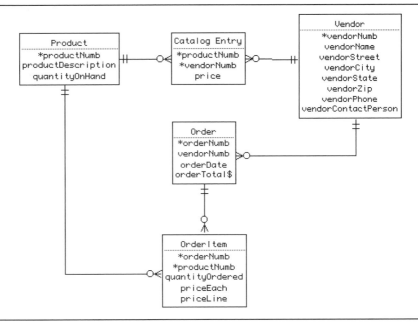

Figure 1-2:   The simple network data model

entities could be stored using hashing to provide direct access to instances of those entities. However, the remaining entities would probably be accessible only through their parents.

> *Note: Hashing is a technique in which a key value (much like the primary key of a relation) is put through a transformation process (a* hashing *algorithm) to generate a location for the instance of an entity in a data file. When the user supplies the key value, the DMBS can recompute the hash value and use it to access the data directly. This is a very fast form of access.*

Simple network databases therefore perform well when access follows the relationships but perform poorly if manual searches that are not based on hash keys or predefined relationships must be coded into an application program. Depending on the design of the database, ad hoc queries can be very difficult to satisfy.

> *Note: As relational databases began to supplant simple networks, many people designed their simple networks as if they*

were relational, including foreign keys in related entities. As a result, some vendors of simple network DBMSs were able to add ad hoc query languages to their products to allow ad hoc querying in a "relational-like" manner. However, this worked well only if the database design was normalized.

The national standard for the simple network data model was initially proposed by the Database Task Group (DBTG) or the Committee on Data Systems Languages (CODASYL), the same committee that developed COBOL. Although some legacy databases based on the CODASYL standard are still in use, few new CODASYL databases are being installed at this time.

The Complex Network Data Model

The complex network data model is similar to the simple network, but it allows the direct implementation of many-to-many relationships. As an example, consider Figure 1-3, which contains a many-to-many relationship.

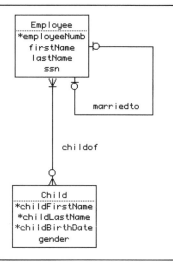

Figure 1-3:   The complex network data model

The many-to-many relationship is between employees and children; the second relationship in the diagram is a one-to-one relationship indicating who is married to whom. As long as there are no relationship data, the direct many-to-many relationship in this case presents no problems and eliminates the need for a composite entity that serves only to represent a relationship. However, when there are relationship data, even a complex network database must include the composite entity. In addition, as you will see in Chapter 3, there are situations in which a direct many-to-many relationship actually causes the database to lose information.

There have been no commercially successful complex network DBMSs, primarily because the many-to-many relationships become very complicated and nearly impossible to maintain. This data model therefore is of theoretical interest only and generally continues to exist only in college database textbooks.

A Major Change: The Relational Data Model

If you look carefully at the evolution of data modeling from the hierarchical through the complex data models, you'll notice that they are basically similar, with each successive data model removing restrictions on the types of relationships allowed. In contrast, the relational data model was a major change. Although an ER diagram for a relational design of the products and vendors database would look exactly like Figure 1-2, the implementation is significantly different.

In particular, the relationships explicitly shown in Figure 1-2 do not become a part of a relational database. Logical relationships are represented only by primary key–foreign key matches that are connected as needed by the join operation. Relational databases are therefore not navigational and provide superior ad hoc query support to any of the earlier data models. A relational database schema is also easier to modify because in most cases modifications can be made while the database is in use.

The traditional drawback to a relational database is performance. Because the hierarchical and network data models are so closely tied to their physical data storage and because the data structures for relationships are actually part of the database, access to related data is much faster. Nonetheless, as business uses of databases began to rely more heavily on ad hoc queries, the relational data model replaced the older data models for new database installations. Add to that the speed of today's computers, and the performance issue becomes much less of a problem.

Enter the Object-Oriented Data Model

The development of the object-oriented paradigm, which is discussed in depth in Chapter 2, brought about a fundamental change in the way we look at data and the procedures that operate on data. Traditionally, data and procedures have been stored separately, the data and their relationships in a database, the procedures in an application program. Object orientation, however, combines an entity's procedures with its data.

This combination is generally considered to be a step forward in data management. Entities become self-contained units that can be reused and moved around with relative ease. Rather than an entity's behaviors being tied to a specific application program, the behaviors are part of the entity itself, so that no matter where the entity is used, it behaves in a predictable, known way.

As you will read in Chapter 3, the object-oriented data model also supports direct many-to-many relationships, the first data model to do so. This is a mixed blessing. You will see that you must be careful when designing such relationships to avoid losing information.

In addition, object-oriented databases are navigational: Access to data is through relationships stored within the data themselves. This, therefore, is the step backward. Object-oriented databases are not as well suited to ad hoc querying as relational databases, although ad hoc queries are typically supported. An object-oriented database's navigational nature, however, means that queries must follow predefined relationships and cannot insert new relationships on the fly.

By the time you finish reading this book, you will understand why the current crop of object-oriented databases are unlikely to replace relational databases for all applications in the same way that relational databases have replaced earlier data models. You will also have a feeling about the circumstances in which object-oriented databases make a great deal of sense.

Object Roles in Databases

Objects have entered the database world in two ways:

- *Pure object-oriented DBMSs*: A pure object-oriented DBMS is based solely on the object-oriented data model. There are a number of industrial-strength pure object-oriented DBMSs available today, some of which are being used in mission-critical applications.
- *Hybrid,* or *post-relational, DBMSs:* A hybrid DBMS is primarily relational but stores objects in relations.

There is a great deal of disagreement between both theorists and practitioners as to which of these approaches will survive. Unlike the Beta–VHS competition, in this case there may well be room for both strategies to coexist, each being used where appropriate. The difference between pure object orientation and hybrids is discussed in much more detail in Chapter 3.

Sample Uses for Object-Oriented Databases

Object-oriented databases are being used today in a wide range of organizations for a wide range of purposes, including the following:

- F. A. Davis Company, publishers of *Taber's Cyclopedic Medical Dictionary* and other technical reference materials, is using an object-oriented database to manage the content of its publications. The company uses XML and SGML to format its documents and found that the hierarchical nature of those documents mapped more closely to an object-oriented model than to a relational database.

♦ Adidas AG uses an object-oriented database to handle its CD-ROM catalog, content for its Web site, and sales at its retail outlets. The consulting firm hired by Adidas to develop the information system decided that an object-oriented database was the best way to handle the high volume of multimedia data (text, audio, still pictures, and video). The navigational nature of the object-oriented data model provides excellent performance for the retrieval of large multimedia files.

♦ The Federal Aviation Administration (FAA) uses a system based on an object-oriented database to simulate passenger and baggage traffic. Because object-oriented databases store procedures with data, modeling the complex and varied interactions between passengers, baggage, and their environment was easier than it would have been using the relational data model.

♦ Sales Media, Inc., a developer of software for the insurance industry, has switched to an object-oriented database as the foundation for its product Automated Agent. The combination of an object-oriented backend and an object-oriented application development language makes it easier for Sales Media to deliver updates to their software quickly. (You will read more about the advantages of object-oriented programming in Chapter 2.)

♦ Radio Computing Services provides automation software for radio stations. Its original program, Selector, supported the selection, sequencing, and monitoring of songs played by a station. Today, the company is using an object-oriented database as the underlying data storage for a more comprehensive station automation package, including musical selections and commercials. The object-oriented environment saves development time because it allows programmers to handle all program material the same way, regardless of what it is.

- Wandel * Goltermann Technologies, Inc. uses an object-oriented database as the underlying data storage for DominoWIZARD, its network baselining software. This software measures and stores various characteristics of a network so that the baseline statistics can be compared with measurements taken later for use in troubleshooting or by those selling network equipment. In the latter case, for example, the salesperson can demonstrate performance with the current network and then install new switches or routers and take measurements again, hopefully to show a performance improvement.
- Echelon uses an object-oriented database as the foundation for its control network software. (A control network is a network that monitors or controls a process with minimal human control, such as robotic systems in factories, elevators, and climate control in tall buildings.) The software models each element being controlled, along with the behaviors it is expected to exhibit, making it easier to look for exceptions to normal network performance.

Note: For more details on any of the preceding object-oriented database applications, see http://www.poet.com.

- Interface and Control Systems, Inc. used object-oriented technology to create a database that supports a flight control system for spacecraft. Tracking and controlling a spacecraft requires analyzing a very large volume of data, something that object-oriented databases are able to do without suffering significant performance degradation.
- The French National Centre for Space Studies is also using object-oriented database technology in the aerospace industry. In particular, it has developed a multimedia database that can help model the integrated systems needed in the design of a spacecraft. The organization felt that an object-oriented database was well suited to an environment where many types of entities interact in complex ways.

- Switzerland's largest health insurance company, Swiss Social Christian, has an object-oriented database at the heart of its claims processing system. The company felt an object-oriented database was appropriate because the rules for deciding how much to pay on specific claims are very complex. The system can also handle a high volume of traffic, estimated to be 18,000 claims a day in the year 2000.
- STERIA has used an object-oriented database to support a commercial software application for the design and planning of large data communications networks. Such networks can quickly become so complex that it is difficult to keep track of exactly what hardware is installed in what configuration. The object-oriented database allows a network designer to model the interaction of the various elements of the network and to be continually aware of the structure of the network.
- The French electric company, Électricité de France, uses an object-oriented database to manage overhead power lines. The database is able to map the electrical lines throughout the utility's service area. It can also be used to determine all the equipment needed to install a new power line.

Note: For more details on any of the preceding object-oriented database applications, see http://www.advantasoft.com.

Looking at all these applications of object-oriented database technology, some common themes begin to appear:

- Many of the applications involve the interrelationship of many parts, such as spacecraft systems or large computer networks. The parts each have specific behaviors that interact with the behaviors of other parts.
- Many of these systems must manipulate large amounts of data.
- Many of these applications involve predictable types of data access, so that the navigational nature of an object-oriented database is not a major drawback.

♦ A good portion of the applications have limited need for ad hoc querying.

The preceding characteristics can help identify appropriate applications for object-oriented databases. However, when an environment has access patterns that cannot be easily anticipated, then a relational database is probably a better choice.

2

Introducing the Object-Oriented Paradigm

The object-oriented paradigm was the brainchild of Dr. Kristen Nygarrd, a Norwegian who was attempting to write a computer program to model the behavior of ships, tides, and fjords. He found that the interactions were extremely complex and realized that it would be easier to write the program if he separated the three types of program elements and let each one model its own behavior against each of the others.

The object-oriented programming languages in use today (most notably C++, SmallTalk, and Java) are a direct outgrowth of Nygarrd's early work. The object-oriented data model is an extension of object-oriented programming.

Note: This is in direct contrast to the relational data model, which was designed specifically to model data relationships, although much of its theoretical foundations are found in mathematical set theory.

To understand the object-oriented data model, you therefore must first understand the object-oriented paradigm as it is used in object-oriented programming. In this chapter, you will read about the fundamental concepts of that paradigm. Do not worry if you cannot program: You *do not* need to be a programmer to understand this material. If you *are* fluent in an object-oriented programming language, however, you can skim this chapter and begin reading in depth with Chapter 3, which discusses how object-oriented programming has been extended into a data model.

The easiest way to understand what object-oriented programming is all about is to begin with an example that has absolutely nothing to do with programming at all.

Writing Instructions

Assume that you have a 16-year-old daughter (or sister, whichever is more appropriate) named Jane and that your family is going to take a long car trip. Like most 16-year-olds, Jane is less than thrilled about a trip with the family and in particular with spending so much time with her 12-year-old brother. In self-defense, Jane needs something to keep her 12-year-old brother busy so he won't bother her as she reads while her parents are driving. She therefore decides to write up some instructions for playing solitaire card games for him.

The first set of instructions is for the most common solitaire game, Klondike. As you can see in Figure 2-1, the deal involves seven piles of cards of increasing depth, with the top card turned over. The rest of the deck remains in the draw pile. Jane decides to break the written instructions into two main parts: information about the game and questions her brother might ask. She therefore produces instructions that look something like Listing 2-1. She also attaches the illustration of the game's deal.

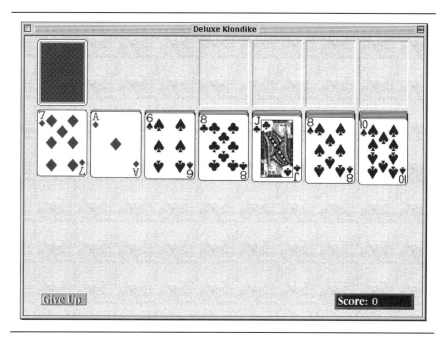

Figure 2-1:   The initial deal for Klondike

The next game she tackles is Canfield. Like Klondike, it is played with one deck, but the deal and play are slightly different (see Figure 2-2). Jane uses the same pattern for the instructions as she did for Klondike because it cuts down the amount of writing she has to do (see Listing 2-2).

And finally, just to make sure her brother doesn't get too bored, Jane prepares instructions for Forty Thieves (see Figure 2-3). This game uses two decks of cards and plays in a very different way from the other two games (see Listing 2-3). Nonetheless, preparing the instructions for the third game is fairly easy, because she has the template for the instructions down pat.

After completing three sets of instructions, it becomes clear to Jane that having the template for the instructions makes the process extremely

```
Information about the Game
   Name: Klondike
   Illustration: See next page
   Decks: One
   Dealing: Deal from left to right.
      First pass: First card face up, six cards down.
      Second pass: First card face upon top of card #2, five cards down.
      Third pass: First card on top of card #3, four cards down.
      ... repeat pattern for total of seven passes ...
   Playing: One or three cards can be turned at a time.
      As encountered, put aces on top. Build up in suits.
      Build down from deal, opposite suit colors.
      Can move cards from the middle of a stack, moving card and all cards
   built below it.
      Move kings only into empty spots.
      If turning one card, make only one pass through the deck.
      If turning three cards, make as many passes as you like through the
   deck.
   Winning: All cards built on top of their aces.
Questions to Ask
   What is the name of the game?
      Read Name section.
   How many decks do I need?
      Read Decks section.
   What does the deal look like?
      Read Illustration section.
   How do I deal the game?
      Read the Dealing section.
   How do I play the game?
      Read the Playing section.
   How do I know when I've won?
      Read the Winning section.
```

Listing 2-1:   Instructions for playing Klondike

easy. Jane can use the template to organize any number of sets of instructions for playing solitaire. All she has to do is photocopy the template and fill in the values for the information about the game.

Objects

If someone were writing an object-oriented computer program to manage the instructions for playing solitaire, each game would be known as an *object*. It is a self-contained element used by the program.

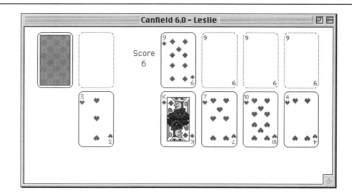

Figure 2-2:   The initial Canfield deal

Information about the Game
    Name: Canfield
    Illustration: See next page
    Decks: One
    Dealing: Deal four cards face up.
        Place on additional card face up above the first four as the starting card for building suits.
        The remaining cards stay in the draw pile.
    Playing: Turn one card at a time, going through the deck as many times as desired.
        Build down from deal, opposite suit colors.
        Can move cards from the middle of a stack, moving card and all cards built below it.
        Place cards of the same value as the initial foundation card above the deal as encountered.
        Build up in suits from the foundation cards.
        Any card can be placed in an empty slot.
    Winning: All cards built on top of the foundation cards.
Questions to Ask
    What is the name of the game?
        Read **Name** section.
    How many decks do I need?
        Read **Decks** section.
    What does the deal look like?
        Read **Illustration** section.
    How do I deal the game?
        Read the **Dealing** section.
    How do I play the game?
        Read the **Playing** section.
    How do I know when I've won?
        Read the **Winning** section.

Listing 2-2   The instructions for playing Canfield

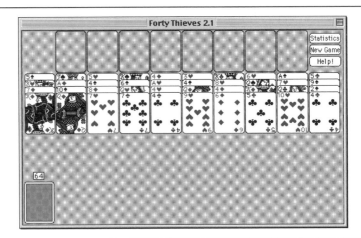

Figure 2-3:   The initial deal for Forty Thieves

Information about the Game
  Name: Forty Thieves
  Illustration: See next page
  Decks: Two
  Dealing: Make ten piles of four cards, all face up.
      Jog cards so that the values of all cards can be seen.
      Remaining cards stay in the deck.
  Playing: Turn one card at a time. Make only one pass through the deck.
      Build down in suits.
      Only the top card of a stack can be moved.
      As aces are encountered, place at top of deal and build up in suits
  from the aces.
      Any card can be moved into any open space in the deal.
  Winning: All cards built on top of their aces.
Questions to Ask
  What is the name of the game?
      Read **Name** section.
  How many decks do I need?
      Read **Decks** section.
  What does the deal look like?
      Read **Illustration** section.
  How do I deal the game?
      Read the **Dealing** section.
  How do I play the game?
      Read the **Playing** section.
  How do I know when I've won?
      Read the **Winning** section.

Listing 2-3   The instructions for playing Forty Thieves

It has things that it knows about itself: its name, an illustration of its layout, the number of decks needed to play, how to deal, how to play, and how to determine when the game is won. In object-oriented terms, the values that an object stores about itself are known as *attributes* or *variables* or occasionally, *properties*.

The solitaire game object also has some things it knows how to do: explain how to deal, explain how to play, explain how to identify a win, and so on. In object-oriented programming terminology, actions that objects know how to perform are called *methods*, *services*, *functions*, *procedures*, or *operations*.

> *Note: It is unfortunate, but there is no single accepted terminology for the object-oriented paradigm. Each programming language or DBMS chooses which terms it will use. You therefore need to recognize all of the terms that might be used to describe the same thing.*

An object is very security minded. It typically keeps the things it knows about itself private and releases that information only through a method whose purpose is to share data values. For example, a user or program using the Klondike game object cannot access the contents of the Dealing variable directly. Instead, the user or program must execute the How Do I Deal the Game? method to see that data.

Objects also keep the details of the procedures for the things they know how to do private, but they make it easy for someone to ask them to perform those actions. Users or programs cannot see what is inside any of the methods. They see only the result of executing the method. This characteristic of objects is known as *information hiding* or *data encapsulation*.

An object presents a public interface to other objects that might use it. This provides other objects with a way to ask for data values or for actions to be performed. In the example of the solitaire games, the questions that Jane's little brother can ask are the game's public interface. The instructions below each question represent the procedure to be used to answer the question. A major benefit of data encapsulation is that as long as the object's public interface remains the same, you can change the details of the object's methods without needing to inform any other objects that might be using those methods. For example, the card game objects currently tell the user to "read" the contents of an attribute. However, there is no reason that the methods couldn't be changed to tell the user to "print" the contents of an attribute. The user would still access the method in the same way, but the way in which the method operates would be slightly different.

An object requests data or an action by sending a *message* to another object. For example, if you were writing a computer program to manage the instructions for solitaire games, the program (an object in its own right) could send a message to the game object asking the game object to display the instructions for dealing the game. Because the actual procedures of the method are hidden, your program would ask for the instruction display and then you would see the instructions on the screen. However, you would not need to worry about the details of how the screen display was produced. That is the job of the game object rather than the object that is asking the game to do something.

An object-oriented program is made up of a collection of objects, each of which has attributes and methods. The objects interact by sending messages to one another. The trick, of course, is figuring out exactly which objects a program needs and the attributes and methods those objects should have.

Classes

The template on which the solitaire game instructions are based is the same for each game. Without data, it might be represented as in Listing 2-4. The nice thing about this template is that it provides a consistent way of organizing all the characteristics of a game. When you want to create the instructions for another game, you make a copy of the template and "fill in the blanks": You write the data values for the attributes. The procedures that make up the answers to the questions someone might ask about the game have already been completed.

```
Information about the Game (Variables)
    Name:
    Illustration:
    Decks:
    Dealing:
    Playing:
    Winning:
Questions to Ask (Methods)
    What is the name of the game?
        Read Name section.
    How many decks do I need?
        Read Decks section.
    What does the deal look like?
        Read Illustration section.
    How do I deal the game?
        Read the Dealing section.
    How do I play the game?
        Read the Playing section.
    How do I know when I've won?
        Read the Winning section.
```

Listing 2-4:   The solitaire game instruction template

In object-oriented terminology, the template on which similar objects like the solitaire game instructions are based is known as a *class*. When a program creates an object from a class, it provides data for the object's variables. The object can then use the methods that have been written for its class. All of the objects created from the same class share the same procedures for their methods. They also have the same types of data, but the values for the data may differ, for example, just as the names of the solitaire games are different.

A class is also a data type. In fact, a class is an implementation of what is known as an *abstract data type*, which is just another term for a user-defined data type. The implication of a class being a data type is that you can use a class as the data type of an attribute.

Suppose, for example, you were developing a class to handle data about the employees in your organization. The attributes of the class might include the employee ID, the first name, the last name, and the address. The address itself is made up of a street, city, state, and zip. Therefore, you would probably create an address class with those attributes and then, rather than duplicating those attributes in the employee class, simply indicate that an object of the employee class will include an object created from the address class to contain the employee's address.

Types of Classes

There are three major types of classes used in an object-oriented program:

- *Control classes*: Control classes neither manage data nor have visible output. Instead, they control the operational flow of a program. For example, *application classes* represent the program itself. In most cases, each program creates only one object from an application class. The application class's job includes starting the execution of the program, detecting menu selections, and executing the correct program code to satisfy the user's requests.
- *Entity classes*: Entity classes are used to create objects that manage data. The solitaire game class, for example, is an entity class. Classes for people, tangible objects, and events (for example, business meetings) are entity classes. Most object-oriented programs have at least one entity class from which many objects are created. In fact, in its simplest sense, the object-oriented data model is built from the representation of relationships between objects created from entity objects.
- *Interface classes*: Interface classes handle the input and output of information. For example, if you are working with a graphic user interface, then each window and menu used by the program is an object created from an interface class.

In an object-oriented program, entity classes do not do their own input and output (I/O). Keyboard input is handled by interface objects that collect data and send it to entity objects for storage and processing. Screen and printed output is formatted by interface objects that get data for display from entity objects. When entity objects become part of a database, the DBMS takes care of file I/O; the rest of the I/O is handled by application programs or DBMS utilities.

Why is it so important to keep data manipulation separate from I/O? Wouldn't it be simpler to let the entity object manage its own I/O? It might be simpler, but if you decided to change a screen layout, you would need to modify the entity class. If you keep them separate, then data manipulation procedures are independent of data display. You can change one without affecting the other. In a large program, this can not only save you a lot of time but also help you avoid programming errors. In a database environment, the separation of I/O and data storage becomes especially critical, because you do not want to modify data storage each time you decide to modify the look and feel of an application program.

Many object-oriented programs also use a fourth type of class: a *container class*. Container classes exist to "contain," or manage, multiple objects created from the same type of class. Because they gather objects together, they are also known as *aggregations*. For example, if you had a program that handled the instructions for playing solitaire, then that program would probably have a container class that organized all the individual card game objects. The container class would keep the objects in some order, list them for you, and probably search through them as well. As you will see, many pure object-oriented DBMSs require container classes, known as *extents*, to provide access to all objects created from the same class.

Types of Methods

Several types of methods are common to most classes, including the following:

- ◆ *Constructors*: A constructor is a method that has the same name as the class. It is executed whenever an object is created from a class. A constructor therefore usually contains instructions to initialize an object's variables in some way.

♦ *Destructors:* A destructor is a method that is executed when an object is destroyed. Not all object-oriented languages support destructors, which are usually used to release system resources (for example, main memory) allocated by the object.

♦ *Accessors:* An accessor, also known as a *get method*, returns the value of a private attribute to another object. This is the typical way in which external objects gain access to encapsulated data.

♦ *Mutators:* A mutator, or *set method*, stores a new value in an attribute. This is the typical way in which external objects can modify encapsulated data.

The remaining methods defined for a class depend on the specific type of class and the specific behaviors it needs to perform.

Method Overloading

One of the characteristics of a class is its ability to contain *overloaded* methods, methods that have the same name but require different data to operate. Because the data are different, the public interfaces of the methods are distinct.

As an example, assume that a human relations program has a container class named AllEmployees that aggregates all objects created from the Employees class. Programs that use the AllEmployees class create one object from the class and then relate all employee objects to the container using some form of program data structure (for example, an array, linked list, or binary tree).

To make the container class useful, there must be some way to locate specific employee objects. You might want to search by the employee ID number, by first and last name, or by telephone number. The AllEmployees class therefore contains three methods named find. One of the three requires an integer (the employee number) as input, the second requires two strings (the first and last name), and the third requires a single string (the phone number). Although the methods have the same name, their public interfaces are different because the combination of the name and the required input data is distinct.

Many classes have overloaded constructors. One might accept interactive input, another might read input from a file, and a third might get its data by copying the data in another object (a *copy constructor*). For example, most object-oriented environments have a Date class that supports initializing a date object with a string, three integers (day, month, year), the current system date, another Date object, and so on.

The benefit of method overloading is that the methods present a consistent interface to the programmer. Whenever a programmer wants to locate an employee, he or she knows to use a method named `find`. Then, the programmer just uses whichever of the three types of data he or she happens to have. The object-oriented program locates the correct method by using its entire public interface (its *signature*), made up of the name and the required input data.

Naming Classes, Attributes, and Methods

There are a few naming conventions used throughout the object-oriented world. Although there is absolutely nothing that says you have to name your classes, attributes, and methods in this way, you will be consistent with other programmers and database designers if you do so.

- ◆ Class names start with uppercase letters, followed by lowercase letters. If a class name is more than one word, it either uses an underscore (_) to separate the words — as in Merchandise_item — or uses embedded uppercase letters, as in MerchandiseItem.
- ◆ Attribute and method names start with lowercase letters and contain uppercase letters, lowercase letters, and numbers. If an attribute or method name is more than

one word, it either uses an underscore to separate the words (for example, product_numb or display_label) or uses embedded uppercase letters, as in productNumb or displayLabel.

♦ Accessor method names begin with the word *get* followed by the name of the attribute whose value is to be retrieved. For example, a method to retrieve a product number would be *getProductNumb*.

♦ Mutation method names begin with the word *set* followed by the name of the attribute whose value is to be modified, as in *setProductNumb*.

An Introduction to Inheritance

As you are developing an object-oriented program, you will run into situations where you need to use similar—but not identical—classes. If these classes are related in general to specific relationships, then you can take advantage of one of the major features of the object-oriented paradigm known as *inheritance*.

Inheriting Attributes

To see how inheritance works, assume that you are writing a program to manage a pet shop. One of the entity classes you will use is Animal, which will describe the living creatures sold by the shop. The data that describe objects created from the Animal class include the English and Latin names of the animal, the animal's age, and the animal's gender. However, the rest of the data depends on what type of animal is being represented. For example, for reptiles, you want to know the length of the animal, but for mammals, you want to know the weight. And for fish, you don't care about the weight or length, but you do want to know the color. All the animals sold by the pet shop share some data, yet have pieces of data that are specific to certain subgroups.

You could diagram the relationship as in Figure 2-4. The Animal class provides the data common to all types of animals. The subgroups—Mammals, Reptiles, and Fish—*add* the data specific to themselves. They don't need to repeat the common data because they *inherit* them from Animals. In other words, Mammals, Reptiles, and Fish all include the four pieces of data that are part of Animal.

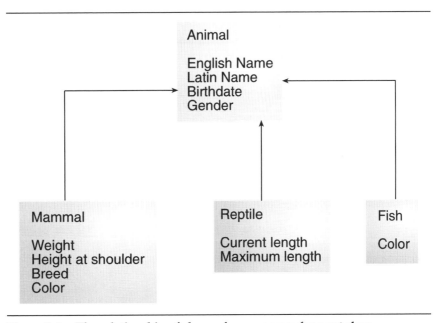

Figure 2-4:   The relationship of classes for a program for a pet shop

If you look closely at Figure 2-4, you'll notice that the lines on the arrows go from the subgroups up to Animal. This is actually contrary to what is happening: The data from Animal are flowing down the lines into the subgroups. Unfortunately, the direction of the arrows is dictated by convention, even though it may seem counterintuitive.

In object-oriented terminology, the subgroups are known as *subclasses* or *derived* classes. The Animal class is a *superclass* or *base* class.

The trick to understanding inheritance is to remember that sub-classes represent a more specific occurrence of their superclass. The relationships between a base class and its derived classes therefore can be expressed using the phrase "is a":

- ♦ A mammal is an animal
- ♦ A reptile is an animal
- ♦ A fish is an animal

If the "is a" phrasing does not make sense in a given situation, then you are not looking at inheritance. As an example, assume that you are writing a program to handle the rentals of equipment at a ski shop. You create a class for a generic merchandise item and then subclasses for the specific types of items being rented, as in the top four rectangles in Figure 2-5. Inheritance works properly here because skis are a specific type of merchandise item, as well as boots and poles.

However, you run into trouble when you begin to consider the specific items being rented and the customer doing the renting (the renter). Although there is a logical database-style relationship between a renter and an item being rented, inheritance does not work because the "is a" test fails. A rented item is not a renter!

The situation with merchandise items and rental inventory is more complex. The Merchandise Item, Skis, Boots, and Poles classes represent descriptions of types of merchandise but not physical inventory. For example, the ski shop may have many pairs of one type of ski in inventory and many pairs of boots of the same type, size, and width. Therefore, what is being rented is individual inventory items, represented by the Item Rented class. A given inventory item is either skis, boots, or poles. It can only be *one*, not all three as shown in Figure 2-5. Therefore, an item rented is not a pair of skis, a pair of boots, and a set of poles. (You also have the problem of having no class that can store the size and/or length of an item.)

One solution to the problem is to create a separate rented item class for each type of merchandise, as in Figure 2-6. When you are looking at this diagram, be sure to pay attention to the direction of the

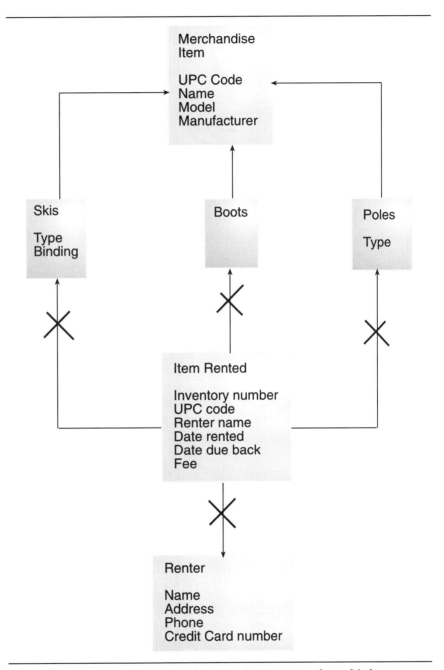

Figure 2-5: Inheritance and no inheritance in a program for a ski shop

arrows. The physical layout of the diagram does not correspond to the direction of the inheritance. Remember that by convention, the arrows point from the derived class to the base class.

The Ski Item class inherits information about the type of item it is from the Skis class. It also inherits information about an item being rented from the Item Rented class. A ski item "is a" pair of skis; a ski item "is a" rented item as well. Now the design of the classes passes the "is a" test for appropriate inheritance. (Note that this also gives you a class that can contain information such as the length and size of a specific inventory item.) The Renter class does not participate in the inheritance hierarchy at all.

Multiple Inheritance

When a class inherits from more than one base class, you have *multiple inheritance*. The extent to which multiple inheritance is supported in programming languages and by DBMSs varies considerably from one product to another. You will read much more about this concept throughout this book.

Not every class in an inheritance hierarchy is necessarily used to create objects. For example, in Figure 2-6 it is unlikely that any objects are ever created from the Merchandise Item or Item Rented classes. These classes are present simply to provide the common attributes and methods that their derived classes share.

Such classes are known as *abstract*, or *virtual*, classes. In contrast, classes from which objects are created are known as *concrete* classes.

> *Note: Many computer scientists use the verb "instantiate" to mean "creating an object from a class." For example, you could say that abstract classes are never instantiated. However, this author finds that term rather contrived (although not quite as bad as saying "we now will motivate the code" to mean "we will now explain the code") and prefers to use the more direct "create an object from a class."*

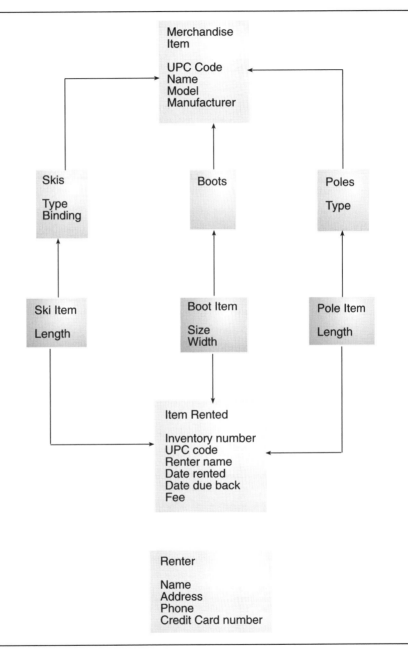

Figure 2-6: Multiple inheritance in a program for a ski shop

Interfaces

Some object-oriented languages (in particular, Java) do not support multiple inheritance. Instead, they allow a class to be derived from only one base class but allow a class to *implement* multiple *interfaces*.

An interface is a specification for a class without any instructions for the methods. In other words, the class has signatures for its methods, but the methods have no contents. It is up to the class implementing the interface to provide the programming language instructions for each method in the interface. An interface may include both attributes and methods, just methods, or just attributes.

In most cases, an interface is designed to provide additional functionality to a class. For example, if the hierarchy in Figure 2-6 was needed in an environment that did not support multiple inheritance, then the BootItem class could inherit from Boot but implement an interface named ItemRented. The ItemRented interface would provide the attributes that describe a rental and also methods for renting the item, computing the charge for the rental, and returning the item to inventory. Any class that represented something that could be rented would implement the interface, giving objects from that class the behaviors necessary to be rented.

Inheriting Methods: Polymorphism

In general, methods are inherited by subclasses from their superclass. A subclass can use its base class's methods as its own. However, in some cases it may not be possible to write a generic method that can be used by all subclasses. For example, assume that the ski rental shop's Merchandise Item class has a method named printCatalogEntry, the intent of which is to print a properly formatted catalog entry for each distinct type of merchandise item. The subclasses of Merchandise Item, however, have attributes not shared by all subclasses, and the printCatalogEntry method therefore must work somewhat differently for each subclass.

To solve the problem, the ski rental shop can take advantage of *polymorphism*, the ability to write different bodies for methods of the same name that belong to classes in the same inheritance hierarchy. The Merchandise Item class includes a *prototype* for the print-CatalogEntry method, indicating just the method's public interface. There is no body for the method, no specifications of how the method is to perform its work (a *virtual method*). Each subclass then redefines the method, adding the program instructions necessary to execute the method.

The beauty of polymorphism is that a programmer can expect methods of the same name and same type of output for all the subclasses of the same base class. However, each subclass can perform the method according to its own needs. Encapsulation hides the details from all objects outside the class hierarchy.

> *Note: It is very easy to confuse polymorphism and overloading. Just keep in mind that overloading applies to methods of the same class that have the same name but different signatures, whereas polymorphism applies to several subclasses of the same base class that have methods with the same signature but different implementations.*

Benefits of Object Orientation

There are several reasons why the object-oriented paradigm has become so pervasive in programming. Among the perceived benefits are the following:

- An object-oriented program consists of modular units that are independent of one another. These units can therefore be reused in multiple programs, saving development time. For example, if you have a well-debugged employee class, you can use it in any of your business programs that require data about employees.
- As long as a class's public interface remains unchanged, the internals of the class can be modified as needed without

requiring any changes to the programs that use the class. This can significantly speed up program modification. It can also make program modification more reliable, as it cuts down on many unexpected side effects of program changes.

♦ An object-oriented program separates the user interface from data handling, making it possible to modify one independent of the other.

♦ Inheritance adds logical structure to a program by relating classes in a general to specific manner, making the program easier to understand and therefore easier to maintain.

3

The Object-Oriented Data Model

As you read in Chapter 1, the object-oriented data model is a direct outgrowth of the object-oriented paradigm. The entity objects used by object-oriented programs are directly analogous to database entities used by pure object-oriented databases, with one major difference: Program objects disappear once a program stops running; database objects must stick around.

The idea that an object continues to exist once the program that created it has finished running is known as *persistence*. Most pure object-oriented DBMSs today are based on the concept of persistent objects and use class declarations very similar to those used by object-oriented programming languages.

However, those class declarations must not only indicate that objects created from the classes are persistent but also in some way indicate relationships between objects.

In this chapter you will read about the types of relationships available and how those relationships are represented in pure object-oriented databases. You will also see how those relationships are represented in entity–relationship (ER) diagrams, using modeling techniques best suited for object-oriented designs. Finally, you will be introduced to the way in which objects have been included in hybrid object–relational databases.

> *Note: Object–relational databases are often known as "post-relational" databases. Throughout this book, however, they will simply be known as "hybrids."*

Object-Oriented Data Relationships

An object-oriented database must be able to not only represent the traditional database relationships (one-to-many and many-to-many) but also the "is a" relationship implied by inheritance. In this section you will read about how pure object-oriented DBMSs represent data relationships of all types.

Object Identifiers

A relational database represents data relationships by having matching primary key–foreign key data. There are no data structures within the database that form links between the tables; the relationships are used as needed by joining tables. In direct contrast, a pure object-oriented database "hard codes" its relationships by including object identifiers within an object to indicate other objects to which it is related.

An *object identifier* is an internal database identifier for each individual object. Users, whether they be programmers or end users working with an interactive query tool, never see or manipulate these identifiers directly. Object identifiers are assigned and used only by the DBMS.

The meaning of the identifier is unique to each DBMS. It may be an arbitrary value or it may include the information necessary to locate the object in a database file. For example, an object identifier might include the page number and the offset from the beginning of the page for the file in which the object is stored.

Suppose, for example, you were relating objects of an Employee class to objects of a Child class. Each employee object would be related to one or more child objects. To see how this type of relationship is handled by an object-oriented DBMS, take a look at Figure 3-1. Each rectangle in the diagram is an employee object and each hexagon is a child object, all of which have their own unique object identifiers. Notice that every object identifier is different and, at least in this example, is totally unrelated to the class from which the object was created.

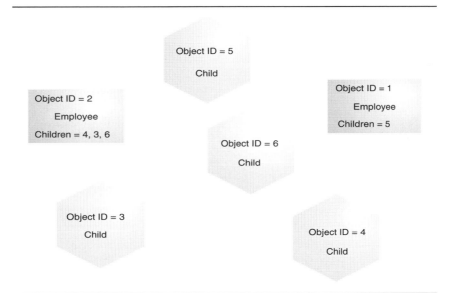

Figure 3-1: **Using object identifiers to represent object relationships**

The two employee objects have attributes named Children. The values of those attributes are the object identifiers of the employee's offspring.

There are two important aspects to this method of representing data relationships:

- ♦ For this mechanism to work, an object's identifier must not change while the object is a part of the database. If it were to change, the DBMS would be unable to locate related objects because the identifiers would not indicate the correct related objects.
- ♦ The only relationships that can be used for querying or traversing the database are those that have been predefined by storing the object identifiers of related objects in attributes. A pure object-oriented database is therefore *navigational*, a property found in the earlier hierarchical and network data models. In this respect, the object-oriented data model is a step backward because it limits the flexibility of the programmer/user to those predefined relationships. Object-oriented databases are therefore generally not as well suited to ad hoc querying as relational databases. On the other hand, if your access patterns closely follow the paths defined by the data relationships, then performance will generally be better than with a relational database, because using object identifiers to locate objects is much faster than joining tables.

One-to-Many Relationships

In direct contrast to the relational data model, the object-oriented data model allows multivalued attributes, aggregations known as *sets* or *bags*. This ability is essential if a pure object-oriented database is going to represent any type of "many" relationship.

> Note: For purposes of this discussion, a one-to-one relationship
> is merely a special case of a one-to-many relationship in which
> the cardinality of the relationship is one on both sides.

To represent a one-to-many relationship, you define an attribute of the class at the "many" end of the relationship to hold the object identifier of its parent. The class of the parent objects contains an attribute that will hold a set of values, the object identifiers of the many objects to which it is related. When the DBMS sees an attribute with a data type that is another class, it knows that the attribute will hold an object identifier rather than actual data values.

For example, to relate employees to their children, the Child class would contain an attribute with a data type of Employee. The Employee class would contain an attribute whose data type was Child, with the attribute being declared to hold a set of values. It is important to keep in mind that although the relationship is defined by attributes in the class, in the database itself, relationships are between objects, just as primary key–foreign key relationships are between specific rows rather than entire tables.

Many-to-Many Relationships

Because an object-oriented database allows objects to have multi-valued attributes, it can directly represent many-to-many relationships, without the need to create composite entities to remove the relationships. To represent the relationship, each class that participates in the relationship defines an attribute that will contain a set of values of the other class to which it will be related.

At first, the ability to represent directly many-to-many relationships may seem like a huge advantage for an object-oriented database. Unfortunately, you must be very careful when you use it.

First, if you have relationship data, such as the price of a merchandise item that varies depending on the vendor from which you order it, you will need to create a composite entity to hold that relationship data. The many-to-many relationship will then be replaced with two one-to-many relationships, just as it would be in a relational database.

Second, it is possible to create a database design that contains many-to-many relationships that either lose information or make it impossible to determine relationships accurately. As an example, consider the instance diagram in Figure 3-2. Each of the shapes represents objects of a different class. In this particular case, there are three classes: Store, Customer, and Product. The lines between the objects in the diagram indicate which objects are related to one another. (The dashes on the lines have no significance other than to make it easier for you to distinguish between the three Customer objects and their relationships.)

The intent of the database is to represent the customers that purchased products at specific stores and the products that they purchased at those stores. There is a many-to-many relationship between a customer and a store and a many-to-many relationship between a customer and a product. (There is also a many-to-many relationship between a product and a store, but that relationship has no meaning in this database unless it is associated with the customer that purchased the product.)

From the diagram, you can determine that Customer #1 purchased Product #1 and Product #2 at Store #1 (one customer purchasing many products from one store). By the same token, you can see that Customer #2 made purchases at both Store #1 and Store #2 and that both purchases were of a single product (one customer purchasing one product at many stores). When you look at Customer #3, however, the picture is not as clear.

Customer #3 shopped at both Store #2 and Store #3. By the same token, Customer #3 purchased Product #2 and Product #3 (one customer purchasing many products at many stores). At which store did Customer #3 purchase each product? There is absolutely no way to tell given the relationships in Figure 3-2. By taking advantage of the ability to represent direct many-to-many relationships, we have lost some very important information: the store from which a specific product was purchased.

In this case, the only solution is to remove the many-to-many relationship between customers and products, inserting a three-way

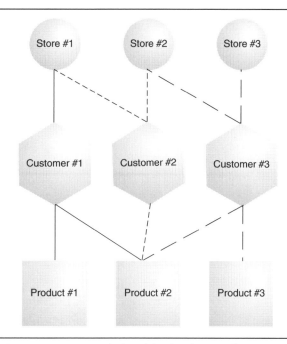

Figure 3-2:   A many-to-many relationship that loses information

composite entity to represent the purchase of a product by a customer from a store. As you can see in Figure 3-3, the new class (Purchase) relates one or more products to a specific customer and store.
There is now no question that Customer #3 purchased Product #2
from Store #2 and that Product #3 came from Store #3.

The moral to this, as you might expect, is that you must examine
many-to-many relationships very carefully, especially in the context
of other many-to-many relationships with which a given class
many participate. All that being said, you can use direct many-to-
many relationships in the object-oriented data model. It is up to you
to ensure that their use does not cause any loss of meaning in the
database.

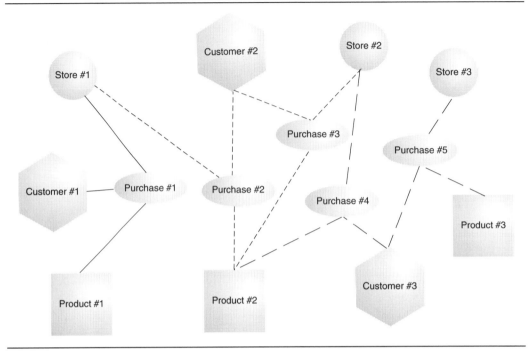

Figure 3-3:   Solving the many-to-many information loss problem

The "Is A" Relationship

Because the object-oriented paradigm supports inheritance, an object-oriented database can also use the "is a" relationship between objects. For example, assume that you are modeling a human resources database. You declare a generic Employee class with attributes such as name, address, social security number, date of hire, and department.

However, recording how an employee is paid presents a bit of a dilemma: Not all employees are paid in the same way; some are paid hourly and some are salaried. The class for hourly employees needs attributes for the hourly wage, overtime wage, and the typical number of hours worked. The class for salaried employees needs only an attribute for annual salary.

In an object-oriented database, the correct way to handle this situation is to create two subclasses of employee, one for each type of employee. Although the DBMS may never create objects directly from the Employee class, the presence of Employee in the design clarifies the logical design of the database and helps application programmers by allowing them to write methods used by both subclasses only once, for the Employee class.

The "Extends" Relationship

In theory, an object-oriented database should support two types of inheritance, the "is a" relationship about which you have been reading and an "extends" relationship. The "is a" relationship, also known as a *generalization–specialization* relationship, or *gen-spec*, creates an inheritance hierarchy where subclasses are specific types of their superclass.

With the *extends* relationship, however, a subclass expands on its superclass rather than narrowing it to a more specific type. For example, assume that you are working with the Employee class hierarchy mentioned in the previous section. As well as classes about employees working in specific jobs, you also need to record additional data for managers, who are employees but also have some special characteristics.

The database will include a Manager class that adds an attribute for the Employees that the manager manages. In this sense, a manager is not a more specific employee but an employee with additions. The Manager class therefore extends the definition of each of the salary-type classes rather than making them more specific.

The "Whole–Part" Relationship

One of the things that is awkward for a relational database to represent is the idea of parts of a whole, such as where a manufacturing database needs to keep track of the parts and subassemblies used to create specific products. An object-oriented database, however, can take advantage of a relationship known as *whole–part*, in which objects of a class are related to objects of other classes that are a part of it. In the case of a manufacturing database, a Product class would be related to Part and Subassembly classes using the whole–part relationship.

A whole–part relationship is a many-to-many relationship with a special meaning. A product can be made up of many parts and subassemblies. By the same token, the same part or subassembly may be used in many different products. When a whole–part relationship is implemented in a database, it is therefore implemented as any other many-to-many relationship using sets of object identifiers in two classes being related. However, the meaning of the relationship is more specific than a normal many-to-many relationship and can be included in design documentation as a whole–part relationship to make the design easier to understand.

> *Note: The product, part, and subassemblies relationship is actually a bit more complex than just mentioned, in particular because subassemblies are made up of parts and may also be part of larger subassemblies.*

Relationship Integrity

If relationships are going to work in pure object-oriented databases, then the object identifiers on both sides of the relationship must match. For example, if employees are being related to their children, then there must be some way to ensure that when the object identifier of a child object is inserted into an employee object, the object identifier of the same employee object is inserted into the child object. This type of relationship integrity, which is somewhat analogous to referential integrity in the relational data model, is handled by specifying *inverse relationships*.

The Employee class has an attribute called children (Employee.children, defined as a set). At the same time, the Child class has an attribute called parent (Child.parent). To ensure the integrity of the relationship, a pure object-oriented DBMS will allow the database designer to include syntax specifying where the inverse object identifier should appear, such as

```
children : (set) Child
    inverse is Child.parent
```

for the Employee class and

```
parent : Employee
    inverse is Employee.children
```

for the Child class.

Whenever a user or application program inserts or removes an object identifier from the children attribute in an employee object, the DBMS will automatically update the parent attribute in the related child object. When a modification is made to the child object, the DBMS will automatically propagate it to the employee object.

Just as it is up to the database designer to specify referential integrity rules for a relational database, it is the responsibility of an object-oriented database designer to identify inverse relationships to the DBMS when creating a database schema.

ER Diagramming Models for Object-Oriented Relationships

An object-oriented database design can be modeled using an entity–relationship (ER) diagram, just like a relationship database design. However, the modeling techniques must include the ability to represent classes and the added class relationships that object orientation provides. This section therefore discusses several of the data modeling techniques that have been designed specifically for object-oriented scenarios. As you will see, each type of notation has its own strengths and weaknesses.

The database used in this section is a simple parts and suppliers database for a firm that manufactures shoes and hats. The Footwear and Headgear classes are subclasses of a generic MerchandiseItem class. In addition, the database contains classes for raw materials, sources of those materials, and which materials are used in making specific products.

Coad/Yourdon Notation

Peter Coad and Edward Yourdon are generally credited as having written the definitive works on object-oriented analysis and design. Their notation for representing classes and class relationships is one of the most commonly used.

In Figure 3-4 you can see an ER diagram for the sample database drawn using Coad/Yourdon notation. A few attributes and methods have been included as examples, but in that respect the diagram is not complete.

The notation has the following characteristics:

  ◆ A class is represented by a round-cornered rectangle.
  ◆ Classes from which objects are created have a dashed outline outside the inner border of the class. Abstract classes, such as Product in Figure 3-4, have only a single-line outline.
  ◆ The name of the class appears at the top of the round-cornered rectangle.
  ◆ The middle of the class round-cornered rectangle contains the attributes defined for the class.
  ◆ The bottom of the class round-cornered rectangle contains the methods defined for the class.

  ◆ The symbol ⌂ represents the "is a" relationship. Therefore, in Figure 3-4, a piece of Footwear "is a" product, just as "is a" piece of Headgear.

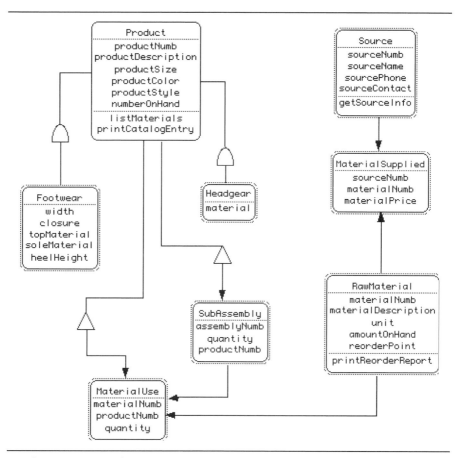

Figure 3-4:   An object-oriented database design using Coad/Yourdon notation

♦ The symbol △ represents the "whole–part" relationship. For example, in Figure 3-4 a SubAssembly is a part of a product.
♦ A line without an arrow represents zero or one.
♦ A line with an arrow represents zero, one, or more.

Coad/Yourdon notation has two strong points. First, it provides good support for the special class relationships that are present in an object-oriented environment. Second, it clearly identifies concrete and abstract classes. However, Coad/Yourdon notation cannot distinguish between mandatory and optional database relationships, nor does it provide a great of documentation about the meaning of database relationships. There is also no intrinsic ability to represent aggregate classes, which are therefore not included in Figure 3-4.

Shlaer/Mellor Notation

An alternative to Coad/Yourdon notation is Shlaer/Mellor notation. As you can see in Figure 3-5, classes are represented as rectangles, with the same divisions for class name, attributes, and methods as in Coad/Yourdon notation.

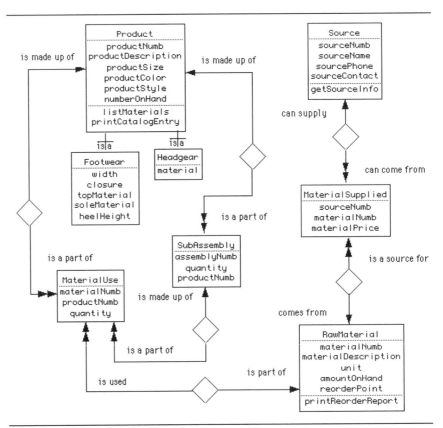

Figure 3-5: An object-oriented database design using Shlaer/Mellor notation

To represent the "is a" relationship, the Shlaer/Mellor relationship uses a vertical line with a labeled horizontal line through it. Database relationships are represented by small diamonds to which lines with arrows are attached. A single arrow means zero or one; a double arrow means one or more. Each relationship is labeled to indicate the meaning of the relationship in both directions.

Shlaer/Mellor notation provides more information about database relationships than does Coad/Yourdon notation. However, it has no explicit support for the whole–part relationship. It also cannot distinguish between optional and mandatory database relationships, nor does it support any easy way to represent aggregations.

OMT (Rombaugh) Notation

Object Modeling Technique (OMT) was developed by a team of computer scientists led by J. Rombaugh. Although like Shlaer/Mellor. it has no direct support for whole–part relationships, it does support aggregations and some mandatory database relationships.

The sample database is represented in OMT notation in Figure 3-6. Once again, classes are rectangles with class name, attributes, and methods each in its own section within the class rectangle. The "is a" relationship is represented using the △ symbol, exactly the opposite of the same symbol's use in Coad/Yourdon notation.

> *Note: The lack of consistency in terminology and notation within the object-oriented paradigm is enough to drive you crazy. This situation is probably the result of two things: Object-oriented technologies are still fairly new, and there is no accepted standard.*

Relationships, which are known as *associations,* are indicated by line ends as follows:

♦ ————————: A plain-ended line means "exactly one" and therefore is used at the "one" end of a mandatory one-to-many relationship.

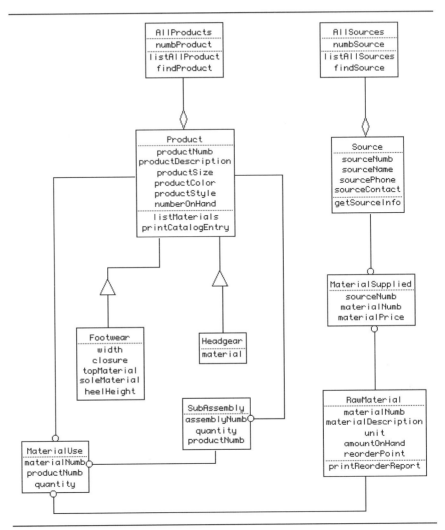

Figure 3-6:   An object-oriented database design using OMT notation

- ◆ ○─────────: A line with an open circle at the end means "zero or one." This notation is used at the "one" end of a relationship that is not mandatory.
- ◆ ●─────────: A line with a filled circle at the end means "zero or more" and therefore is used at the "many" end of a one-to-many relationship or at either

end of a many-to-many relationship. OMT has no symbol for "one or more."

♦ ◁◇————————: An open diamond represents a mandatory aggregation, such as the membership of objects created from the Product and Source classes in their respective aggregate classes.

♦ ○◇————————: An open diamond with an open circle at its tip stands for an optional aggregation.

♦ ●◇————————: An open diamond with a filled circle at its tip represents many aggregations.

♦ n ————————: If the cardinality of a relationship is fixed and known, you can represent that cardinality by placing an integer over a straight line. For example, assume that every employee had two business phone numbers stored in an employee object, one for the office and the other for a cell phone. The relationship between an employee object and a phone number object would therefore be 2 ————————.

Booch Notation

Booch notation provides yet another variation on using an ER diagram to represent classes and their associations. As you can see in Figure 3-7, classes are simple round-cornered rectangles with the typical three sections: name, attributes, and methods.

Associations between classes are represented by a variety of notations on the lines that connect the classes, including the following:

♦ ———— $\frac{1}{n}$ ————: A line with no terminator represents an association whose cardinality is specified by numbers on the line. In Figure 3-7, all the associations are 1:n, indicating a mandatory one-to-many relationship.

♦ ————————▶: A line terminated with a single arrow indicates inheritance. As you can see in Figure 3-7, the arrow points from the derived class to its base class.

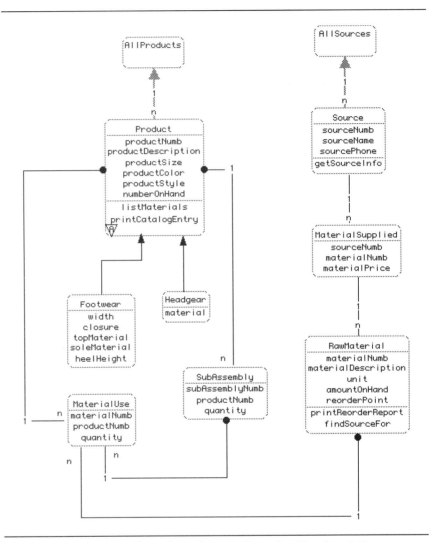

Figure 3-7:   An object-oriented database design using Booch notation

♦ ———————●: A line terminated with a solid circle represents the has association. In Figure 3-7, this is used to indicate whole–part relationships.

♦ ⟩⟩⟩⟩⟩⟩⟩⟩⟩⟩⟩⟩▷: A gray single-headed arrow represents a metaclass, a class of classes. This type of relationship is used to connect the Product and Source classes to their aggregate classes.

Special types of classes, objects, attributes, and methods are indicated by markers in the lower left corner of the class:

- ♦ : An *A* indicates an abstract class (a class from which objects cannot be created). You can see this marker in use in Figure 3-7 in the Product class.

- ♦ : An *S* indicates an attribute that has a single value for all objects created for the same class, that the attribute is *static*. For example, if you were to define a static attribute numbEmployees for an Employee class, the computer would maintain only one copy of that attribute, rather than separate copies for each object. All the employee objects would share that single copy.

- ♦ : A *U* stands for a base class shared by many subclasses (in Booch terminology, a *virtual* class).

- ♦ : An *F* indicates a class that allows *friend* access to other classes, allowing them free access to the typically private portions of the class.

Note: Because friend access defeats encapsulation, some people believe that it violates the basic principles of object orientation and therefore should not be used.

Unified Modeling Language (UML)

If anything even approaches a standard for diagramming data models and other elements of a system design in an object-oriented environment, it is the Unified Modeling Language (UML). This notation combines many of the elements you have seen in the previous diagramming methods and includes provisions that the others lack. UML will therefore be used throughout the remainder of this book for all ER diagrams.

Note: The similarity of UML to other object-oriented modeling notations is not an accident. It is designed to be a successor to methods such as OMT. Its primary designers—Grady Booch, Ivar Jacobson, and Jim Rumbaugh—were all authors of their own modeling languages, which they proceeded to unify with UML. (The Jacobson model is not discussed in this chapter because it does not adapt well to representing database relationships but is better suited for describing programming systems.)

Note: Because of space constraints, this book cannot contain complete coverage of UML. To download documentation of the entire modeling language, go to http://www.rational.com and follow the links to UML documentation.

An example of an ER diagram using UML can be found in Figure 3-8. The major features of this diagram are as follows:

- A regular class is represented by a rectangle, divided into the three parts you have seen before (name, attributes, methods).
- An aggregate class is represented by a rectangle containing its name and the rectangles of the classes whose objects it aggregates. For example, in Figure 3-8, the Product and Source classes are within their aggregate classes, AllProducts and AllSources, respectively.
- Associations are shown with lines with plain ends. The cardinality of a relationship is expressed as n, n..n, or n..*. For example, if the cardinality is 1, it is simply written as 1. If the cardinality is 0 or 1, it is written 0..1. If the cardinality is 0 or more, it appears as 0..*; 1 or more appears as 1..*. Notice in Figure 3-8 that there are several direct many-to-many relationships, shown with 0..* at either end of the association line.
- Inheritance is shown by a line with an open arrow pointing toward the base class. In Figure 3-8, the Footwear and Headgear classes have such arrows pointing toward Product.
- What we call composite entities in a relational database are known as *association classes*. They are connected to the relationship to which they apply with a dashed line. As

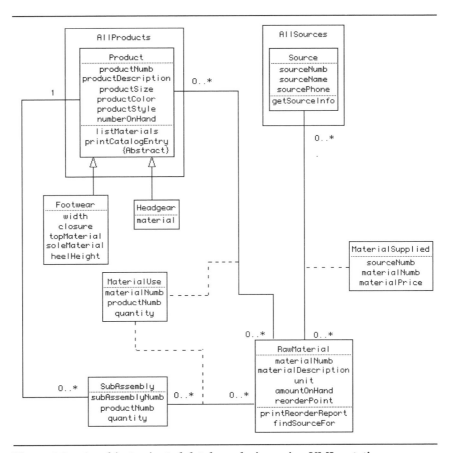

Figure 3-8: An object-oriented database design using UML notation

you can see in Figure 3-8, the MaterialSupplied and MaterialUse classes are each connected to at least one many-to-many relationship by the required dashed line.

In addition to the basic features shown in Figure 3-8, UML diagrams can include any of the following:

◆ An attribute can include information about its visibility (public, protected, or private), data type, default value, and domain. In Figure 3-9, for example, you can see four classes and the data types of their attributes. Keep in mind that in an object-oriented environment, data types can be other classes. Therefore, the Source class uses an object of the TelephoneNumber class for its phoneNumber attribute and an object of the Address class for its sourceAddress attribute. In turn, Source, Address, and Telephone number all contain attributes that are objects of the String class.

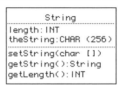

Figure 3-9:   UML classes showing their data types

Note: The idea of building classes from a small set of primitive data types is integral to the object-oriented data model. You will read about this in Chapter 4, where we discuss the proposed object database standard.

♦ Methods (officially called *operations* in UML) can include their complete signature and return data type. If you look at Figure 3-9, for example, you can see each operation's name followed by the types of data that it requires to perform its job (*parameters*). Together, the method's name and its parameters make up the method's signature. If data are returned by the operation, then the operation's signature is followed by a colon and the data type of the return value, which may be an object of another class or a simple data type such as an integer.

♦ Solid arrows can be used at the end of associations to indicate the directions in which a relationship can be navigated. There are three possible ways to use the arrows:

- Use arrows on the ends of all associations where navigation is possible. If an association has a plain end, then navigation is not possible in that direction. This would indicate, for example, a relationship between two objects that is not an inverse relationship, where only one of the two objects in a relationship contains the object identifier of a related object.

- Show no arrows at all, as was done in Figure 3-9. In that case, the diagram provides no information about how the database design can be navigated.

- Show no arrows on associations that can be navigated in both directions, but use arrows on associations that can be navigated in only one direction. The drawback to this approach is that you cannot differentiate associations that can be navigated in both directions from associations that cannot be navigated at all.

♦ An association that ends in a filled diamond indicates a whole–part relationship. For example, if you were representing a spreadsheet in a database, the relationship between the spreadsheet and its cells could be diagrammed as in Figure 3-10. The filled diamond can also be used to show aggregation instead of placing one object within another, as was done in Figure 3-8.

♦ When an association is between more than two objects, UML uses a diamond to represent the relationship. If an association class is present, it will be connected to the diamond, as in Figure 3-11. The four classes in the illustration represent entities from a poetry reading society's database. A "reading" occurs when a single person reads

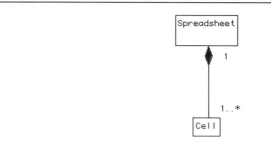

Figure 3-10: Using UML to diagram a whole–part relationship

a single poem that was written by one or more poets. The association entity indicates when and where the reading took place.

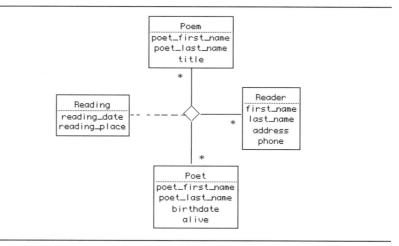

Figure 3-11: Using UML to diagram a relationship between more than two classes

Integrating Objects into a Relational Database

Throughout this chapter, you have been viewing a class as an entity, the element that is involved in data relationships. However, when we look at merging objects into the relational data model, a class takes on an entirely different role: It becomes a domain, acting as the data type for a column.

There are two very important implications of using a class as a domain:

♦ It becomes possible to store multiple values in the same column in the same row because an object usually contains multiple values. However, if a class is a domain assigned to a column, then any given column in a row can contain only one object created from that class. The relation therefore technically still conforms to the relational constraint of there being no multivalued attributes.

♦ It becomes possible to store procedures in a relation, because an object is linked to the program code for the processes that it knows how to do.

As you will see throughout the latter parts of this book, a hybrid DBMS is really a relational DBMS with the ability to store objects in its tables. The database is still subject to the constraints that apply to all relational databases and still has the ability to use the join operation to implement relationships on the fly.

For Further Reading

If you would like to delve further into the theory of object-oriented analysis and design, see any of the following:

Booch, G. *Object-Oriented Analysis and Design—With Applications*. 2nd Ed. Benjamin/Cummings, 1994.

Jacboson, I. *Object-Oriented Software Engineering*. Addison-Wesley, 1992.

Rombaugh, J., Blaha, M., Premerlani, W., Eddy, F., and Lorenson, W. *Object-Oriented Modeling and Design*. Prentice-Hall, 1991.

Shlaer, S. and Mellor, Stephen J. *Object-Oriented Systems Analysis: Modeling the World in Data.* Prentice-Hall, 1988.

Shlaer, S. and Mellor, Stephen J. *Object-Lifecycles: Modeling the World in States.* Prentice-Hall, 1992.

Yourdon, E. and Coad, P. *Object-Oriented Analysis.* Prentice-Hall, 1991.

Yourdon, E. and Coad, P. *Object-Oriented Design.* Prentice-Hall, 1991.

For a complete (but opinionated) look at the integration of objects into the relational data model, see:

Date, C. J. and Darwen, Hugh. *Foundation for Object/Relational Databases: The Third Manifesto.* Addison-Wesley, 1998.

4

The Proposed Object Database Standard

At the time this book was written, there was no accepted standard for the object-oriented data model. However, there is an independent group of industry representatives known as the Object Database Management Group (ODMG) who have been working to prepare a proposed standard.

> Note: The ODMG's Web site can be found at
> http://www.odmg.org.

The chair of the committee, Rick Cattell, states in his introduction to the documentation of the proposed standard:

> "We have worked outside of traditional standard bodies for out efforts in order to make quick progress."

Version 2.0 of the proposed standard was released in 1997 but has not yet been submitted to standard-making bodies. Nonetheless, most major OODBMS vendors have committed to adhering to the proposed standard. It is therefore important that you are familiar with this standard before you go searching for software.

In this chapter you will be introduced to the provisions of the proposed standard as they relate to the logical design elements of an object-oriented database. The data definition language will be presented in Chapter 5.

Basic OODBMS Terminology

As mentioned in Chapter 2, the terminology of the object-oriented paradigm varies a great deal depending on the specific environment with which you are working. You will find that the proposed standard uses many of the words to which you have already been introduced in the context of object-oriented programming, but that it sometimes uses them in somewhat different ways. Therefore, the best way to start examining the proposed standard for object-oriented databases is to understand the precise terminology used in the standard's documentation:

♦ The basic components of an object-oriented database are the *object* and the *literal*. An object is the self-contained instance of an entity about which you have been reading. It has some type of unique object identifier. An literal is a specified value, such as "female" or 31. As you would expect, a literal has no identifier.

Note: A literal is not necessarily a single value. It may be a structure, *a collection of related values stored under a single name.*

♦ Objects have *properties*, which include both their *attributes* and the relationships they have with other objects. The current values for an object's properties make up the object's current *state*.

♦ All objects and literals have *types*. Each type has a specific domain shared by all objects and literals of that type. Types can also have behaviors. For a type that has behaviors, all objects of that type share the same behaviors. In a practical sense, a type can be a class from which an object is created, an interface, or a data type for a literal (for example, integer). An object can be thought of as an *instance* of a type.

♦ The things that an object knows how to do are its *operations*. Each operation can require data as input (*input parameters*) and may return some value with a known type.

♦ A *database* is a collection of objects that are managed so that they can be accessed by multiple users.

♦ The definition of a database is contained in a *schema* that has been created with Object Definition Language (ODL), the data manipulation language that is defined as a part of the proposed object-oriented database standard.

Understanding Types

One of the major characteristics of the object-oriented paradigm is the distinction between a class's public interface and its private elements (encapsulation). The proposed standard for object-oriented databases makes this distinction by talking about a type's *external specification* and its *implementations*.

External Specifications

A type's external specification includes the following:

♦ The operations that can be performed on an instance of the type

♦ The properties of the type (those that are accessible through some mechanism)

♦ *Exceptions* that can be raised by the type's operations

In programming terms, an exception is a predictable error. For example, when a program is trying to open a file to read its contents, an exception will occur (the exception would be "raised") if the file cannot be found. The program "tries" to perform the file open operation; if the exception is raised, the program can then "catch" the exception and take appropriate action. In this example, appropriate action might be displaying an alert notifying the user that the file cannot be found. By including exception handling in their operations, types can simplify the job of the application programmer and provide tighter control over data integrity.

The external specification of a type should be implementation independent. It contains only the information necessary to invoke an operation on an instance of the type, to retrieve the value of a property, and to identify exceptions. The writers of the proposed object database standard refer to this as an *abstract* description, something that has no implementation details. An interface contains only abstract operations. A class contains both abstract operations and the abstract state of a type. A literal contains only an abstract state.

> Note: The writers of the proposed object database standard define an interface as something that has only operations and no properties. However, programming languages such as Java do allow interfaces to have properties and do not require them to have operations.

Implementations

An implementation of a type consists of two parts. The *representation* is a programming language-dependent data structure containing the type's properties. The specifics of the implementation come from a *language binding*. This means that the internal representation of a type will be different depending on the programming language being used and that a given type therefore may have more than one representation.

The details of a type's operations are specified by a set of *methods*. (Yes, this is a slightly different use of the term than you read about before; it is specific to this proposed standard.) There must be at least one method for each operation in the external specification. However, a type may include methods that are never seen outside the type itself. Such methods usually perform utility functions for other methods of the type.

Methods will be written in the same programming language used to express a type's representation. If a database will support application programming in C++, Java, and SmallTalk, for example, then there will need to be three implementations of each type, one for each language. However, typically only one implementation is used in any given application program.

Primitive Types

Every element in an object-oriented database is build from a small group of primitive data types:

- `boolean`: A value of either true or false
- `char`: A single ASCII or UNICODE character
- `short`: A signed integer, usually 8 or 16 bits long
- `long`: A signed integer, usually 32 or 64 bits long
- `float`: A single-precision floating point value
- `double`: A double-precision floating point value

Note: Integer sizes and floating point ranges are implementation and machine dependent.

- `octet`: Eight-bit storage
- `string`: A string of characters
- `enum`: An enumerated type where the values are specified explicitly when the type is declared
- `any`: Any data type. The `any` type is analogous to using a `void` parameter in C++ and using the `Object` class as a parameter in Java.

From these data types, you can build larger types (both literals and classes) that can be used to build even larger types. For example, the

Address class that you saw earlier in this book is made up of a collection of strings. The Address class can then be used as a type for attributes in any class that requires an address.

Inheritance

The proposed standard for object-oriented databases supports simple inheritance and multiple inheritance through interfaces. As you will see, the rules for inheritance are somewhat different from those presented in Chapter 2, which are characteristic of object-oriented programming languages.

> *Note: These conflicting definitions are truly unfortunate because they make understanding the way in which a specific object-oriented environment works more difficult. Hopefully, the time will come when there is a single, accepted standard that will eliminate much of this redefinition of terms.*

In the terms of the proposed standard, an *interface* is the declaration of a type from which objects *cannot* be created. This is the equivalent of an *abstract class* in most object-oriented programming languages. A *class* is a type from which objects *can* be created, the equivalent of a *concrete class*.

Interfaces and Inheritance

Inheritance, the "is a" relationship, applies to interfaces only. Because interfaces that are part of the object database model contain only declarations of behaviors, only behaviors are inherited through this mechanism. Interfaces from which other interfaces inherit are known as *supertypes*; the interfaces doing the inheriting are *subtypes*.

For example, if you are creating a database for a retail establishment, then you might have an interface named Merchandise Item from which you would derive an interface named Furniture, from which in turn you would derive interfaces named Chair, Desk, Sofa, and so on. In the object database model, you could write this as

```
interface MerchandiseItem {…};
interface Furniture : MerchandiseItem {…};
interface Chair : Furniture : MerchandiseItem {…};
interface Desk : Furniture : MerchandiseItem {…};
interface Sofa : Furniture : MerchandiseItem {…};
```

The "lowest "interface in an inheritance hierarchy is known as the *most specific type*. Because it inherits the behaviors of all the types above it in the hierarchy, it is the most complete interface. In the preceding example, Chair, Desk, and Sofa are the most specific types.

One of the practical benefits of inheritance is that you can refer to subtypes as their supertype. For example, an application program could refer to chairs, desks, and sofas as furniture, or even as merchandise items. This makes it easy to handle subtypes as a group when necessary.

Subtypes can be specialized as needed by adding behaviors. Subtypes of the specialized subtype will inherit the behaviors added to its supertype.

Given that interfaces cannot be used to create objects, there are some special rules about the organization of an inheritance hierarchy:

- ◆ Interfaces can inherit from other interfaces.
- ◆ Classes can inherit from interfaces.
- ◆ Interfaces cannot inherit from classes.
- ◆ Classes cannot inherit from other classes.

The practical implication of this is that classes will be the lowest elements in an inheritance hierarchy.

The object database model supports multiple inheritance. However, it does not allow method overloading as part of inheritance, which might occur when two supertypes have operations with the same name but different signatures. No two interfaces in the same inheritance hierarchy may have operations with the same name. However, overloading within a single class or interface is permissible.

Classes and Extensions

The object database model uses the *extends* relationship to indicate inheritance of both state and behavior. Classes that extend another class gain access to all the states and behaviors of the supertype, including anything the supertype may have acquired through inheriting from interfaces.

A class can extend at most one other class. However, if you build up a hierarchy of extensions, the classes at the bottom of the hierarchy inherit everything their supertypes inherited from classes above them. As an example, consider Figure 4-1, which represents an inheritance hierarchy for a combined elementary and middle school.

The Person interface represents behaviors common to all people in the database. However, the people in the database fall into a number of more specific categories. Some, for example, are employees. The Employee interface therefore handles behaviors related to those who work for the school. Classes for specific types of employees, such as the Teachers and MaintenanceWorkers shown in Figure 4-1, inherit from the Employee interface.

The Guardian class inherits directly from the Person interface. (There is absolutely no requirement that the levels in an inheritance hierarchy be balanced.) The Student class also inherits from the Person interface. Although it is a class and objects can theoretically be created from it, in practice we would not do so. The ElementaryStudent and MiddleSchoolStudent classes extend the Students class. They are the classes from which student objects are actually generated.

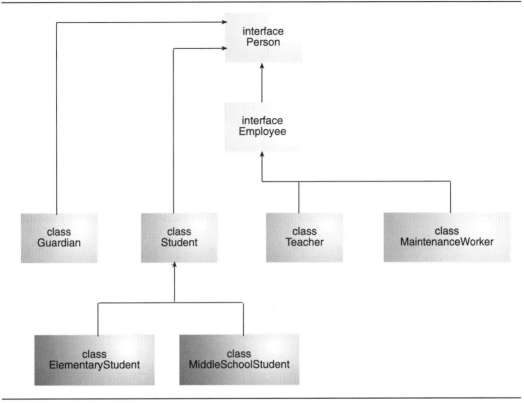

Figure 4-1: Inheritance according to the proposed standard for the object database model

Objects

The proposed standard for object-oriented databases includes the following characteristics of objects:

♦ If the database designer desires, the DBMS can maintain an *extent* for each type that includes all the instances created from the type. For example, the extent of the class Guardian would contain all guardian objects. An extent can be indexed to provide faster access to its contents. However, the proposed standard cautions that there is a great deal of overhead in maintaining the index and that its presence is optional.

♦ As with rows in a relation, it is possible to give a type a unique identifier, its *key*. When a key is made up of a single property, it is known as a *simple key*; a key made up of multiple properties is known as a *compound key*. Unlike those in the relational data model, however, unique keys are not required.

♦ Every object has a unique *object identifier*, generated by the DBMS with characteristics like those described in Chapter 3. The precise contents of the object identifier are left up to each specific DBMS, giving DBMS software developers the freedom to use whatever physical access methods they wish to locate objects.

♦ Each type has a name that is accessible to the entire database environment; it is *global* to the database. The DBMS takes care of mapping the name to the internal representation of the type.

♦ Objects can be *transient* or *persistent*. Transient objects exist for the life of the application program that created them. Such objects are used either for temporary storage or to support the currently running application program. Persistent objects are those that are stored in the database itself.

Collection Objects

Collection objects, which are derived from the interface Collection, are the proposed object database standard's equivalent of container classes. These are the elements that allow an object to contain multiple values of a single property. The collection objects identified by the proposed standard include the following:

♦ *Set*: A set contains an unordered group of objects of the same type. No duplicates are allowed.

♦ *Bag*: A bag contains an unordered group of objects of the same type. Duplicates are allowed.

♦ *List:* A list is an ordered group of objects of the same type.

- *Array:* An array is an ordered group of objects of the same type that can be accessed by position. It is similar to an array in a programming language. However, its size is dynamic rather than fixed. Elements can be inserted in and removed from any position.
- *Dictionary*: A dictionary is very much like an index. It is made up of ordered keys, each of which is paired with a single value. For example, if you have a dictionary of objects created from a Book class, then you might use some characters from the title as the key paired with the full title as the value. Then you could search using the keys to find the full titles quickly.

When we speak of "objects of the same type," keep in mind that subtypes that inherit or extend the same supertype can be handled as if they were created directly from the supertype. Therefore, if the collection object is declared to hold objects of a supertype, any objects created from subtypes of that supertype can be part of the collection.

The Collection interface provides every collection with operations that return information about the contents of the collection. These operations are summarized in Table 4-1. As you will see shortly, collections are used to hold references to related objects.

Structured Objects

A DBMS that adheres to the proposed object database standard supports four *structured objects*.

- Date
- Interval
- Time
- Timestamp

The structure and function of these objects are the same as those of the data types with the same name defined by the SQL-92 standard.

Operation	Action
InvalidCollectionType	Raises an exception if a collection type is not valid
ElementNotFound	Raises an exception if a specific element is not part of a given collection
cardinality	Returns the number of elements in a collection
is_empty	Returns *true* if a collection is empty, *false* if it is not
is_ordered	Returns *true* if the elements of a collection are ordered in some way, *false* if they are not
allows_duplicates	Returns *true* if the collection allows duplicates, *false* if it does not
contains_element	Returns *true* if a specific element is part of a given collection, *false* if it is not
insert_element	Inserts an element into a collection
remove_element	Removes an element from a collection
create_iterator	Creates an object that can be used to access the element of a collection in forward order (from first to next, and so on)
create_bidirectional_iterator	Creates an object that can be used to access the elements of a collection in forward and backward order (from first to next or from last to prior, and so on)

Table 4-1:   Operations available through the Collection interface

Creating and Destroying Objects

Creating objects for an object-oriented database is closely related to the programming language being used to write the application program that is creating the objects. Each language binding provides *factory interfaces* for each type that contain an operation for creating new instances of the type. The operation is called new and always returns a new instance of its type.

To remove an object from a database, a programmer uses the `delete` operation.

Representing Logical Relationships

The proposed object database standard represents relationships between types using the method first introduced in Chapter 3, by placing the object identifiers of related objects within one another. Relationships are defined between two types (most typically, classes); relationships involving more than two types are not allowed.

Relationships themselves are not objects. They have no names and no database identifiers. Every relationship has two parts—the type at each end of the relationship—and relationships must therefore always be declared in pairs. The connection between two types creates a *traversal path*, a way by which an application can traverse, or navigate, the database.

As you will see in Chapter 5, the data manipulation language defined in the proposed standard uses inverses to indicate the two halves of a relationship. Once a relationship has been declared, it is up to the DBMS to manage the integrity of that relationship, ensuring that when a relationship is stored in one type of a pair, the inverse relationship is stored in the other half.

The DBMS must also ensure that deletions cascade. In other words, if an application deletes an object that is related to other objects, the relationships in the other objects must be deleted as well. The related objects can remain in the database, but the database identifier that creates the traversal path must be deleted from the remaining objects.

To indicate a "many" relationship, the attribute that will hold the object identifiers of related objects is declared as a collective attribute. It can be any of the collections discussed earlier in this chapter but is most commonly a set.

For Further Reading

The complete OODBMS proposed standard is documented in:

Cattell, R. G. G. and Barry, Douglas K., eds. *Object Database Standard: ODMG 2.0*. Morgan Kaufmann, 1997.

5

The Proposed Standards for Object Database Definition

One of the reasons that relational databases are so widely used is the existence of a standard data manipulation language (SQL). The framers of the proposed standard for object databases have therefore defined two languages, Object Definition Language (ODL) and Object Query Language (OQL), with the intent that together they will play the same role with object databases as SQL does with relational databases.

> *Note: OQL syntax is very similar to the SQL-92 standard with extensions to support object concepts. A discussion of OQL is therefore beyond the scope of this book.*

ODL is used to declare the structure of classes, including properties and operation signatures. The implementation of operations, however, requires a specific programming language and therefore is not part of ODL. To complete a object database schema, a programmer must write the implementation of the operations in C++, Java, and/or SmallTalk. It is therefore possible that a single object database schema will have implementations of the same class in more than one programming language.

Note: The sample database used for the examples in this chapter is based on the combined elementary and middle school database diagrammed in Figure 4-1.

Basic interface and Class Structure

The ODL syntax for declaring interfaces and classes is similar to the C++ and Java syntax, but not quite identical. The boundaries of a class or interface declaration, however, are taken directly from C++:

```
class class_name
{
    // class elements go here
};

interface interface_name
{
    // interface elements go here
};
```

Each declaration begins with either the keyword `class` or `interface` to identify which element is being declared. The keyword is followed by the name of the interface or class. By convention, class and interface names begin with uppercase letters.

If a class implements one or more interfaces, those interfaces are separated from the class name by a colon:

```
class class_name : interface_name
{
    // class elements go here
};
```

When a class inherits from another class, it *extends* the class:

```
class class_name extends superclass_name : interface_name
{
    // class elements go here
};
```

If a class has an extent (an object to which all objects created from a single class belong), then you specify the name of the extent in parentheses following the class name.

```
class class_name extends superclass_nam : interface_name
(extent extent_name)
{
    // class elements go here
};
```

Combining all of the syntax you have seen so far, the interfaces and classes in the school database have the basic structure shown in Listing 5-1. There are three major new classes in this version of the database. The GradeReceived class is a composite entity between a student and a teacher. For elementary school students, the relationship represents just a student's transcript. However, for middle school student there is a second relationship that indicates current class enrollments.

There are now also two types of teachers, elementary and middle school, making it easier to assign elementary students to a single teacher and middle school students to different teachers for different subjects.

Declaring Attributes

Attributes are declared by providing names and domains. Domains can be taken from any of the primitive data types discussed in Chapter 4 or from any other class in the database. Because objects cannot be created from interfaces, interfaces cannot be used as domains.

```
interface Person
{

};

interface Employee : Person
{

};

class Guardian: : Person
(extent guardians)
{

];

class Student : Person
{

};

class ElementaryStudent extends Student
(extent elementarystudents)
{
};

class MiddleSchoolStudent extends Student
(extent middelschoolstudents)
{

};

class GradeReceived
{

};

class Teacher : Employee
(extent teachers)
{

};

class ElementaryTeacher extends Teacher
{

};
```

Listing 5-1:   The major classes in the school database

```
class MiddleSchoolTeacher extends Teacher
{

};

lass MaintenanceWorker : Employee
(extent maintenanceworkers)
{

};

class MiddleSchoolStudent extends Student
(extent middelschoolstudents)
{

};

class GradeReceived
{

};

class Teacher : Employee
(extent teachers)
{

};

class ElementaryTeacher extends Teacher
{

};

class MiddleSchoolTeacher extends Teacher
{

};

class MaintenanceWorker : Employee
(extent maintenanceworkers)
{

};
```

Listing 5-1: (Continued)   The major classes in the school database

Attribute declarations have the following syntax:

```
attribute domain attribute_name;
```

The school database will need two additional classes that can be used as domains. The partial declarations of those classes can be found in Listing 5-2.

```
class Address
{
    attribute string street;
    attribute string city;
    attribute string state;
    attribute string zip;
};

class Phone
{
    attribute string areaCode;
    attribute string phoneNumber;
};
```

Listing 5-2:   Additional classes with attributes for the school database

Adding all the attributes and domains to the school database produces the partial class declarations in Listing 5-3. Notice that attributes are declared as high up in the inheritance hierarchy as possible to avoid data duplication.

There are two additional considerations about declaring attributes to keep in mind.

♦ If you want to store multiple values in an attribute, you follow the keyword `attribute` with the keyword that identifies the type of collection, such as `set` or `bag`. Then, you place the data type of the elements in the collection within < and >. For example,

```
attribute set <Phone> phoneNumbers;
```

identifies a set of Phone objects, allowing you to store multiple numbers in the same attribute. This, by the way, is not the same as storing relationships to Phone objects.

```
interface Person
{
    attribute string id;
    attribute string firstName;
    attribute string lastName;
    attribute string ssn;
    attribute date birthDate;
    attribute string gender;
    attribute Address homeAddress;
    attribute Phone homePhone;
    key id;
};

interface Employee : Person
{
    attribute date dateHired;
    attribute float payRate;
    attribute integer numbExemptions;
    attribute float healthPlanDeduction;
    attribute float retirementContribution;
};

class Guardian: : Person
(extent guardians)
{
    attribute string employer;
    attribute Address workAddress;
    attribute Phone workPhone;
    attribute Phone cellPhone;
];

class Student : Person
{
    attribute integer currentGrade;
};

class ElementaryStudent extends Student
(extent elementarystudents)
{
    attribute string classroom;
};

class MiddleSchoolStudent extends Student
(extent middelschoolstudents)
{
    attribute float gpa;
};
```

Listing 5-3:   Attributes for the interfaces and classes in the school database

```
class Teacher : Employee
(extent teachers)
{
    attribute string classroom;
};

class ElementaryTeacher extends Teacher
({

};

class MiddleSchoolTeacher extends Teacher
{
    attribute set<string> subjectsTaught;
};

class GradeReceived
{
    attribute integer year;
    attribute integer gradingPeriod;
    attribute string subject;
    attribute string grade;
};

class MaintenanceWorker : Employee
(extent maintenanceworkers)
{
    attribute string assignment;
    attribute integer hoursPerWeek[2];
    attribute float sickDays;
    attribute float vacationDays:
};
```

Listing 5-3: (Continued)   Attributes for the interfaces and classes in the school database

Instead, the entire Phone objects themselves are stored in the attribute. (Remember that relationships store only object identifiers.) You use this type of design when you would never need to search the stored objects or access them outside the context of their parent.

♦ To give a class or interface a key, use the keyword key followed by a list of the attribute or attributes that make up the key. As every concrete class in the school database ultimately implements the Person interface, it is enough to declare the key in that interface. It will then be propagated down the hierarchy.

Specifying Relationships

Relationships are different from attributes in that they store object identifiers rather than data. A relationship declaration must also include a specification of the other end of the relationship (the inverse).

The general syntax for the "one" end of a relationship is as follows:

```
relationship class_related_to relationship_name
    inverse class_related_to::relationship_name_in_related_class;
```

For example, because an elementary school student has only one teacher, the relationship would be

```
relationship Teacher teacher
    inverse Teacher::students;
```

Relationships on the "many" end use a slightly different syntax.

```
relationship collection_type<class_related_to> relationship_name
    inverse class_related_to::relationship_name_in_related_class;
```

Because an elementary school teacher has multiple students in his or her class, the inverse side of the student-to-teacher relationship would be

```
relationship set<ElementaryStudent> students
    inverse ElementaryStudent::teacher;
```

The design for the school database that we have been building appears with relationships added in Listing 5-4. As with attributes, relationships have been declared at the highest level possible in the inheritance hierarchy.

For example, the relationship between a student and grades received can be declared between the Student class and the GradeReceived class because the relationship is the same for both elementary and middle school students. However, the relationship involving current class enrollments is different for middle school and elementary school. Therefore, those relationships are declared at the lowest level in the hierarchy.

```
interface Person
{
    attribute string id;
    attribute string firstName;
    attribute string lastName;
    attribute string ssn;
    attribute date birthDate;
    attribute string gender;
    attribute Address homeAddress;
    attribute Phone homePhone;
    key id;
};

interface Employee : Person
{
    attribute date dateHired;
    attribute float payRate;
    attribute integer numbExemptions;
    attribute float healthPlanDeduction;
    attribute float retirementContribution;

};

class Guardian: : Person
(extent guardians)
{
    attribute string employer;
    attribute Address workAddress;
    attribute Phone workPhone;
    attribute Phone cellPhone;
    relationship set<Student> guardians_of
        inverse Student::children_of;
];

class Student : Person
{
    attribute integer currentGrade;
    attribute set <GradeReceived> grades;
    relationship set<Guardian> children_of
        inverse Guardian::guardians_of;
    relationship set<GradeReceived> transcript
        inverse GradeReceived::grade_for;
};
```

Listing 5-4:   The school database schema including relationships

```
class ElementaryStudent extends Student
(extent elementarystudents)
{
    attribute string classroom;
    relationship ElementaryTeacher current_teacher
        inverse ElementaryTeacher::current_students;
};

class MiddleSchoolStudent extends Student
(extent middelschoolstudents)
{
    attribute float gpa;
    relationship set<GradeReceived> classes_enrolled_in
        inverse GradeReceived::students_taking;
};

class GradeReceived
{
    attribute integer year;
    attribute integer gradingPeriod;
    attribute string subject;
    attribute string grade;
    relationship Student grade_for
        inverse Student::transcript;
    relationship Teacher assigned_by
        inverse Teacher::grades_given
    relationship MiddleSchoolStudent currently_enrolled
        inverse MiddleSchoolStudent::classes_enrolled_in;
};

class Teacher : Employee
(extent teachers)
{
    attribute string classroom;
    attribute set<string> subjectsTaught;
    relationship set<GradeReceived> grades_given
        inverse GradeReceived::assigned_by;
};

class ElementaryTeacher extends Teacher
{
    relationship set<ElementaryStudent> current_students
        inverse ElementaryStudent::current_teacher;
};
```

Listing 5-4: (Continued)   The school database schema including relationships

```
class MiddleSchoolTeacher extends Teacher
{
    attribute set<string> subjectsTaught;
    relationship set<GradeReceived> currentStudents
        inverse GradeReceived::currently_enrolled;
};

class MaintenanceWorker : Employee
(extent maintenanceworkers)
{
    attribute string assignment;
    attribute integer hoursPerWeek[2];
    attribute float sickDays;
    attribute float vacationDays:

};

class Address
{
    attribute string street;
    attribute string city;
    attribute string state;
    attribute string zip;
};

class Phone
{
    attribute string areaCode;
    attribute string phoneNumber;
};
```

Listing 5-4: (Continued)   The school database schema including relationships

Adding Operation Signatures

The final element of a class declaration is the operation signatures. Each signature must have a return data type (or void if it does not return a value), a name, and a parameter list. The signature optionally can list the exceptions that operation may trigger, or *raise*. The basic syntax for an operation is therefore

```
return_data_type operation_name (parameter_list)
    raises (exception_list);
```

Parameter Lists

A parameter list contains declarations for one or more values that will either be sent to the operation when it is invoked or returned from the operation when it finishes. Parameters are of three types.

- ♦ `in`: An `in`, or input, parameter is used only as input to the operation. If its value is modified during the execution of the operation, the change is not returned to the object that initiated the operation.
- ♦ `out`: An `out`, or output, parameter is a storage location given to an operation when it begins execution. During execution, the operation places a value in the output parameter that be accessed by the object that initiated the operation.
- ♦ `inout`: An `inout` parameter contains a value that is used as input to an operation but any value placed in it during the operation's run will also be available to the object that initiated the operation.

The entries in a parameter list are separated by commas. Each entry contains its type, its data type, and its name.

```
parameter_type parameter_data_type parameter_name
```

For example, an operation to set the grade for a student would need the grade, the year, the grading period, and the subject as input parameters:

```
in string iGrade, in integer iYear, in integer iPeriod,
    in string iSubject
```

If an operation has no parameters, then the parameter list is left empty, as in

```
()
```

Parameters can include the following types of elements:

- ♦ Primitive data types, such as integers and strings.
- ♦ Arrays, named containers for multiple values of the same data type. To declare an array parameter, you follow the

name of the parameter with brackets ([ ]), inside of which is the maximum number of elements the array can hold. For example,

```
integer values[10]
```

declares a single parameter that holds 10 integer values. When arrays are used as return values, you do not need to indicate the number of elements. For example,

```
integer[] operation_name …
```

indicates that an operation will return an array of integer values.

♦ Structures, named containers for multiple values of different data types.
♦ Objects.

You can also use structures and arrays that contain objects.

Return Values versus Output Parameters

At first, it may seem redundant for an operation to have both a return value and output parameters. However, the two means of sending values out of an operation work in different ways.

Each operation can return a single piece of data (an object, data structure, or primitive data type). Typically, a programming language sends this value back to the object that invoked the operation by including a `return` statement in its implementation. When an object needs to invoke an operation that returns a value, it first sets aside storage to receive that value.

```
float theGrossPay;
```

Then, the operation that is going to invoke an operation belonging to another object assigns the return value to the storage location.

```
theGrossPay = theEmployee.computeGrossPay();
```

Note to C++ programmers: Yes, in most cases you would use dynamic binding and pointers rather than static binding, but because this notation is found in both C++ and Java, it will be used in this book so that it is accessible to more readers.

When the operation being invoked encounters a `return` statement, it *copies* the return value from wherever it is stored into the place the invoking object has prepared. The operation knows nothing about the location into which the return value will be placed; it has no access to that storage location.

Output parameters work differently. When an object invokes an operation that uses output parameters, the programming language controlling the actions must first allocate storage space for the output parameters. The operation receives the *location* of the output parameters in main memory, which can then be used within the operation as if the operation had declared them. The operation loads the output parameters with values and, when the operation finishes, the output parameters stay in memory so that the object initiating the operation can use them. There is no copying of the parameters. The operation manipulates the storage locations directly.

Output parameters have one major benefit: There is no limit to the number that can be used. If an operation needs to send more than one value back to the object that invoked the operation, then output parameters are the only way to do so.

An operation to return a phone number does so by using output parameters.

```
void getHomePhone (out string oAreaCode, out string oPhoneNumber);
```

Notice that there is no return value, indicated by the presence of `void`. However, the two pieces of the phone number can be returned through the two output parameters.

Exceptions

As you know, an exception is a predictable error that an operation can handle. In programming language terms, we say that an operation *raises* an exception. The declaration of an object database operation can therefore include the names of exceptions that any or all methods can raise. Assuming that the exceptions are given meaningful names, then programmers writing the implementations of the operations will know which exceptions to expect and program for.

For example, any operation that expects a date as an input parameter probably wants to check that the date is within some valid range. In the school database, anyone born prior to 1988 is not likely to be a student at the school. The operation to set a student's birthdate might have the following signature:

```
void setBirthDate (in date iBirthDate)
    raises (invalidDate);
```

If more than one exception is possible, the exception names are separated by commas within the parentheses.

The Completed Schema

A generally complete schema for the school database can be found in Listing 5-5. (More needed operations would probably come to light as programmers began to write application programs that use the database.)

There are several characteristics of an object-oriented database schema that appear in this example.

```
interface Person
{
    attribute string id;
    attribute string firstName;
    attribute string lastName;
    attribute string ssn;
    attribute date birthDate;
    attribute string gender;
    attribute Address homeAddress;
    attribute Phone homePhone;
    key id;
    string getID ();
    string getFirstName ();
    string getLastName ();
    string getWholeName ();
    string getSsn ();
    date getBirthDate ();
    string getGender ();
    string getAddress ();
    string getMailingLabel ();
    void getHomePhone (out string oAreaCode, out string oPhoneNumber);
    void changeName (in string iFirst, in string iLast);
    void changeHomeAddress (in string iStreet, in string iCity, in string iState,
        in iZip);
    void changeHomePhone (in string iAreaCode, in string iPhoneNumber);
    void setSsn (in string iSsn);
    void setBirthDate (in date iBirthDate)
        raises (invalidDate);
    void setGender (in string iGender)
        raises (invalidGender);
};

interface Employee : Person
{
    attribute date dateHired;
    attribute float payRate;
    attribute integer numbExemptions;
    attribute float healthPlanDeduction;
    attribute float retirementContribution;
    date getDateHired ();
    float getPayRate ();
    void setDateHired (in date iHireDate)
        raises (invalidDate);
    void setPayRate (in float iRate)
        raises (invalidPayRate);
    float printPayCheck (in float iGrossPay);
    };
```

Listing 5-5:   The completed school database schema

```
    boolean removeGuardian (in Guardian iGuardian)
        raises (noSuchGuardian);
    Guardian[] getGuardians ();
    float getSingleGrade (in integer iYear, in integer iGradingPeriod,
        in string Subject);
};


class Guardian: : Person
(extent guardians)
{
    attribute string employer;
    attribute Address workAddress;
    attribute Phone workPhone;
    attribute Phone cellPhone;
    relationship set<Student> guardians_of
        inverse Student::children_of;
    string getEmployer ();
    string getWorkAddress ();
    void getWorkPhone (out oAreaCode, out oPhoneNumber);
    void getCellPhone (out oAreaCode, out oPhoneNumber);
    void setEmployer (in string iEmployer);
    void setWorkAddress (in string iStreet, in string iCity, in string iState,
        in iZip);
    void setWorkPhone (in string iAreaCode, in string iPhoneNumber);
    void setCellPhone (in string iAreaCode, in string iPhoneNumber);
    boolean addStudent (in Student iStudent);
    boolean removeStudent (in Student iStudent)
        raises (noSuchStudent);
    Student[] getStudents ();
];


class Student : Person
{
    attribute integer currentGrade;
    attribute set <GradeReceived> grades;
    relationship set<Guardian> children_of
        inverse Guardian::guardians_of;
    relationship set<GradeReceived> transcript
        inverse GradeReceived::grade_for;
    void printTranscript ()
        raises (noGradesRecorded);
    void printTranscript (in iYear)
        raises (noSuchYear);
    void printTranscript (in iYear, in iGradingPeriod)
        raises (noSuchYearPeriod);
```

Listing 5-5: (Continued)   The completed school database schema

```
        void printTranscript (in iSubject)
            raises (noSuchSubject);
        void recordGrade (in integer iYear, in integer iGradingPeriod,
            in string iSubject, in string grade);
        boolean addGuardian (in Guardian iGuardian);
};


class ElementaryStudent extends Student
(extent elementarystudents)
{
    attribute string classroom;
    relationship ElementaryTeacher current_teacher
        inverse ElementaryTeacher::current_students;
    string getClassroom ();
    Teacher getTeacher ();
};

class MiddleSchoolStudent extends Student
(extent middelschoolstudents)
{
    attribute float gpa;
    relationship set<GradeReceived> classes_enrolled_in
        inverse GradeReceived::students_taking;
    void computeGPA ();
    float getOverallGPA ();
    float getGradingPeriodGPA (in integer iYear, in integer iGradingPeriod)
        raises (noSuchYear, nosuchPeriod);
};

class GradeReceived
{
    attribute integer year;
    attribute integer gradingPeriod;
    attribute string subject;
    attribute string grade;
    key year, gradingPeriod;
    relationship Student grade_for
        inverse Student::transcript;
    relationship Teacher assigned_by
        inverse Teacher::grades_given
    relationship MiddleSchoolStudent currently_enrolled
        inverse MiddleSchoolStudent::classes_enrolled_in;
    string getSubject ();
    string getGrade ();
```

Listing 5-5: (Continued)   The completed school database schema

```
    integer getYear ();
    integer getGradingPeriod ();
    void setSubject (in string iSubject);
    void setGrade (in string iGrade);
    void setYear (in integer iYear);
    void setGradingPeriod (in integer iPeriod);
};


class Teacher : Employee
(extent teachers)
{
    attribute string classroom;
    attribute set<string> subjectsTaught;
    relationship set<GradeReceived> grades_given
        inverse GradeReceived::assigned_by;
    float getGrossPay ();
    string getClassroom ();
    void setClassroom (in string iClassroom);
};

class ElementaryTeacher extends Teacher
{
    relationship set<ElementaryStudent> current_students
        inverse ElementaryStudent::current_teacher;
    void printClassList ();
};

class MiddleSchoolTeacher extends Teacher
{
    attribute set<string> subjectsTaught;
    relationship set<GradeReceived> currentStudents
        inverse GradeReceived::currently_enrolled;
    void printClassLists();
    void printClassLists (in string iSubject)
        raises (noSuchSubject);
};

class MaintenanceWorker : Employee
(extent maintenanceworkers)
{
    attribute string assignment;
    attribute integer hoursPerWeek;
    attribute float sickDays;
    attribute float vacationDays:
```

Listing 5-5: (Continued)   The completed school database schema

```
    string getAssignment ();
    integer getHoursPerWeek ();
    void setAssignment (in string iAssignment);
    void setHoursPerWeek (in integer iHours)
        raises (invalidHours);
    float computeGrossPay (in float iHoursWorked)
        raises (invalidHours);
};


class Address
{
    attribute string street;
    attribute string city;
    attribute string state;
    attribute string zip;
    string displayAddress ();
    void changeAddress (in string iStreet, in string iCity, in string iState,
        in iZip);
};

class Phone
{
    attribute string areaCode;
    attribute string phoneNumber;
    string displayPhone ();
    string getAreaCode ();
    string getPhoneNumber ();
    void changePhone (in string iAreaCode, in string iPhoneNumber);
};
```

Listing 5-5: (Continued)   The completed school database schema

- ◆ Attributes and operations are declared at the highest possible level in the inheritance hierarchy. For example, operations to retrieve and modify personal data are part of the Person interface. An ID number is also assigned to someone in the Person interface.
- ◆ Operation overloading is used where appropriate to simplify work for the programmer. For example, there are four operations with the name printTranscript in the Student class. Each, however, has a different parameter list and thus a different signature. The operation without parameters prints a complete transcript. The rest print transcripts for one year, one grading period within one year,

and one subject. The operation that prints transcripts for one grading period within one year can be used to create report cards. The benefit of the overloading is that all a programmer needs to remember is one operation name, regardless of the criteria used to restrict the data that are to be printed.

Note: In this case, "print" means either display on the screen or print on paper.

♦ All attributes have "get" operations and "set" operations. These ensure that programmers can retrieve and modify every piece of data in the database.
♦ Exceptions are defined wherever possible to provide additional data validation beyond that provided by the automatic domain checking performed by a DBMS.
♦ Input parameters are named beginning with an i. Output parameter names begin with o. This is a convention used by many object-oriented programmers for clarity but is not required by the proposed standard.

Part Two

Practice

The second part of this book provides examples of the state of the art in object database technology. Chapters 6 through 8 revisit the case studies originally presented in Relational Database Design Clearly Explained *and present both pure object-oriented and hybrid designs. If you have read the relational design book, you can skip over the first part of each chapter, which discusses the environment of the case; that material is identical to the original book to provide background for those who are beginning with this book.*

The database designs in the three case studies are presented in ER diagrams and using the proposed standard ODL discussed in Chapter 5. The material is accessible to all readers; you do not need to know how to program in C++ or Java to understand them. Chapters 9 and 10, however, turn to actual implementations of object-oriented databases.

Unlike relational DBMSs, which typically use the standard nonprocedural language SQL, OODBMSs and the proposed object database standard are closely tied to object-oriented programming languages or to their own proprietary languages. If you are not a programmer, you can certainly read the implementa-tion chapters and learn a great deal, but to gain full benefit from them, you do need some programming knowledge.

6

Database Design Case Study #1: Mighty-Mite Motors

It is not unusual for a database designer to be employed to reengineer the information systems of an established corporation. As you will see from the company described in this chapter, information systems in older companies have often grown haphazardly, with almost no planning and integration. The result is a hodgepodge of data repositories that cannot provide the information needed for the corporation to function because they are isolated from one another. In such a situation, it is the job of the database designer to examine the environment as a whole and to focus on the integration of data access across the corporation as well as the design of one or more databases that will meet individual department needs.

On the bright side, an organization such as Mighty-Mite Motors, which has a history of data processing of some kind, knows quite well what it needs in an information system, even if the employees are unable to articulate those needs immediately. There will almost certainly be a collection of paper forms and reports that the organization uses regularly. Such documents specify the input and output needs of the organization and can greatly simplify a database designer's task.

Corporate Overview

Mighty-Mite Motors, Inc. (MMM) is a closely held corporation, established in 1980, that designs, develops, manufactures, and markets miniature ridable motor vehicles for children. Products include several models of cars, trucks, all-terrain vehicles, and trains (see Figure 6-1). Vehicles are powered by car batteries and achieve top speeds of about 5 mph.

At this time, MMM is organized into three divisions: Product Development, Manufacturing, and Marketing & Sales. Each division is headed by a vice president who reports directly to the CEO. (An organization chart appears in Figure 6-2.) All three divisions are housed in a single location that the corporation owns outright.

Product Development Division

The Product Development division is responsible for designing and testing new products. The division employs design engineers who use computer-aided design (CAD) software to prepare initial designs for new vehicles. Once a design is completed, between 1 and 10 prototypes are built. The prototypes are first tested in house using robotic drivers–passengers. After refinement, the prototypes are tested by live children in a variety of settings. Feedback from the testers is used to refine product designs and to make decisions about which designs should actually be manufactured for mass marketing.

Mighty-Mite Motors

Product Catalog

Winter Holiday Season 2001

Figure 6-1: Mighty-Mite Motors product catalog

Model # 001

All Terrain Vehicle: Accelerator in the handlegrip lets young riders reach speeds of up to 5 miles per hour. Vehicle stops immediately when child removes his or her hand from the handlegrip. Can carry one passenger up to 65 lbs. **Suggested retail price: $124.95**

Model #002

4 Wheel Drive Cruiser: Two-pedal drive system lets vehicle move forward at 2 ^{1}/2 mph on hard surfaces, plus reverse. Electronic speed reduction for beginners. Includes one 6v battery and one recharger. Ages 3–7 (can carry two passengers up to 65 lbs. each). **Suggested retail price: $149.99**

Figure 6-1: (Continued)   Mighty-Mite Motors product catalog

Model # 003

Classic roadster: Sounds include engine start-up, rev, shifting gears, and idle. Two forward speeds—2 $1/2$ mph and 5 mph; reverses at 2 $1/2$ mph. High-speed lockout. On/off power pedal. Power-Lock electric brake. Includes two 6v batteries and recharger. Ages 3–7 (can carry two passengers up to 65 lbs. each). **Suggested retail price: $189.99.**

Model #004

Sports car #1: Two forward speeds, 2 $1/2$ and 5 mph. Reverses at 2 $1/2$ mph. High-speed lockout. Power-Lock electric brake. Includes two 6v batteries and one recharger. Ages 3–6 (can carry two passengers up to 90 lbs. combined). **Suggested retail price: $249.99.**

Model #005

Sports car #2: Phone lets child pretend to talk while he or she drives. Two forward speeds—2 $1/2$ and 5 mph; reverses at 2 $1/2$ mph. High-speed lockout. Power-Lock electric brake. Includes two 6v batteries and one recharger. Ages 3–6 (can carry two passengers up to 90 lbs. combined). **Suggested retail price: $249.99.**

Figure 6-1: (Continued)   Mighty-Mite Motors product catalog

Model #006

Turbo Injected Porsche 911: Working stick shift—3 and 6 mph forward; 3 mph reverse. High-speed lockout. Adjustable seat. Doors, trunk, and hood open. Simulated car phone. Includes one 18v battery and recharger. Ages 3–8 (can carry two passengers up to 120 lbs combined). **Suggested retail price: $299.99.**

Model #007

Indy Car: Dual motors for cruising on a variety of surfaces, even up hills. Two forward speeds (2 $1/2$ and 5 mph), plus reverse (2 $1/2$ mph). Adjustable seat. Includes two 6v batteries and recharger. Ages 3–7 (can carry one passenger up to 80 lbs.). **Suggested retail price: $269.99.**

Model #008

2-Ton Pickup Truck: In metallic teal color. Simulated chrome engine covers and headlight with over-size wheels. 2 $1/2$ mph forward speed. Includes one 6v battery and recharger. Ages 3–7 (can carry one passenger up to 65 lbs.). **Suggested retail price: $189.99.**

Figure 6-1: (Continued)   Mighty-Mite Motors product catalog

Model #009

Santa Fe Train: Soundly engineered by a little guy or gal. A hand-operated on/off button controls the 6v battery-operated motor. Reaches speeds to 3 mph. Even includes a battery-powered "whoo whoo" whistle to greet pass-ersby. Rides on 76" x 168" oval track (sold separately) or carpet or sidewalk, indoors or outdoors. Plastic body and floorboard; steel axles and coupling pins. Bright red, blue, and yellow body features a large lift-up seat and trailing car for storage. Includes battery and charger. Ages 3–6. **Suggested retail price: $159.90.**

Model #010

Oval Track: Measures 76" by 168". **Suggested retail price: $39.90.**

Model #011

Additional 6-Pc Straight Track: Six straight sections 19" each (total 105"). **Suggested retail price: $19.90.**

Figure 6-1: (Continued) Mighty-Mite Motors product catalog

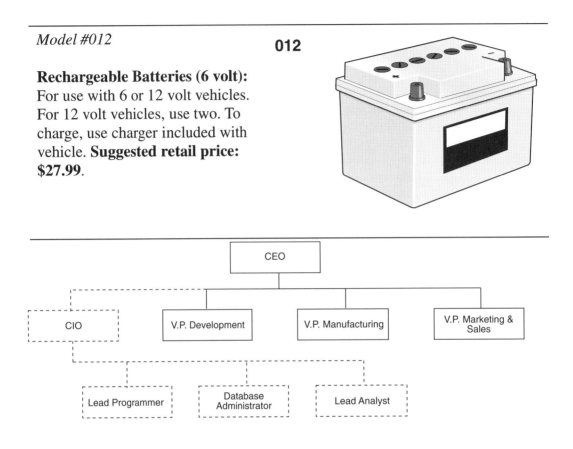

Model #012

012

Rechargeable Batteries (6 volt):
For use with 6 or 12 volt vehicles.
For 12 volt vehicles, use two. To
charge, use charger included with
vehicle. **Suggested retail price:
$27.99**.

Figure 6-2:   Mighty-Mite Motors organization chart

Manufacturing Division

The Manufacturing division is responsible for producing products
for mass market sales. Manufacturing procures its own raw materials and manages its own operations, including personnel (hiring,
firing, scheduling) and assembly line management. Manufacturing
maintains the inventory of products ready for sale. It also handles
shipping of products to resellers, based on sales information received from Marketing & Sales.

Marketing & Sales Division

MMM sells directly to toy stores and catalog houses; the corporation has never used distributors. Marketing & Sales employs a staff of 25 salespeople who make personal contacts with resellers. Salespeople are responsible for distributing catalogs in their territories, visiting and/or calling potential resellers, and taking reseller orders. Order accounting is handled by Marketing & Sales. As noted earlier, Marketing & Sales transmits shipping information to Manufacturing, which takes care of actual product delivery.

Current Information Systems

MMM's information systems are a hodgepodge of computers and applications that have grown up with little corporate planning. The Product Development division relies primarily on stand-alone CAD workstations. In contrast to the sophistication of the CAD workstations, testing records are kept and analyzed manually. Product Development employs product designers (some of whom function as project leaders) and clerical support staff, but no information systems personnel. Attempts to have clerical staff develop simple database applications to store data about children who test new products and the results of those tests have proved futile. It has become evident that Product Development needs information systems professionals, and although the division is willing to hire IS staff, corporate management has decided to centralize the IS staff, rather than add to a decentralized model.

Manufacturing uses a stand-alone minicomputer to track purchases and inventory levels of raw materials, personnel scheduling, manufacturing line scheduling, and finished product inventory. Each of these applications was written in COBOL in the early 1980s, shortly after the corporation was established. The data used by a Manufacturing application are contained in files that do not share information with any of the other applications. Manufacturing employs a data processing staff of five, most of whom are COBOL maintenance programmers. Although these programmers are talented, the basic applications no longer meet the needs of the Manufacturing division and management has determined that it isn't cost effective to rewrite them from scratch.

Marketing & Sales, which wasn't computerized until 1987, has a local area network (LAN) consisting of one server and 15 workstations. The server provides shared applications such as word processing and spreadsheets. It also maintains a marketing and sales database, which has been developed using dBase III Plus. The database suffers from several problems, including a limit of 10 users at one time and concurrency control problems that lead to severe data inconsistencies. The marketing and sales database was developed by one member of the division's three-person IS staff. However, that individual left the company in 1992 and no current staff member totally understands the software. Regardless of the amount of time spent trying to maintain the database, inaccurate data continue to be introduced.

The Marketing & Sales LAN has no data communications capabilities. Salespeople therefore must transmit hard copies of their orders to the central office, where the orders are manually keyed into the existing database. (Some of the salespeople do have laptop computers, but because the LAN has no modems, the salespeople cannot connect to it.)

Reengineering Project

Because MMM seems to have lost its strategic advantage in the marketplace, the CEO has decided to undertake a major systems reengineering project. The overall thrust of the project is to provide an integrated information system that will support better evaluation of product testing, better analysis of sales patterns, and better control of the manufacturing process. New information systems will be based on a client–server model and include one or more databases running on a network of servers, workstations, and PCs.

New Information Systems Division

The first step in the reengineering project is to establish an Information Systems division. This new division will also be housed in the corporate headquarters, along with the three existing divisions. To accommodate the new division, MMM will be constructing a 10,000 square foot addition to its building.

MMM is in the process of searching for a Chief Information Officer (CIO). This individual, who will report directly to the CEO, will manage the new division and be responsible for overseeing the reengineering of computer-based information systems that will handle all of the corporation's operations.

All current IS personnel (those who work for the Manufacturing and Marketing & Sales divisions) will be transferred to the new IS division. The division will hire (either internally or externally) three management-level professionals: a Lead Programmer (responsible for overseeing application development), a Database Administrator (responsible for database design and management), and a Lead Analyst (responsible for overseeing systems analysis and design efforts). Retraining in the client–server model and client–server development tools will be provided for all current employees who are willing to make the transition. Those who are unwilling to move to the new development environment will be laid off.

Basic System Goals

The CEO has defined the following goals for the reengineering project:

- ◆ Develop a corporation-wide data administration plan that documents all databases to be developed for the corporation. This documentation will include ER diagrams, schemas, and data dictionaries.
- ◆ Provide an application road map that documents all application programs that will be needed to provide access to corporate databases.

- Create a time line for the installation of corporate data-bases and the development of application programs.
- Specify hardware changes and/or acquisitions that will be necessary to support access to the databases from within the headquarters building and by salespeople who are traveling. Although not every employee will have access to every database, the equipment should nonetheless make universal access possible, providing maximum flexibility for future growth.
- Develop and implement a security plan that supports access restrictions to the corporate databases.
- Install the databases and develop application programs.
- Acquire and install necessary hardware upgrades.

Current Business Processes

To aid the systems analysts in their assessment of MMM's information systems needs, the CEO of MMM asked all existing division heads to document the way in which information is currently processed. This documentation, which also includes some information about what an improved system should do, provides a starting point for the redesign of both business and IS processes.

The Sales and Ordering Processes

MMM receives orders at its plant in two ways: either by telephone directly from customers or from members of the sales staff who have visited customers in person. Orders from the remote sales staff usually arrive by fax or overnight courier.

Each order is taken on a standard order form (Figure 6-3). If the order arrives by fax, it will already be on the correct form. Telephone orders are written directly onto the form. Several times a day a clerk enters the orders into the dBase III database application. Unfortunately, if the sales office is particularly busy, order entry may be delayed. This backup has a major impact on production line scheduling and thus on the company's ability to fill orders. The new information system must streamline the order entry process, including the electronic transmission of orders from the field and the direct entry of in-house orders into electronic form.

The in-house sales staff has no access to the computer files that show the current finished goods inventory. They are therefore unable to tell customers when their orders will ship. They can, however, tell customers how many orders are ahead of theirs to be filled and, based on general manufacturing timetables, come up with an approximation of how long it will take to ship a given order. One of the goals of the information systems reengineering project is to provide better company-wide knowledge of how long it will take to fill customer orders.

The Manufacturing, Inventory, and Shipping Processes

The MMM Manufacturing division occupies a large portion of the MMM facility. The division controls the actual manufacturing lines (three assembly lines), a storage area for finished goods, a storage area for raw materials, and several offices for supervisory and clerical staff.

The manufacturing process is triggered when a batch of order forms is received each morning by the manufacturing office. (The batch consists of all orders that were entered into the sales database the previous working day.) A secretary takes the individual order forms and compiles a report summarizing the number ordered by model (Figure 6-4). This report is then given to the Manufacturing Supervisor, whose responsibility it is to schedule which model will be produced on each manufacturing line each day.

The scheduling process is somewhat complex, because the Manufacturing Supervisor must take into account previously placed orders, which have determined the current manufacturing schedule, and current inventory levels as well as the new orders when adjusting the schedule. The availability of raw materials and the time it takes to modify a manufacturing line to produce a different model also enter into the scheduling decision. This is one function that MMM's management understands will be almost impossible to automate; there is too much human expertise involved to translate it

Mighty-Mite Motors

Customer Order Form

Customer #:

Order date:

Name:

Street:

City: State: Zip:

Voice phone #:   Fax:

First name: Contact person   Last name:

Item #	Quantity	Unit Price	Line Total

Order total:

Figure 6-3:   Mighty-Mite Motors order form

Mighty-Mite Motors
Order Summary

mm/dd/yyyy

Model #	Quantity Ordered
001	75
002	150
004	80
005	35
008	115
009	25
010	25
011	15

Figure 6-4:   Mighty-Mite Motors order summary report format

into an automatic process. However, it is vital that the Manufacturing Supervisor have access to accurate, up-to-date information about orders, inventory, and the current line schedule so that judgements can be made based on as much hard data as possible.

As finished vehicles come off the assembly line, they are packed for shipping, labeled, and sent to finished goods storage. Each shipping carton contains one vehicle, which is marked with its model number, serial number, and date of manufacturing. The Shipping Manager, who oversees finished goods storage and shipping, ensures that newly manufactured items are entered into the existing inventory files.

The Shipping Manager receives customer order forms after the order report has been completed. (Photocopies of the order forms are kept in the Marketing & Sales office as backup.) The orders are placed in a box in reverse chronological order so that the oldest orders can be filled first. The Shipping Manager checks orders against inventory levels by looking at the inventory level output screen (Figure 6-5). If the manager sees that there is enough inventory to

fill an order, then the order is given to a shipping clerk for processing. If there isn't enough inventory, then the order is put back in the
box, where it will be checked again the following day. Under this
system, no partial orders are filled because they would be extremely
difficult to track. (The reengineered information system should allow handling of partial shipments.)

Current Finished Goods Inventory Levels
mm/dd/yy

INV#	NUMBER ON HAND
001	215
002	35
003	180
004	312
005	82
006	5
007	212
008	189
009	37
010	111
011	195
012	22

Figure 6-5:   Mighty-Mite Motors inventory screen layout

Shipping clerks are given orders to fill. They create shipping labels
for all vehicles that are part of a shipment. The cartons are labeled
and set aside for pickup by UPS. The shipping clerks create UPS
manifests (which also serve as packing slips), ensure that the items
being shipped are removed from the inventory file, and return the
filled orders to the Shipping Manager. The orders are then marked
as filled and returned to Marketing & Sales. The reengineered information system should automate the generation of pick-lists, packing slips, and updating of finished goods inventory.

MMM's raw materials inventory is maintained on a just-in-time basis. The Manufacturing Supervisor checks the line schedule (Figure
6-6) and the current raw materials inventory (Figure 6-7) daily to determine what raw materials need to be ordered. This process relies
heavily on the Manufacturing Supervisor's knowledge of which

materials are needed for which model vehicle. MMM's CEO is very concerned about this process because the Manufacturing Supervisor, while accurate in scheduling the manufacturing line, is nowhere near as accurate in judging raw materials needs. The result is that occasionally manufacturing must stop because raw materials have run out. The CEO would therefore like to see ordering of raw materials triggered automatically. The new information system should keep track of the raw materials needed to produce each model and, based on the line schedule and a reorder point established for each item, generate orders for items when needed.

Raw materials are taken from inventory each morning as each manufacturing line is being set up for the day's production run. The inventory files are modified immediately after all raw materials have been removed for a given manufacturing line. There is no way to automate the reduction of inventory; however, the new information system should make it easy for nontechnical users to update inventory levels.

The Product Testing and Support Function

MMM's top management makes decisions about which model vehicles to produce based on data from three sources: product testing, customer registrations, and problem reports.

Customer registrations are received on cards packaged with sold vehicles (Figure 6-8). Currently, the registration cards are filed by customer name. However, MMM would also like access to these data by model and serial number to make it easier to notify customers if a recall occurs. Management would also like summaries of the data by model purchased, age of primary user, gender of primary user, and who purchased the vehicle for the child.

Problem reports (Figure 6-9) are taken by customer support representatives who work within the product testing division. These reports include the serial number and model experiencing problems along with the date and type of problem. Currently, the problem descriptions are nonstandard, written in whatever language the customer support representative happens to use. It is therefore difficult

Line Schedule
mm/dd/yy

mm/dd/yy
Line #1: Model 005	100 units
Line #2: Model 007	150 units
Line #3: Model 010	100 units

mm/dd/yy
Line #1: Model 003	200 units
Line #2: Model 005	150 units
Line #3: Model 008	300 units

mm/dd/yy
Line #1: Model 006	150 units
Line #2: Model 008	100 units
Line #3: Model 002	300 units

:
:
:

Total production scheduled:

Model 002	300 units
Model 003	200 units
Model 005	250 units
Model 006	150 units
Model 007	150 units
Model 008	400 units
Model 010	100 units

Figure 6-6:   **Mighty-Mite Motors line schedule report format**

to summarize problem reports to get an accurate picture of which models are experiencing design problems that should be corrected. MMM would therefore like to introduce a standardized method for describing problems, probably through a set of problem codes. The result should be regular reports on the problems reported for each model that can be used to help make decisions about which models

```
┌─────────────────────────────────────────────────────────────┐
│              Current Raw Materials Inventory Levels           │
│                         mm/dd/yy                              │
│       ITEM#          ITEM              QUANTITY ON HAND        │
│       001       Plastic #3                 95 lbs             │
│       002       Red dye 109                25 gals            │
│       003       Wheel 12"                  120 each           │
│       004       Plastic #4                 300 lbs            │
│       005       Yellow dye 110             5 gals             │
│       006       Yellow dye 65              30 gals            │
│       007       Strut 15"                  99 each            │
│       008       Axle 18"                   250 each           │
│       009       Blue dye 25                18 gals            │
│       010       Plastic #8                 350 lbs            │
│       011       Cotter pin small           515 each           │
│       012       Cotter pin medium          109 each           │
└─────────────────────────────────────────────────────────────┘
```

Figure 6-7:   Mighty-Mite Motors raw materials inventory screen layout

to continue, which to discontinue, which to redesign, and which to recall.

MMM does not repair its own products. When a problem report is received, the customer is either directed to return the product to the store where it was purchased for an exchange (during the first 30 days after purchase) or directed to an authorized repair center in the customer's area. In the latter case, the problem report is faxed to the repair center so that it is waiting when the customer arrives. MMM does not plan to change this procedure because it currently provides quick, excellent service to customers and alleviates the need for MMM to stock replacement parts. (Replacement parts are stocked by the authorized repair centers.)

Product test results are recorded on paper forms (Figure 6-10). After a testing period is completed, the forms are collated manually to produce a summary of how well a new product performed. MMM would like the test results stored within an information system so that the testing report can be produced automatically, saving time and effort. Such a report will be used to help decide which new models should be placed in production.

Please register your Mighty-Mite Motors vehicle

By registering you receive the following benefits:

- Validation of the warranty on your vehicle,
  making it easier to obtain warranty service
  if ever necessary.
- Notification of product updates relating to your vehicle.
- Information mailings about enhancements to your vehicle
  and other products that may be of interest.

First name

Last name

Street

City   State   Zip

Phone #:

Model #   Serial #

Age of primary user of vehicle: _____

Gender: ☐ Male   ☐ Female

Fold Here. Tape closed; do not staple.

Date of purchase: ☐☐ ☐☐ ☐☐

Place of purchase:

Where did you first learn about Mighty-Mite Motors?

☐ Advertisement in a magazine or newspaper
☐ Friend's recommendation
☐ In-store display
☐ Catalog
☐ Other

What features of the vehicle prompted your purchase?

☐ Size
☐ Color
☐ Speed
☐ Safety features
☐ Cost
☐ Other

What is the relationship of the purchaser to the primary user?

☐ Parent
☐ Grandparent
☐ Aunt/Uncle
☐ Friend
☐ Other

Figure 6-8:   Mighty-Mite Motors purchase registration form

Designing the Database

The most effective approach to the design of a database (or collection of databases) for an environment as diverse as that presented by Mighty-Mite Motors usually involves breaking the design into components indicated by the organization of the company. As the design evolves, the designer can examine the entities and their relationships to determine where parts of the organization will need to share data. Working on one portion of the design at a time also sim-

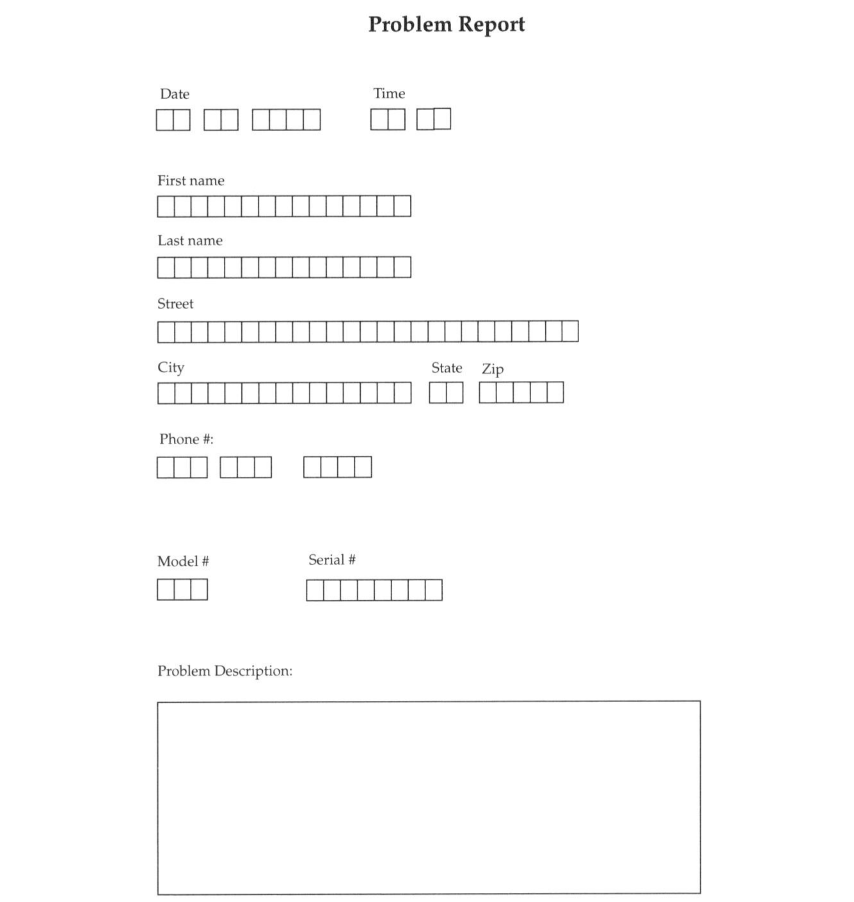

Problem Report

Date   Time

First name

Last name

Street

City   State   Zip

Phone #:

Model #   Serial #

Problem Description:

Figure 6-9:   Mighty-Mite Motors problem report

plifies dealing with what might at first seem to be an overwhelmingly large database environment.

The Mighty-Mite Motors database environment seems to fall naturally into the following areas:

♦ Manufacturing (including finished goods inventory and raw materials ordering)
♦ Sales to toy stores and shipping of products ordered
♦ Reported purchases

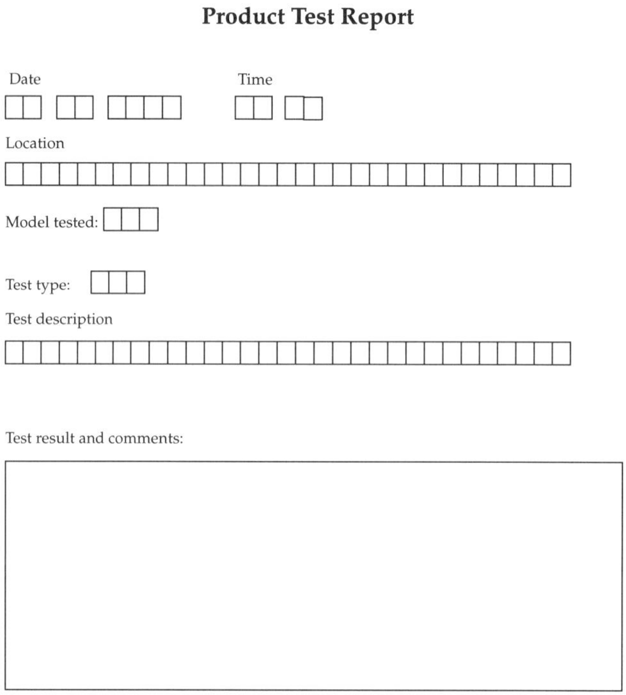

Product Test Report

Date   Time

□□ □□ □□□□   □□ □□

Location

□□□□□□□□□□□□□□□□□□□□□□□□□□□□□□□□□

Model tested: □□□

Test type: □□□

Test description

□□□□□□□□□□□□□□□□□□□□□□□□□□□□□□□□

Test result and comments:

Figure 6-10: Mighty-Mite Motors product test report

   ♦ Testing
   ♦ Problem handling

Examining the Data Flows

In this particular situation, a data flow diagram can be of enormous use in identifying where data are shared by various parts of an organization. The top-level DFD (the *context diagram*) in Figure 6-11 actually tells us very little. It indicates that three sources outside the company provide data: customers (the stores to which the company sells), purchasers (the individuals who purchase products from the stores), and raw materials suppliers. Somehow, all that data is used by a general process named "Manufacture & Sell Products" to keep the company in business.

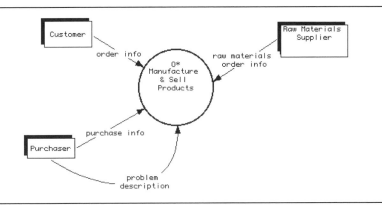

Figure 6-11:   Context DFD for Mighty-Mite Motors

However, the level 1 DFD (Figure 6-12) is much more telling. As the data handling processes are broken down, five data stores emerge:

♦ Raw materials: This data store holds both the raw materials inventory and the orders for raw materials.

♦ Product data: The product data store contains data about the products being manufactured and the finished goods inventory.

♦ Customer orders: This data store contains customer information as well as order data.

♦ Purchaser data: The purchaser data store contains information about the individuals who purchase products and the products they have purchased.

♦ Problem data: This final data store contains problem reports.

As you examine the processes that interact with these five data stores, you will find a number of processes that manipulate data in more than one data store as well as data stores that are used by more than one process:

♦ The raw materials data store is used by the raw materials ordering and the manufacturing processes.

♦ Product data are used by manufacturing, sales, shipping, and purchaser registration.

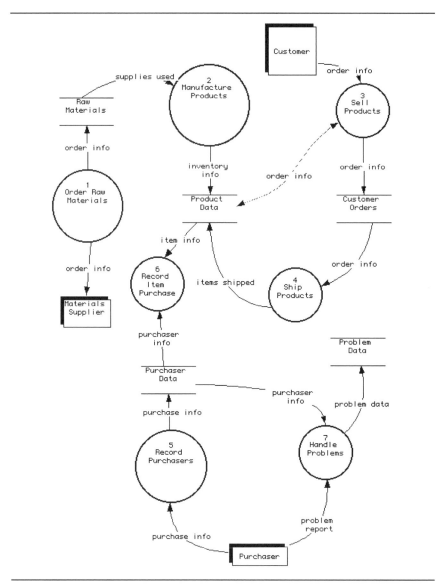

Figure 6-12: Level 1 DFD for Mighty-Mite Motors

♦ Customer order data are used by sales and shipping.
♦ The purchaser data store is used by purchaser registration and problem handling.

♦ The problem data store, used only by problem handling, is the only data store not shared by multiple processes.

The raw materials ordering process is the only process that uses only a single data store. Nonetheless, the level 1 DFD makes it very clear that there is no instance in which a single process uses a single data store without interaction with other data stores and processes. Given that each process in the DFD probably represents all or part of an application program, this suggests that the database designer should probably consider a single database, rather than a set of databases.

The DFD makes it very clear that the need for the integration of the various data stores is very strong. In addition, Mighty-Mite Motors is a relatively small business and therefore a single database that manages all needed aspects of the company will not grow unreasonably large. Ultimately, the database designer may decide to distribute the database onto multiple servers, placing portions of it that are used most frequently in the divisions where that use occurs. The database design, however, will be the same regardless of whether the final implementation is centralized or distributed. The essential decision is to create a single database rather than several smaller, isolated databases that must somehow share data.

For Reference: The Relational Design

The relational design of the MMM database contains the following tables:

```
model (model numb, model_description, suggested_retail_price,
    shipping_weight, time_to_manufacture)
test (model_numb, test_date, test_location, test_code, test_results)
test_types (test_code, test_description)
customers (customer_numb, customer_name, customer_street, customer_
    street, customer_city, customer_state, customer_zip, contact_
    person, contact_phone, contact_fax)
orders (order_numb, customer_numb, order_date, order_total, order_
    filled)
order_line (order_numb, model_numb, quantity_ordered, unit_price,
    line_total, all_shipped)
```

```
shipments (order_numb, model_numb, shipping_date, quantity_shipped)
product (serial_numb, model_numb, date_manufactured, status_code,
    order_numb, date_shipped)
product_status (status_code, status_description)
raw_material (material_id_numb, material_name, unit_of_measurement,
    quantity_in_stock, reorder_point)
supplier (supplier_numb, supplier_name, supplier_street, supplier_
    city, supplier_state, supplier_zip, supplier_contact, supplier_
    phone)
material_order (po_numb, supplier_numb, material_order_date,
    material_order_total)
material_order_line (po_numb, material_id_numb, material_quantity,
    material_cost_each, material_line_cost)
material_needed (model_numb, material_id_numb, quantity_needed)
manufacturing_line (line_numb, line_status)
line_schedule (line_numb, production_date, model_numb, quantity_to_
    produce)
owner (owner_numb, owner_first_name, owner_last_name, owner_street,
    owner_city, owner_state, owner_zip, owner_phone)
purchase (serial_numb, owner_numb, age, gender, purchase_date,
    purchase_place, learn_code, relationship)
purchase_feature (serial_numb, feature_code)
learn_about (learn_code, learn_description)
feature (feature_code, feature_description)
problem_report (serial_numb, problem_date, problem_time, problem_
    type_code, problem_description)
problem_type (problem_type_code, problem_type_description)
```

Designing the Object-Relational Database

One of the most challenging aspects of having object-oriented capabilities added to a relational DBMS is deciding whether a particular schema can benefit from a design that incorporates objects. Mighty-Mite Motors is one of those schemas that does not benefit greatly from a hybrid approach.

Why not? There are no instances of inheritance in the MMM database environment. In addition, the major entities, such as products and models, participate in multiple relationships.. Therefore, changing them into objects and then placing entire objects into related tables would result in unnecessary duplicated data and the introduction of significant data integrity problems.

The best use of the object technololgy in this particular database environment is to handle complex values, such as addresses and telephone numbers. Such objects can be reused throughout the database, simplifying the formatting, searching, and general handling of these elements.

There is no specific ER diagramming technique that has been adapted for hybrid schemas. Therefore, you will see a slight modification of UML for that purpose. Specifically, an attribute whose domain is a class is connected to its class with a dashed gray line. The line has a single arrow that points to the class.

> Note: The ER diagrams that you will see in the remainder of this chapter share the same data dictionary as the ERD for the pure relational design. Therefore, the names of some entities were changed slightly so that multiple entities with similar, but not identical, structures could exist in the data dictionary.

The first portion of the ER diagram for the hybrid MMM design can be found in Figure 6-13. There are three classes in this illustration: LineCost, Address, and Phone. The LineCost class contains the number of items of something that have been ordered and the cost of each item. One of the class's operations then computes and stores the line cost.

The Address class takes a value that may consume multiple columns in a relation and collapses them down to a single column. The major value in doing this is conceptual clarity. You also gain simplicity in the relational design.

In a typical relational database, a telephone number is stored as a single text string. However, breaking it up into its constitutent parts makes it possible to search the database by any of those parts and therefore enables access that was not previously available. (You could do so by searching in a text string, but such a search would be quite slow.) Marketing personnel, for example, could search for all customers within a specific exchange or map purchases by exchange to see purchasing patterns.

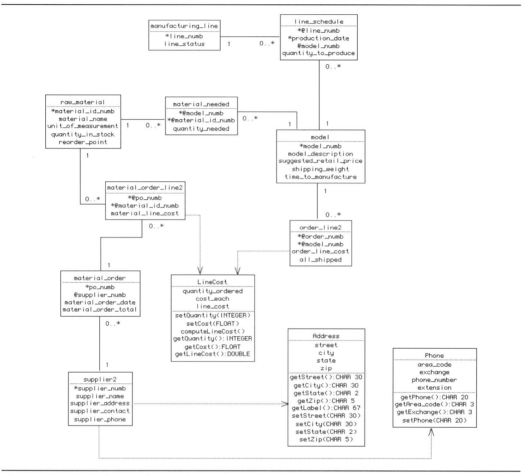

Figure 6-13:   ERD for an object-relational design (part I)

The second portion of the MMM hybrid ER diagram appears in Figure 6-14. Notice that the Customer2 entity has two lines going from the entity to the Phone class. This occurs because the customer_ phone and customer_fax attributes have the same domain: the Phone class. The remainder of this portion of the design is exactly the same as the pure relational design.

Figure 6-15 contains the final portion of the ER diagram. The Owner2 relation is the most significantly changed relation when compared with the pure relational design. The owner's name is

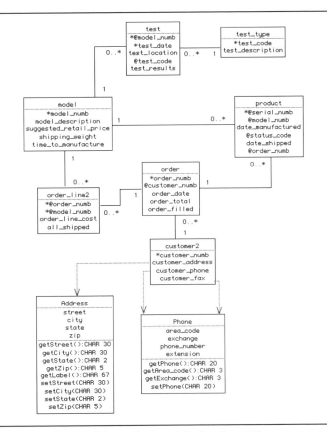

Figure 6-14:   ERD for an object-relational design (part II)

now an object of the Name class. The owner's address and telephone number are now objects of the Address and Phone classes,
respectively.

The resulting relations are as follows:

```
model (model numb, model_description, suggested_retail_price,
    shipping_weight, time_to_manufacture)
test (model numb, test date, test_location, test_code, test_results)
test_types (test_code, test_description)
customers (customer numb, customer_name, customer_address, contact_
    person, contact_phone, contact_fax)
orders (order numb, customer_numb, order_date, order_total, order_
    filled)
order_line (order numb, model numb, order_line_cost, all_shipped)
shipments (order numb, model numb, shipping date, quantity_shipped)
```

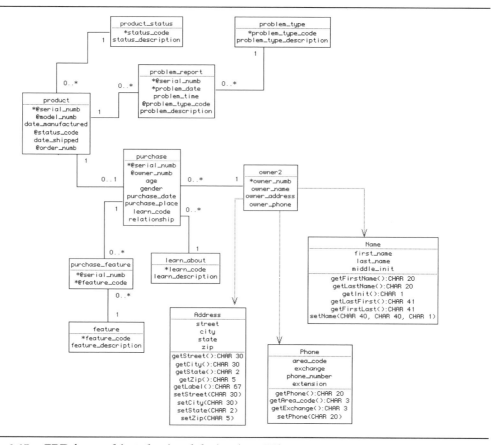

Figure 6-15:   ERD for an object-rleational design (part III)

```
product (serial_numb, model_numb, date_manufactured, status_code,
    order_numb, date_shipped)
product_status (status_code, status_description)
raw_material (material_id_numb, material_name, unit_of_measurement,
    quantity_in_stock, reorder_point)
supplier (supplier_numb, supplier_name, supplier_address, supplier_
    contact, supplier_phone)
material_order (po_numb, supplier_numb, material_order_date,
    material_order_total)
material_order_line (po_numb, material_id_numb, material_line_cost)
material_needed (model_numb, material_id_numb, quantity_needed)
manufacturing_line (line_numb, line_status)
line_schedule (line_numb, production_date, model_numb, quantity_to_
    produce)
owner (owner_numb, owner_name, owner_address, owner_phone)
```

```
purchase (serial_numb, owner_numb, age, gender, purchase_date,
    purchase_place, learn_code, relationship)
purchase_feature (serial_numb, feature_code)
learn_about (learn_code, learn_description)
feature (feature_code, feature_description)
problem_report (serial_numb, problem_date, problem_time, problem_
    type_code, problem_description)
problem_type (problem_type_code, problem_type_description)
```

When you compare the hybrid design with the traditional relational design, you will notice that the hybrid design is smaller. Because multiple values—such as the parts of an address—can now be stored in a single column, the design is somewhat simpler. In addition, because the classes are common enough to appear in several places in the design, code for commonly performed operations can be written once and reused as needed, saving application development time. Therefore, although the design does not take advantage of any of the more sophisticated characteristics of object-orientation, there is still some justification for using objects.

The major drawback to adding objects to this relational design is the need for programmers to complete the objects. You do not need to be a programmer to use SQL to create and manipulate a pure relational schema. However, to complete the hybrid schema and to make the data stored in objects available to users, a programmer must write the code for the LineCost, Name, Address, and Phone class operations.

Designing the Pure Object Database

A pure object database is a viable option for Mighty-Mite Motors, despite there being no use of inheritance. As you will see, the object-oriented implementation avoids a great deal of duplicated data while at the same time allows reuse of structural elements such as addresses and telephone numbers that are found in many classes.

The ER Diagram

The first part of the ER diagram can be found in Figure 6-16. This diagram includes the data types of the attributes, so you can see where classes have been used as data types. The utility classes (those used only as data types) appear on the diagram in shadowed boxes and do not participate in any relationships.

> Note: These ER diagrams include attributes for all classes but only a few of the operations because of space considerations. You can find the operations later in this chapter in the ODL syntax for the schema.

Unlike a relational database, where relationships are indicated by the presence of additional matching attributes, there is no equivalent of foreign keys in a pure-object database. Therefore, some of the class rectangles in the ER diagram may appear to be missing something.

For example, consider the MaterialNeeded class. Only one attribute appears on the diagram (quantity_needed). If you have been working for some time with a relational database, then you may be thinking that you need to add the material_id_numb and model_numb attributes. However, in an object-oriented database, you store the object identifiers of related objects, not entire objects or foreign key values. Therefore, the raw material and model to which the quantity of material needed applies are not attributes of the Material-Needed class. You instead specify the relationships separately, using the ODL relationship syntax (or whatever syntax is used by your OODBMS).

The utility classes are a different situation. When Address, for example, appears as the data type of an attribute, that indicates that an object of the Address class will actually be stored within the containing object. In other words, the containing object will have the data values for the Address object as part of its data, rather than storing an object identifier of an Address object.

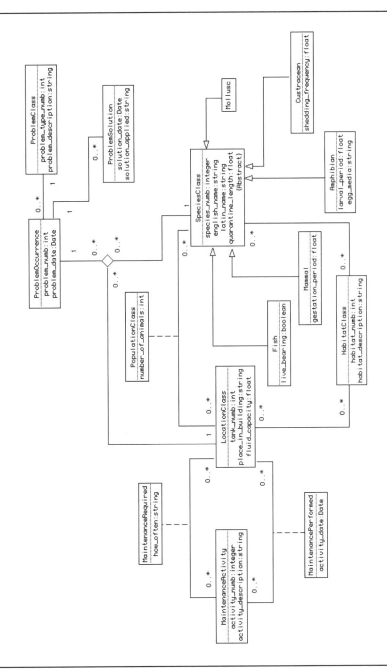

Figure 6-16:   ERD for a pure object design (part I)

In general, you use a relationship when storing data values within objects would result in unnecessary duplicated data because the same data values are needed in more than one place. You use a class as the data type for an attribute when the data should be part of the containing object and those data do not apply to any other object. Another way to look at this is to note that relationships are for shared data; attributes are for data that are not shared.

Figure 6-17 contains the second portion of the object-oriented ER diagram. It contains objects for the purchase of products and for product testing. (Keep in mind that this database is somewhat unusual for a production database because the company is tracking individual products by their serial numbers, much in the same way cars are tracked by their vehicle identification numbers, or VINs.)

The handling of TestClass presents a bit of a dilemma. The TestType class exists for two reasons: to provide a reference list of correct test type names for use in objects created from the TestClass and to make it easier to access tests by type. By the same token, a many-to-many relationship exists between ModelClass and TestType. Should TestClass be a composite entity?

But in Figure 6-17, TestClass is a regular entity. Why? Because a test has an independent existence. It does not depend on TestType for its existence, although it does depend on ModelClass. (You cannot have data about a test if you do not know which model is being tested!) In this particular instance, what appears to be a composite entity—because it just happens to reduce a many-to-many relationship into two one-to-many relationships—is really a regular entity with a real-world existence of its own.

The final portion of the ER diagram can be found in Figure 6-18. Notice that the ProblemReport class is similar to TestClass in that although it does sit in the middle of a many-to-many relationship, it is nonetheless a standard entity because it has an independent existence of its own and depends on only one of its parents. (Problem-Report does *not* depend on ProblemType.)

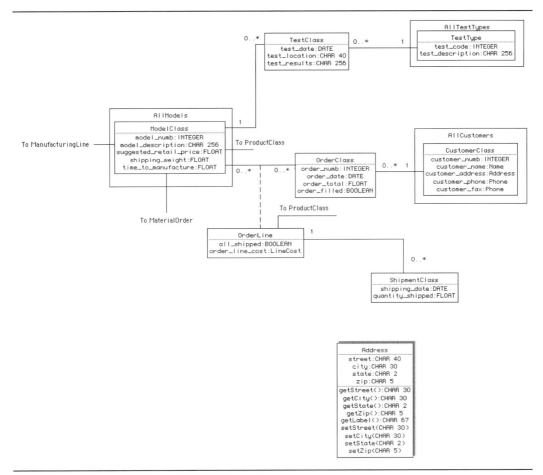

Figure 6-17:   ERD for a pure object design (part II)

Figure 6-18 also contains direct many-to-many relationships, the relationship between FeatureClass and ProductClass and the relationships LearnAbout and ProductClass. Earlier in this book, you read that it is possible to lose information with direct many-to-many relationships. However, in this case, there will not be a problem unless someone tries to extrapolate the relationships and apply them to classes further up the relationship hierarchy.

For example, it is impossible to generalize accurately the features that cause people to purchase a specific model from the relationship

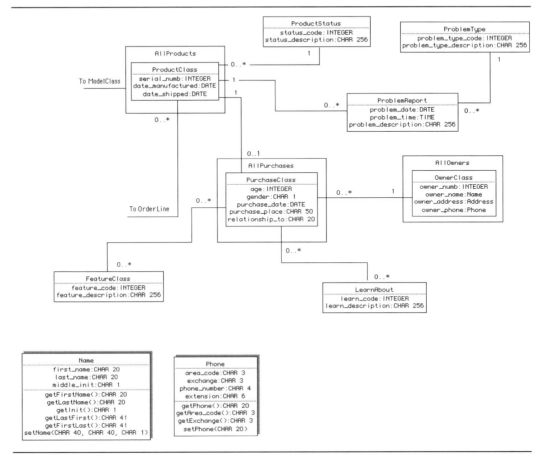

Figure 6-18:   ERD for a pure object design (part III)

between features and products. Because a single feature can be related to products that are different models and each product can be related to many features, there is the chance that we might associate the wrong feature with the wrong model. (See Chapter 3 for details of this problem.)

There are two ways around the problem. The first is to use an application program that checks each product registration to determine its model number and then assembles the features based on common model numbers. The second is to introduce an additional relationship into the database, a direct many-to-many relationship between FeatureClass and ModelClass.

No matter which you do, you add either application complexity (and application development time) or design complexity to the database environment. This is the downside to having direct many-to-many relationships in a database design. If you need to see a grouping of the features by model frequently, then the additional relationship is probably worth the overhead of maintaining the relationship. However, if that access is performed infrequently, then an application program may do the job for you, especially if the program does not take a great deal of effort to develop and test.

The ODL Class Syntax

The ODL syntax for the pure object design can be found at the end of this chapter in Listing 6-1. This design is more complete than the ER diagrams in that it includes many more operations. Notice that each class has accessor (get) and mutator (set) methods. Each class that is at the "one" end of a relationship—it has a set of object identifiers in its relationship variable—also contains methods to display related data.

In addition, many classes have operations that require traversing through one or more relationships. For example, ProductClass has an operation that retrieves the owner of the product and an operation that retrieve's the product's model. Both of these methods return object identifiers, so that when the operation finishes, all information about the owner and model is easily accessible.

Finally, many classes have operations that insert and remove values from relationship attributes. When looking for these operations, keep in mind that because inverses have been declared for all relationships, it may not be necessary to have insert and removal operations at both sides of a relationship. Many DBMSs will automatically insert or remove from the second side of a relationship once an operation has inserted or removed a object identifier on the first side. (This is an implementation-dependent issue and you must therefore check with your particular DBMS to find out how it behaves.)

Beyond these types of operations, there is little more that the objects themselves can do in this particular database. (In the case of ModelClass, however, the operations described earlier are more than enough!) A user working with a query language or an application program will then need to use the extents to access all objects of a specific class and create output by calling one or more operations for each object.

As you are looking at these classes, consider the navigational nature of object-oriented databases. For example, how do you access an object created from PurchaseClass? A purchase has no unique identifier. In fact, there may be many purchase objects with the same data. They are distinguished only by the owner object to which they are related. Unless the database designers give purchases a unique key, the only way to access them will be to navigate from a related object, be it an owner or a product. (You can also access purchases from FeatureClass and LearnAbout, but given the meaning of those relationships, it is more likely for access to go the other way.)

This is not necessarily a significant failing in the design. Think about how the database will be used. When an owner calls in, he or she will need to know either the serial number of the product or the date on which it was purchased. It is much more likely that the owner will remember or be able to find those two pieces of data than it will be to remember a "purchase number."

```
class ModelClass
(extent AllModels}
{
    attribute int model_numb;
    attribute string model_description;
    attribute float suggested_retail_price;
    attribute float shipping_weight;
    attribute float time_to_manufacture;
    key model_numb;
```

Listing 6-1:   ODL syntax for the Might-Mite Motors object-oriented database

```
    relationship set<LineSchedule> production_scheduled
        inverse LineSchedule::which_model;
    relationship set<MaterialNeeded> material_used
        inverse MaterialNeeded::model;
    relationship set<OrderLine> orders_on
        inverse OrderLine::model;
    relationahip set<TestClass> tests_performed
        inverse TestClass::model;
    relationship set<ProductClass> products_made
        inverse ProductClass::model;
    int getModelNumb();
    string getModelDescription();
    float getRetailPrice();
    float getWeight();
    float getTime();
    void setModelNumb (in int iNumb);
    void setDescription (in string iDescription);
    void setWeight (in float iWeight);
    void setTime (in float iTime);
    void displayMaterialsUsed ()
        raises (no_material);
    void displayProductionSchedule ()
        raises (not_scheduled);
    void displayOrdersFor ()
        raises (no_orders);
    void displayTestsFor ()
        raises (no_tests);
    void displayProductsInStock ()
        raises (out_of_stock);
    void displayProductsPurchased ()
        raises (no_purchases);
    void scheduleProduction (in Date iDate, in int iLineNumb,
        in int iNumbToProduce);
    void cancelProduction (in Date iDate, in int iLineNumb);
    void addMaterial (in int iMaterialNumb, in float iQuantity);
    void removeMaterial (in int iMaterialNumb);
    void addProduct (in int serial_numb);
    void addTest (in Date iDate, in string iLocation, in string iResult);
};

class ManufacturingLine
{
    attribute int line_numb;
    attribute string line_status;
    key line_numb;
    relationship set<LineSchedule> schedule_for
```

Listing 6-1: (Continued)   ODL syntax for the Might-Mite Motors object-oriented database

```
        inverse LineSchedule::which_line;
    int getLineNumb();
    string getStatus();
    void setLineNumb(in int iNumb);
    void setStatus(in string iStatus);
    void displaySchedule (in Date iDate)
        raises (no_schedule);
    void displaySchedule (in Date iStart, in Date iEnd)
        raises (no_schedule);
};

class LineSchedule
{
    attribute Date production_date;
    attribute int quantity_to_produce;
    relationship ModelClass which_model
        inverse ModelClass::production_scheduled;
    relationship ManufacturingLine which_line
        inverse ManufacturingLine::schedule_for;
    Date getDate();
    int getQuantity();
    void setDate (in Date iDate);
    void setQuantity (in int iQuantity);
};

class RawMaterial
(extent AllRawMaterials)
{
    attribute int material_id_numb;
    attribute string material_name;
    attribute string unit_of_measurement;
    attribute float quantity_in_stock;
    attribute float reorder_point;
    relationship set<MaterialNeeded> how_much_used
        inverse MaterialNeeded::raw_material;
    relationship set<MaterialOrderLine> ordered_on
        inverse MaterialOrderLine::raw_material;
    key material_id_numb;
    int getNumb();
    string getName();
    string getUnit();
    float getInStock();
    float getReorderPoint();
    void setNumb (in int iNumb);
    void setName (in string iName);
    void setUnit (in string iUnit);
    void setInStock (in float iStock);
```

Listing 6-1: (Continued)   ODL syntax for the Might-Mite Motors object-oriented database

```
        void setReorder (in float iReorder);
        void decrementStock (in float iAmountUsed);
        void incrementStock (in float iAmountAdded);
        boolean needsReorder ();
        void displayModelsUsedIn ()
            raises (not_used);
        void displayOutstandingOrders ()
            raises (no_orders);
        set<SupplierClass> getSuppliers()
            raises (never_ordered);
};

class MaterialNeeded
{
        attribute float quantity_needed;
        relationship ModelClass model
            inverse ModelClass::material_used;
        relationship RawMaterial raw_material
            inverse RawMaterial::how_much_used;
        float getQuantity();
        void setQuantity (in float iQuantity);
};

class SupplierClass
{extent AllSuppliers)
{
        attribute int supplier_numb;
        attribute string supplier_name;
        attribute Address supplier_address;
        attribute Name supplier_contact_name;
        atribute Phone supplier_phone;
        attribute Phone supplier_fax;
        key supplier_numb;
        relationship set<MaterialOrder> orders_placed_with
            inverse MaterialOrder::ordered_from;
        int getSupplierNumb ();
        string getSupplierName ();
        Address getSupplierAddress();
        Name getContact ();
        Phone getVoicePhone ();
        Phone getFax ();
        void setSupplierNumb (in int iNumb);
        void setSupplierName (in string iName);
        void setAddress (in Address iAddress);
        void setContact (in Name iContact);
        void setPhone (in Phone iPhone);
```

Listing 6-1: (Continued)   ODL syntax for the Might-Mite Motors object-oriented database

```
    void setFax (in Phone iFax);
    void displayOrdersPlaced ()
        raises (no_orders);
    void addOrder (in Date iDate, in float iTotal);
    void deleteOrder (in int iNumb);
};

class Address
{
    attribute string street;
    attribute string city;
    attribute string state;
    attribute string zip;
    string getStreet();
    string getCity();
    string getState();
    string getZip();
    void setStreet (in string iStreet);
    void setCity (in string iCity);
    void setState (in string iState);
    void inZip (in string iZip);
    string getLabel ();
};

class MaterialOrder
{
    attribute int order_numb;
    attribute Date material_order_date;
    attribute float material_order_total;
    key order_numb;
    relationship Supplier ordered_from
        inverse Supplier::orders_placed_with;
    relationship set<MaterialOrderLine> items_on
        inverse MaterialOrderLine::order;
    Date getOrderDate ();
    float getOrderTotal ();
    void setOrderDate (in Date iDate);
    void computeTotal ()
        raises (no_line_items);
    void displayOrder ()
        raises (no_line_items);
    SupplierClass getSupplier();
    void addItem (in int raw_material_numb);
    void removeItem (in int raw_material_numb);
};
```

Listing 6-1: (Continued)   ODL syntax for the Might-Mite Motors object-oriented database

```
class MaterialOrderLine
{
    attribute LineCost material_line_cost;
    relationship MaterialOrder order
        inverse MaterialOrder::items_on;
    relationship RawMaterial raw_material
        inverse RawMaterial::ordered_on;
    LineCost getLineCost ();
    void setLineCost (in LineCost iCost);
};
class LineCost
{
    attribute float quantity_ordered;
    attribute float cost_each;
    attribute float line_cost;
    float getQuantity();
    float getCost ();
    float getLineCost ();
    void setQuantity (in float iQuantity);
    void setCost (in float iCost);
    void computeLineCost ()
        raises (missing_data);
};


class TestType
(extent AllTestTypes)
{
    attribute int test_code;
    attribute string test_description;
    relationship set<TextClass> tests_performed
        inverse TestClass::type;
    int getCode();
    string getDescription();
    void setCode (in int iCode);
    void setDescription (in string iDescription);
    void displayTestsPerformed ()
        raises (no_tests);
    set<TestClass> find (in Date iDate)
        raises (no_tests);
    set<TestClass> find (in Date iStart, in Date iEnd)
        raises (no_tests);
};
```

Listing 6-1: (Continued)   ODL syntax for the Might-Mite Motors object-oriented database

```
class TestClass
{
    attribute Date test_date;
    attribute string test_location;
    attribute string test_results;
    relationship TestType type
        inverse TestType::tests_performed;
    relationship ModelClass model
        inverse ModelClass::tests_performed;
    Date getDate ();
    string getLocation();
    string getResults();
    void setDate (in Date iDate);
    void setLocation (in string iLocation);
    void setResults (in string iResults);
};
class CustomerClass
(extent AllCustomers)
{
    attribute int customer_numb;
    attribute Name customer_name;
    attribute Address customer_address;
    attribute Phone customer_phone;
    attribute Phone customer_fax;
    key customer_numb;
    relationship set<OrderClass> orders_placed
        inverse OrderClass::customer;
    int getNumb();
    Name getName();
    Address getAddress();
    Phone getPhone();
    Phone getFax();
    void setNumb (in int iNumb);
    void setName (in Name iName);
    void setAddress (in Address iAddress);
    void setPhone (in Phone iPhone);
    void setFax (in Phone iFax);
    set<OrderClass> find ()
        raises (no_orders);
    set<OrderClass> find (in Date iDate)
        raises (no_orders);
    set<OrderClass> find (in Date iStart, in Date iEnd)
        raises (no_orders);
    void addOrder (in Date iDate, in float iTotal);
    void deleteOrder (in int order_numb);
};
```

Listing 6-1: (Continued) **ODL syntax for the Might-Mite Motors object-oriented database**

```
class Name
{
    attribute string first_name;
    attribute string last_name;
    attribute char middle_init;
    string getFirstName();
    string getLastName();
    string getMiddleInit();
    string getLastFirst();
    string getFirstLast();
    void setName (in string iFirst, in string iLast, in char iMiddle)
        raises (data_missing);
};

class Phone
{
    attribute string area_code;
    attribute string exchange;
    attribute string phone_number;
    attribute string extension;
    string getPhone();
    string getAreaCode();
    string getExchange();
    void setAreaCode(in string iCode);
    void setExchange (in string iExchange);
    void setNumber (in string iNumber);
    void setExtension (in string iExt);
};

class OrderClass
{
    attribute int order_numb;
    attribute Date order_date;
    attribute float order_total;
    attribute boolean order_filled:
    key order_numb;
    relationship CustomerClass customer
        inverse CustomerClass::orders_placed;
    relationship set<OrderLine> line_items
        inverse OrderLine::order;
    int getNumb();
    Date getDate();
    float getTotal();
    boolean getFilled();
    void setNumb (in int iNumb);
    void setDate (in Date iDate);
    void computeTotal ()
        raises (no_order_lines);
```

Listing 6-1: (Continued)   ODL syntax for the Might-Mite Motors object-oriented database

```
    void checkFilled()
        raises (no_order_lines);
    set<OrderLine> getLineItems ()
        raises (no_order_lines);
    void addLineItem (in int iModelNumb, in int iQuantity);
    void deleteLineItem (in int iModelNumb)
        raises (not_on_order);
};

class OrderLine
{
    attribute boolean all_shipped;
    attribute LineCost line_cost;
    relationship OrderClass order
        inverse OrderClass::line_items;
    relationship ModelClass model
        inverse ModelClass::orders_on;
    relationship set<ShipmentClass> shipments
        inverse ShipmentClass::order_line;
    relationship set<ProductClass> products_on
        inverse ProductClass::order_line;
    boolean getShipped ();
    LineCost getLineCost();
    void checkShipped()
        raises (no_shipments);
    void setLineCost(in LineCost iCost)
        raises (missing_data);
    void addShipment (in Date iDate, in int iQuantity);
    void deleteShipment (in Date iDate)
        raises (no_such_shipment);
    void addProduct (in int serial_numb)
        raises (no_such_product);
    void removeProduct (in int serial_numb)
        raises (not_on_shipment);
};

class ShipmentClass
{
    attribute Date shipping_date;
    attribute float quantity_shipped;
    relationship OrderLine order_line
        inverse OrderLine::shipments;
    Date getDate();
    float getQuantity();
    void setDate(in Date iDate);
    void setQuantity (in float iQuantity);
};
```

Listing 6-1: (Continued)   ODL syntax for the Might-Mite Motors object-oriented database

```
class ProblemReport
{
    attribute Date problem_date;
    attribute Time problem_time;
    attribute string problem_description;
    relationship ProductClass product
        inverse ProductClass::problems_with;
    relationship ProblemType type
        inverse ProblemType::problems;
    Date getDate();
    Time getTime();
    string getDescription();
    void setDate (in Date iDate);
    void setTime (in Time iTime);
    void setDescription (in string iDescription);
};
class ProblemType
{
    attribute int problem_type_code;
    attribute string problem_type_description;
    relationship set<ProblemReport> problems
        inverse ProblemReport::type;
    int getCode();
    string getDescription();
    void setCode (in int iCode);
    void setDescription (in string iDescription);
    void displayProblems ()
        raises (no_problems);
    void displayProblems (in string iDescription)
        raises (no_problems);
    void find (in Date iDate)
        raises (no_problems);
};

class ProductClass
(extent AllProducts)
{
    attribute int serial_numb;
    attribute Date date_manufactured;
    attribute Date date_shipped;
    key serial_numb;
    relationship ModelClass model
        inverse ModelClass::products_made;
    relationship ProductStatus status
        inverse ProductStatus::products;
    relationship set<ProblemReport> problems_with
        inverse ProblemReport::product;
```

Listing 6-1: (Continued)   ODL syntax for the Might-Mite Motors object-oriented database

```
    relationship PurchaseClass purchase
        inverse PurchaseClass::product;
    relationship OrderLine order_line
        inverse OrderLine::products_on;
    int getSerialNumb();
    Date getManufacturingDate();
    Date getDateShipped();
    void setSerialNumb (in int iNumb);
    void setManufacturingDate (in Date iDate);
    void setDateShipped (in Date iDate);
    void displayProblems ()
        raises (no_problems);
    OwnerClass getPurchaser ()
        raises (not_purchased);
    ModelClass getModel();
    PurchaseClass getPurchase
        raises (not_purchased);
};

class ProductStatus
{
    attribute int status_code;
    attribute string status_description;
    relationship set<ProductClass> products
        inverse ProductClass::status;
    int getCode();
    string getDescription();
    void setCode (in int iCode);
    void setDescription (in string iDescription);
    void displayProducts ()
        raises (no_products);
};

class PurchaseClass
(extent AllPurchases)
{
    attribute int age;
    attribute char gender;
    attribute Date purchase_date;
    attribute string purchase_place;
    attribute string relationship_to;
    relationship ProductClass product
        inverse ProductClass::purchase;
    relationship set<FeatureClass> features
        inverse FeatureClass::purchases;
    relationship set<LearnAbout> how_learned
        inverse LearnAbout::purchases;
```

Listing 6-1: (Continued)   ODL syntax for the Might-Mite Motors object-oriented database

```
        relationship OwnerClass owner
            inverse OwnerClass::purchases;
        int getAge();
        char getGender();
        Date getPurchaseDate();
        string getPlace();
        string getRelationship();
        void setAge (in int iAge);
        void setGender (in char iGender);
        void setDate (in Date iDate);
        void setPlace (in string iPlace);
        void setRelationship (in string iRelationship);
        void displayFeaturesChosen()
            raises (no_features);
        void displayHowLearned()
            raises (no_reasons);
        OwnerClass getOwner();
        ModelClass getModel();
        ProductClass getProduct();
        void addFeature (in int iCode);
        void deleteFeature (in int iCode);
        void addLearnAbout (in int iCode);
        void deleteLearnAbout (in int iCode);
};

class FeatureClass
{
        attribute int feature_code;
        attribute string feature_description;
        relationship set<PurchaseClass> purchases
            inverse PurchaseClass::features;
        int getCode ();
        string getString();
        void setCode (in int iCode);
        void setDescription (in string iDescription);
};

class LearnAbout
{
        attribute int learn_code;
        attribute string learn_description);
        relationship PurchaseClass purchases
            inverse PurchaseClass::how_learned;
        int getCode();
        string getDescription();
        void setCode (in int iCode);
        void setDescription (in string iDescription);
};
```

Listing 6-1: (Continued)   ODL syntax for the Might-Mite Motors object-oriented database

```
class OwnerClass
(extent AllOwners)
{
    attribute int owner_numb;
    attribute Name owner_name;
    attribute Address owner_address;
    attribute Phone owner_phone;
    key owner_numb;
    relationship set<PurchaseClass> purchases
        inverse PurchaseClass::owner;
    int getNumb ();
    Address getAddress ();
    Name getName ();
    Phone getPhone ();
    void setNumb (in int iNumb);
    void setName (in Name iName);
    void setAddress (in Address iAddress);
    void setPhone (in Phone iPhone);

    void displayPurchases ()
        raises (no_purchases);
    void addPurchase ();
    void deletePurchase();
};
```

Listing 6-1: (Continued)   ODL syntax for the Might-Mite Motors object-oriented database

7

Database Design Case Study #2: East Coast Aquarium

Many-to-many relationships are often the bane of the relational database designer. Sometimes it is not completely clear that you are dealing with that type of relationship. However, failure to recognize the many-to-many can result in serious data integrity problems.

As you have read throughout this book, an OODBMS can implement many-to-many relationships without an intervening composite entity. However, doing so can be dangerous in the sense that it may make it impossible to interpret accurately relationships further up or down a relationship hierarchy. One of the tasks we will tackle in this chapter is a further examination of situations in which direct many-to-many relationships are acceptable.

The organization described in this chapter actually needs two databases, the larger of which is replete with many-to-many relationships. In some cases it will be necessary to create additional entities for composite entities to reference merely to ensure data integrity.

Perhaps the biggest challenge facing a database designer working for East Coast Aquarium is the lack of complete specifications. As you will read, the people who will be using the application programs created to manipulate the aquarium's two new databases have only a general idea of what they need the programs to do. Unlike Mighty-Mite Motors, which had the luxury of working from a large collection of existing forms and documents, East Coast Aquarium has nothing of that sort.

The situation therefore lends itself to a technique known as *prototyping*, in which the designers prepare the user interface of an application program and let the end users evaluate it. Based on user feedback, the designers modify the prototype until the output design matches what the users want. This iterative process helps the end users focus their requirements. The designers also gather the necessary information to create a database design that can provide the outputs the users need. A CASE tool that can model screen forms will therefore be an invaluable tool in preparing the prototype.

Organizational Overview

The East Coast Aquarium is a nonprofit organization dedicated to the study and preservation of marine life. Located on the Atlantic coast in the heart of a major northeastern U.S. city, it provides a wide variety of educational services to the surrounding area. The aquarium is supported by donations, memberships, charges for private functions, gift shop revenues, class fees, and the small admission fees it charges to the public. To help keep costs down, many of the public service jobs (leading tours, staffing the admissions counter, running the gift shop) are handled by volunteers.

The aquarium grounds consist of three buildings: the main facility, a dolphin house, and a marina where the aquarium's research barge is docked.

The centerpiece of the main building is a three-story center tank that is surrounded by a spiral walkway. The sides of the tank are primarily glass, so visitors can walk around the tank, observing the residents at various depths.

> *Note: If you happen to recognize the layout of this aquarium, please keep in mind that only the physical structure of the environment is modeled after something that really exists. The way in which the organization functions is purely a product of the author's imagination and no commentary, positive or negative, is intended with regard to the real-world aquarium.*

The height of the tank makes it possible to simulate the way in which habitats change as the ocean depth changes. Species that dwell on the ocean floor, coral reef fish, and sandbar dwellers therefore are all housed in the same tank, interacting in much the same way as they would in the ocean.

The remaining space on the first floor of the main building (Figure 7-1) includes the gift shop and a quarantine area for newly arrived animals. The latter area is not accessible to visitors.

The second floor (Figure 7-2) contains a classroom and the volunteers office. Small tanks containing single-habitat exhibits are installed in the outside walls. These provide places to house species that have special habitat requirements or that don't coexist well with other species.

The third floor (Figure 7-3) provides wall space for additional small exhibits. It also houses the aquarium's administrative offices.

East Coast Aquarium has two very different areas in which it needs data management. The first is in the handling of its animals—where they are housed in the aquarium, where they came from, what they are to be fed, problems that occur in the tanks, and so on.

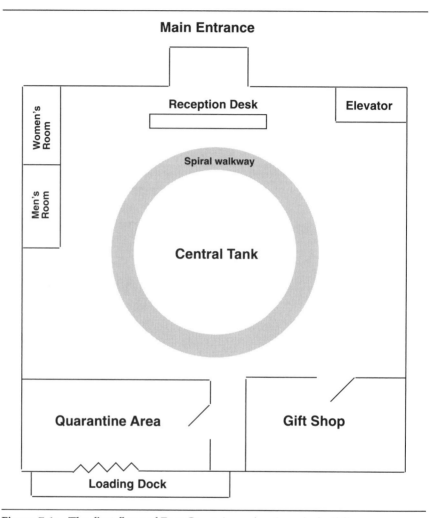

Figure 7-1: The first floor of East Coast Aquarium's main building

The second area concerns the volunteers, including who they are, what they have been trained to do, and when they are scheduled to work. For this particular organization, the two data environments are completely separate; they share no data. A database designer who volunteers to work with the aquarium staff will therefore prepare two database designs, one to be used by the volunteer staff in the volunteers office and another to be used by the administrative and animal-care staff through the aquarium grounds.

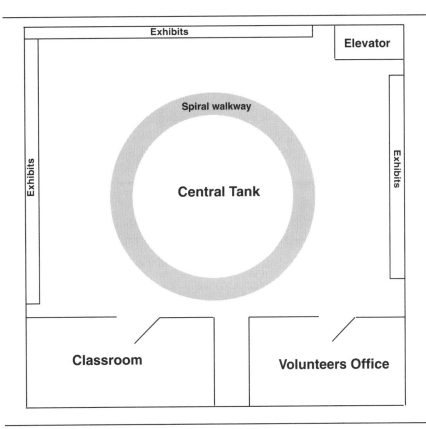

Figure 7-2: The second floor of East Coast Aquarium's main building

Animal Tracking Needs

Currently, East Coast Aquarium uses a general-purpose PC accounting package to handle its data processing needs. The software takes care of payroll as well as purchasing and the accompanying accounts payable. Because the aquarium is a nonprofit organization, it does not have accounts receivable as does a for-profit business. Instead, income from the gift shop, admissions, and donations is handled on a cash basis. Grant income is managed by special-purpose software designed to monitor grant awards and how they are spent.

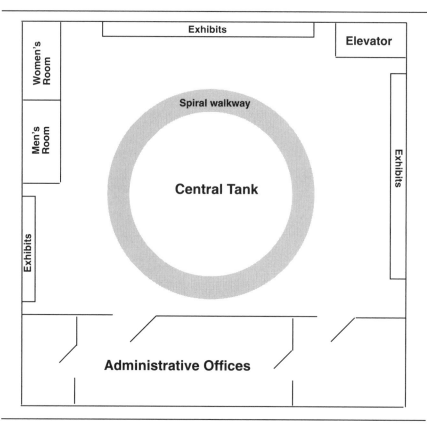

Figure 7-3:   The third floor of East Coast Aquarium's main building

Although the accounting and grant management packages adequately handle the aquarium's finances, there is no data processing that tracks the actual animals housed in the aquarium. The three people in charge of the animals have expressed a need for the following:

♦ An "inventory" of which species are living in which locations in the aquarium. Some species can be found in more than one tank, and several tanks in addition to the central tank contain more than one species. For larger animals, such as sharks and dolphins, the head animal keeper would like a precise count. However, for small fish that are often eaten by larger fish and that breed in large numbers, only an estimate is possible. The animal handling staff would like to be able to search for information about animals using either the animal's English name or its Latin name.

♦ Data about the foods each species eats, including how much should be fed at what interval. The head animal keeper would like to be able to print out a feeding instruction list every morning to give to staff. In addition, the animal-feeding staff would like to store information about their food inventory. Although the purchasing of food is handled by the administrative office, the head animal keeper would like an application program to decrement the food inventory automatically by the amount fed each day and to generate a tickle report whenever the stock level of a type of food drops below the reorder point. This will make it much easier to ensure that the aquarium does not run short of animal feed.

♦ Data about the sizes, locations, and habitats of the tanks on the aquarium grounds. Some tanks, such as the main tank, contain more than one habitat, and the same habitat can be found in more than one tank.

♦ Data about tank maintenance. Although the main tank is fed directly from the ocean, the smaller tanks around the walls of the main building are closed environments, much like a saltwater aquarium someone might have at home. This means that the pH and salinity of the tanks must be monitored closely. The head animal keeper therefore would like to print out a maintenance schedule each day as well as be able to keep track of what maintenance is actually performed.

♦ Data about the habitats in which a given species can live. When a new species arrives at the aquarium, the staff can use this information to determine which locations could possibly house that species.

♦ Data about where species can be obtained. If the aquarium wants to increase the population of a particular species and the increase cannot be generated through in-house breeding, then the staff would like to know which external supplier can be contacted. Some of the suppliers sell animals; others, such as zoos or other aquariums, will trade or donate animals.

♦ Problems that arise in the tanks. When animals become ill, the veterinarian wants to be able to view a history of both the animal and the tank in which it is currently living.

♦ Data about orders placed for animals and, in particular, the shipments in which animals arrive. Because any financial arrangements involved in securing animals are handled by the administrative office, these data indicate only how many individuals of each species are included in a given order or shipment.

The shipment and problem data are particularly important to the aquarium. When animals first arrive, they are not placed immediately into the general population. Instead, they are held in special tanks in the quarantine area at the rear of the aquarium's first floor. The length of the quarantine is determined by the species.

After the quarantine period has passed and the animals are declared disease free, they can be placed on exhibit in the main portion of the aquarium. Nonetheless, animals do become ill after they have been released from quarantine. It is therefore essential that records are kept of the sources of animals so that patterns of illness can be tracked back to specific suppliers, if such patterns appear. By the same token, patterns of illnesses in various species housed in the same tank can be an indication of serious problems with the environment in the tank.

The Volunteer Organization

The volunteer organization (the Friends of the Aquarium) is totally separate from the financial and animal-handling areas of the aquarium. Volunteers perform tasks that do not involve direct contact with animals, such as leading tours, manning the admissions desk, and running the gift shop. The aquarium has provided office space and a telephone line for the volunteer coordinator and her staff. Beyond that, the Friends of the Aquarium organization has been on its own to secure office furniture and equipment.

The recent donation of a PC now makes it possible for the volunteers to automate some of their scheduling. Currently, the scheduling processing works in the following way:

♦ The person on duty in the volunteers office receives requests for volunteer services from the aquarium's administrative office. Some of the jobs are regularly scheduled (for example, staffing the gift shop and the admissions desk). Others are ad hoc, such as the request by a schoolteacher to bring a class of children for a tour.

♦ The volunteer doing the scheduling checks the list of volunteers to see who is trained to do the job requested. Each volunteer's information is recorded on an index card, along with the volunteer's skills. A skill is a general expression of something the volunteer knows how to do, such as lead a tour for elementary school children. The volunteer's information also includes an indication of when that person is available to work.

♦ The volunteer doing the scheduling separates the cards for those people who have the required skill and have indicated that they are available at the required time. Most volunteers work on a regularly scheduled basis either at the admissions desk or in the gift shop. However, for ad hoc jobs, the person doing the scheduling must start making telephone calls until someone who is willing and able to do the job is found.

♦ The volunteer is scheduled for the job by writing in the master schedule notebook. As far as the volunteer coordinator is concerned, a job is an application of a skill. Therefore, a skill is knowing how to lead a tour for elementary school students, and a job that applies that skill is leading a tour of Mrs. Brown's third graders at 10 A.M. on Thursday.

One of the things that is very difficult to do with the current scheduling process is to keep track of the work record of each individual volunteer. The aquarium holds a volunteer recognition luncheon once a year, and the volunteer organization would like to find an easy way to identify volunteers who have put in an extra effort so that they can be recognized at that event. In contrast, the volunteer organization would also like to be able to identify volunteers who rarely participate—the people who stay on the volunteer rolls only to get free admission to the aquarium—as well as people who make commitments to work but do not show up. (The latter are actually far more of a problem than the former.)

The Volunteers Database

In terms of scope, the volunteers database is considerably smaller than the animal tracking database. It therefore makes sense to tackle the smaller project first. The database designers will create the application prototype and review it with the users. When the users are satisfied and the designers feel they have enough detailed information to actually design a database, they will move on to the more traditional steps of creating an ER diagram, tables, and SQL statements.

> *Note: As you will see, there is a lot involved in creating a prototype. It requires very detailed intensive work and produces a significant number of diagrams. We will therefore look at the volunteers prototype in full, but in the interest of length we will look at only selected aspects of the animal tracking prototype.*

Creating the Application Prototype

Given that the specifications of the database are rather general, the first step is to create a prototype of an application program interface. It begins with the opening screen and its main menu bar (Figure 7-4). As you can see, when in browse mode, the CASE tool allows users and designers to pull down the menus in the menu bar.

The complete menu tree (with the exception of the Help menu, whose contents are determined by the user interface guidelines of

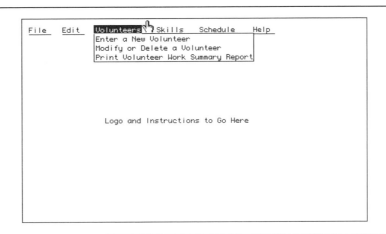

Figure 7-4:   Main menu prototype for the volunteers application

the operating system on which the application is running) can be found in Figure 7-5. Looking at the menu options, users can see that their basic requirements have been fulfilled. The details, however, must be specified by providing users with specific output designs.

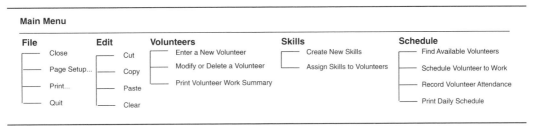

Figure 7-5:   Menu tree of the volunteers database prototype application

Each menu option in the prototype's main menu has therefore been linked to a screen form. For example, to modify or delete a volunteer, a user must first *find* the volunteer's data. Therefore the Modify or Delete a Volunteer menu option leads to a dialog box that allows the user either to enter a volunteer number or to select a volunteer by name and phone number from a list (Figure 7-6). With the prototype, clicking the Find button opens the modify–delete form (Figure 7-7). Users can click in the data entry fields and tab between them, but the buttons at the right of the window are not functional.

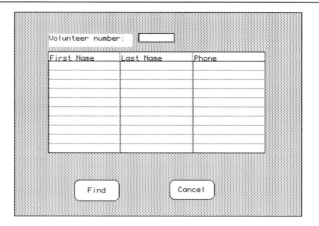

Figure 7-6:   Prototype of a dialog box for finding a volunteer for modification

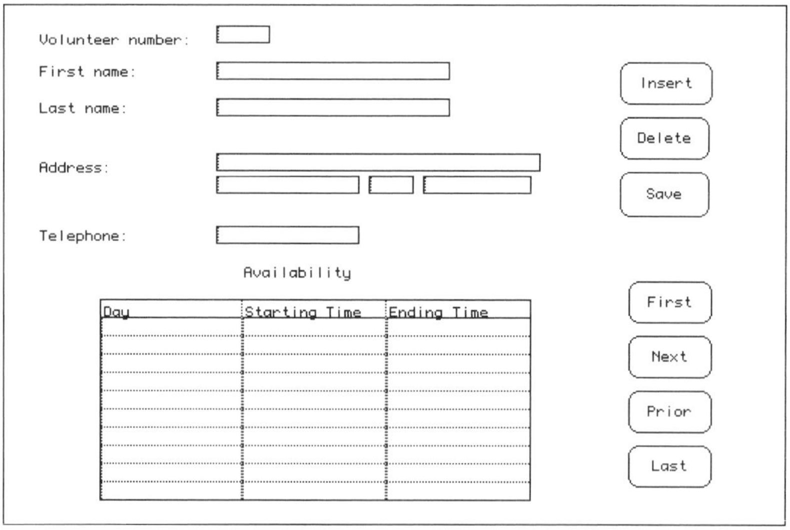

Figure 7-7:   Prototype of a form for modifying and deleting a volunteer

While in browse mode, the CASE tool presents a form as it would appear to the user. However, in design mode, a database designer can see the names of the fields on the form (for example, Figure 7-8). These field names will ultimately guide the design of the database.

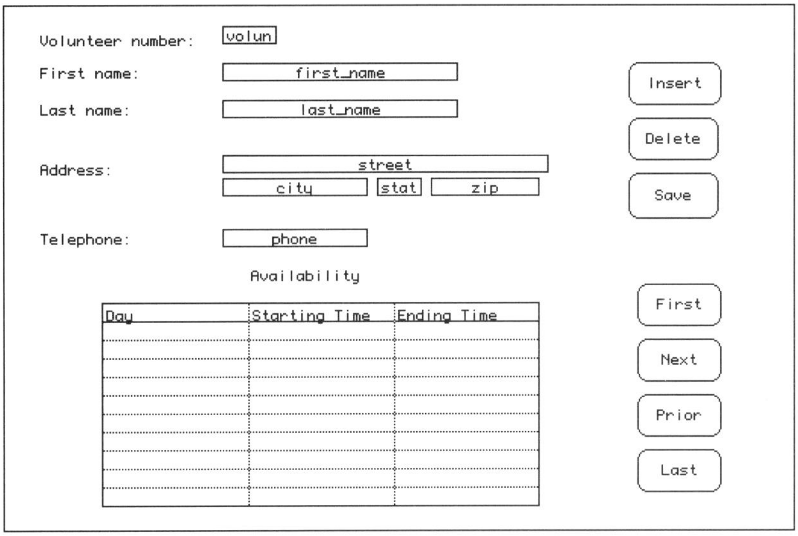

Figure 7-8:   Prototype data modification form showing field names

In the case of the volunteer data, it is apparent to the designers that there are at least two entities (and perhaps three) involved with the data that describe a volunteer. The first entity is represented by the single-valued fields occupying the top half of the form (volunteer number, first name, last name, street, city, state, zip, and phone). However, the availability data—day of the week, starting time, and ending time—are multivalued and therefore must be given an entity of their own. This also implies that there will be a one-to-many relationship between a volunteer and a period of time during which he or she is available.

> *Note: Should you choose, the field names on a screen prototype can become part of the data dictionary. However, if the field names do not ultimately correspond to column names, their inclusion may add unnecessary complexity to the data dictionary.*

The remainder of the prototype application and its forms are designed and analyzed in a similar way:

♦ The volunteer work summary report has been designed to let the user enter a range of dates that the report will cover (see Figure 7-9). The report itself (Figure 7-10) is a control-break report that displays the work performed by each volunteer along with the total hours worked and the number of times the volunteer was a "no-show." The latter number was included because the volunteer coordinator had indicated that it was extremely important to know which volunteers consistently signed up to work and then didn't report when scheduled.

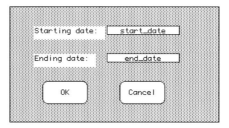

Figure 7-9:   **A dialog box layout for entering dates for the work summary report**

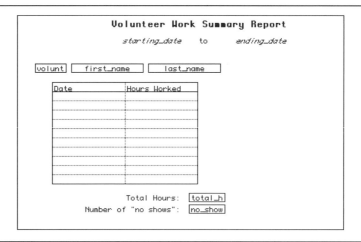

Figure 7-10:   **Prototype layout for the work summary report**

The need to report the no-shows tells the designers that the schedule table needs to include a boolean column that indicates whether a person showed up for a scheduled shift. The report layout also includes some computed fields (total hours worked and number of no-shows) that contain data that do not need to be stored but can be generated when the report is displayed.

- ◆ Entering a new skill into the master list of skills requires only a simple form (Figure 7-11). The end user sees only the description of a skill. However, the database designers know that the best way to handle unstructured blocks of text is to assign each description a skill number, which can then be used as a foreign key throughout the database. Users, however, do not necessarily need to know that a skill number is being used; they will always see just the text descriptions.

Figure 7-11: Entering a new skill

- ◆ To assign skills to a volunteer, the end user must first find the volunteer. The application can therefore use a copy of the dialog box in Figure 7-6. In this case, however, the Find button leads to the form in Figure 7-12.

A database designer will quickly recognize that there is a many-to-many relationship between a skill and a volunteer. There are actually three entities behind Figure 7-12: the skill, the volunteer, and the composite entity that represents the relationship between the two. The skill entry form displays data from the volunteer entity at the top, data from the composite entity in the current skills list, and all skills not assigned from the skills table in the skill description list. Of course, the actual foreign key used in the composite entity is

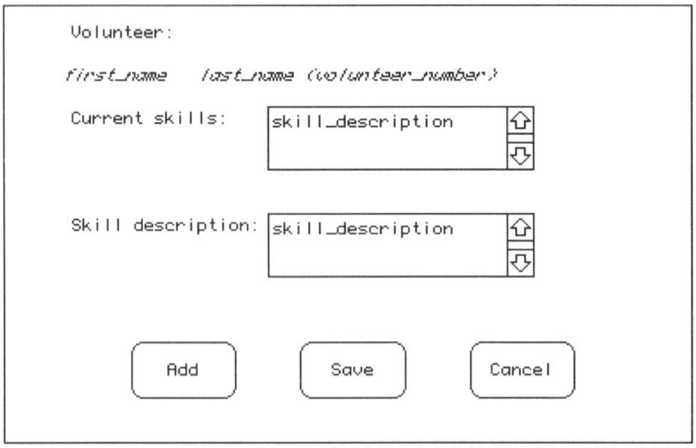

Figure 7-12:   Assigning skills to a volunteer

a skill number, but the user sees only the result of a join back to the skills table that retrieves the skill description.

> *Note: Database integrity constraints will certainly prevent anyone from assigning the same skill twice to the same volunteer. However, it is easier if the user can see currently assigned skills. Then, the application can restrict what appears in the skill description list to all skills not assigned to that volunteer. In this case, it is a matter of user interface design rather than database design.*

♦ To find the volunteers available to perform a specific job, the volunteers application needs a form something like Figure 7-13. The end user enters the date and time of the job and chooses the skill required by the job. Clicking the Search button fills in the table at the bottom of the form with the names and phone numbers of volunteers who are theoretically available.

Of all the outputs produced by this application, finding available volunteers is probably the most difficult to implement. The application program must not only work with overlapping intervals of time but also consider both when a volunteer indicates he or she will be available and when a volunteer is already scheduled to work. In most cases, however, a database designer does not have to

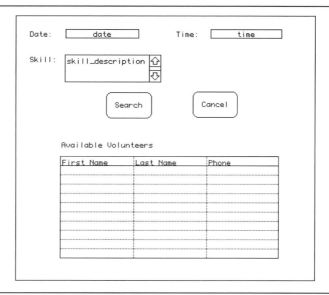

Figure 7-13: Finding available volunteers

write the application program code. The designer needs only to ensure that the data necessary to produce the output are present in the database.

Note: A smart database designer, however, would discuss any output that involves evaluating overlapping time intervals with application programmers to ensure that the output is feasible. There is no point in specifying infeasible output.

♦ Once the person doing the volunteer scheduling has located a volunteer to fill a specific job, then the volunteer's commitment to work needs to become a part of the database. The process begins by presenting the user with a Find Volunteer dialog box like that in Figure 7-6. In this case, the Find button is linked to the Schedule Volunteer window (Figure 7-14). A database designer will recognize that this is not all the data that needs to be stored about a job, however. In particular, someone will need to record whether the volunteer actually appeared to do the scheduled job on the day of the job; this cannot be done when the job is scheduled initially.

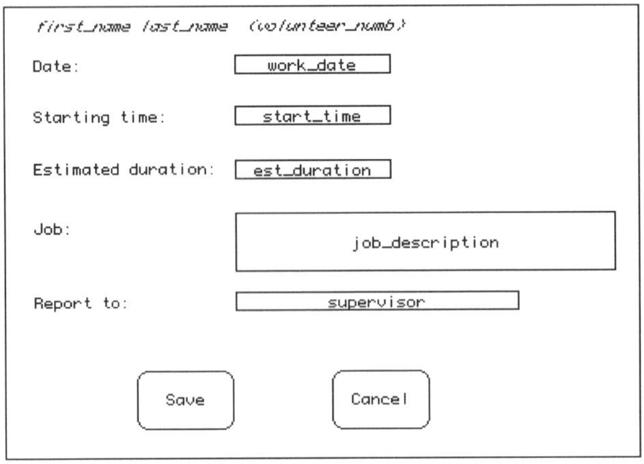

Figure 7-14: Scheduling a volunteer to perform a job

♦ To record attendance, an end user first locates the volunteer using a Find Volunteer dialog box (Figure 7-6), which then leads to a display of the jobs the volunteer has been scheduled to work in reverse chronological order (see Figure 7-15). For those jobs that have not been worked, the End Time and Worked? columns will be empty. The user can then scroll the list to find the job to be modified and enter values for the two empty columns. The fields on this form, plus those on the job scheduling form, represent the attributes that will describe the job entity.

♦ To print a daily schedule, an end user first uses a dialog box to indicate the date for which a schedule should be displayed (Figure 7-16). The application program then assembles the report (Figure 7-17). To simplify working with the program, the application developers should probably allow users to double-click on any line in the listing to open the form in Figure 7-15 for the scheduled volunteer. However, this capability has no impact on the database design.

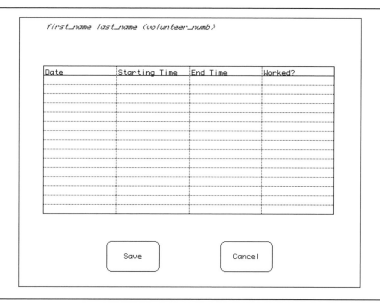

Figure 7-15:   Recording jobs worked

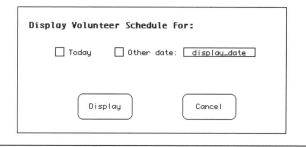

Figure 7-16:   Choosing a date for schedule display

For Reference: The Relational Design

To make it easier for you to compare the hybrid and pure object databases with the relational implementation, the tables in the relational design have been reprinted here.

```
Volunteer (volunteer numb, first_name, last_name, street, city,
    state, zip, phone)
Availability (volunteer numb, day, starting time, ending_time)
```

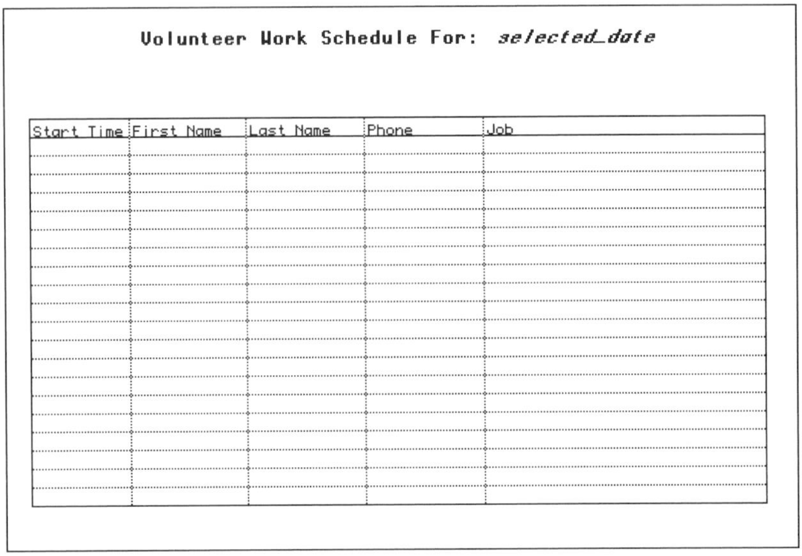

Figure 7-17:   Volunteer work schedule

```
Job (volunteer_numb, job_date, starting_time, estimated_duration,
     supervisor, job_description, ending_time, worked_flag)
Skill (skill_numb, skill_description)
Skills_known (volunteer_numb, skill_numb)
```

Designing the Hybrid Database

Like the database for the Mighty-Mite Motors company, the design for the volunteers database presents only a few simple opportunities to take advantage of the integration of objects into a relational design. The ER diagram in Figure 7-18 contains objects for a name, address, and phone number. When you consider the entities closely, there are no other attributes that it makes sense to group together into objects.

The resulting tables are as follows:

```
Volunteer (volunteer_numb, name, address, zip, phone)
Availability (volunteer_numb, day, starting_time, ending_time)
Job (volunteer_numb, job_date, starting_time, estimated_duration,
     supervisor, job_description, ending_time, worked_flag)
```

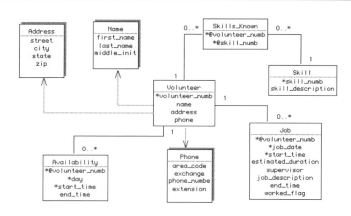

Figure 7-18:   The hybrid design for the volunteers database

```
Skill (skill_numb, skill_description)
Skills_known (volunteer_numb, skill_numb)
```

The only benefit of moving to an object–relational model for this small database is the ability to reuse the Name, Address, and Phone classes, assuming that they have been declared for use elsewhere.

Designing the Pure Object Database

In a database this small, object-orientation has much less impact on the overall design than it does in a larger schema. The design is only minimally simpler than the object–relational design.

The ER Diagram

The ER diagram for the pure object design appears in Figure 7-19. Extents have been omitted to make the diagram easier to read.

The many-to-many relationship between a volunteer and a skill can be represented directly. This is one of the cases in which there is little risk of misinterpretation of relationships because VolunteerClass is at the top of the hierarchy. (In other words, there is no danger of making wrong inferences when moving up a relationship hierarchy.) The remaining two relationships are one-to-many and therefore the same

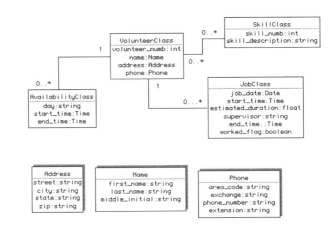

Figure 7-19: The pure object design for the volunteers database

as those in the object–relational design. Notice also that this design reuses the Name, Address, and Phone classes that are part of the Mighty-Mite Motors database.

The ODL Schema

The ODL schema for the volunteers database can be found at the end of this section in Listing 7-1. As you look through this design, you may be wondering why classes such as VolunteerClass contain unique identification numbers. These numbers are required in a relational or object–relational database to provide a good unique key and as primary keys for foreign keys to reference. However, because object-oriented databases define relationships with object identifiers, the arbitrary unique keys are no longer integral to the structure of the database. Why have them at all?

> Note: The Address, Name, and Phone classes are identical to those introduced in Chapter 6 and therefore will not be repeated here.

The unique keys are certainly optional, but they can make using the database easier. For example, most volunteers will very quickly remember their volunteer numbers. Then, when they call with a request or query about their schedule, they can give their number to the volunteer coordinator on the phone. The volunteer coordinator can then use that number to find information about the volunteer, rather than attempting to type a name accurately. The volunteer coordinator could ask for a phone number instead of a name, but there could be more than one volunteer with the same phone number and phone numbers do change. Therefore, having a unique number that never changes to identify a major entity such as a volunteer still makes sense in an object-oriented database.

As with the MMM schema, there are three types of operations: accessor methods to get data values, mutator methods to modify data values, and methods that retrieve related objects. Consider how easy this makes application programming! The program that retrieves volunteer availability needs to find a volunteer object and then simply call a getAvailability method, either with no parameters to see all availability, with a day to see availability on a single day, or with a day and time interval to see availability during a given period on a single day. Once the class's operations are written, the hardest part of the application coding has been done.

```
class VolunteerClass
(extent AllVolunteers)
{
    attribute int volunteer_numb;
    attribute Name name;
    attribute Address address;
    attribute Phone phone;
    key volunteer_numb;
    relationship set<SkillClass> skills_known
        inverse SkillClass::volunteers_with;
    relationship set<AvailabilityClass> when_available
        inverse AvailabilityClass::volunteer;
    relationship set <JobClass>jobs_scheduled
        inverse JobClass::volunteer;
    int getNumb();
    Name getName();
    Address getAddress();
    Phone getPhone();
    void setNamb (in int iNumb);
    void setName (in Name iName);
    void setAddress (in Address iAddress);
    void setPhone (in Phone iPhone);
```

Listing 7-1:   ODL schema for the volunteers database

```
    set<JobClass> getJobs()
        raises (no_jobs);
    set<JobClass> getJobs (in Date iStart, in Date iEnd)
        raises (no_jobs);
    set<JobClass> getJobs (in Date iDate)
        raises (no_jobs);
    set<AvailabilityClass> getAvailability ()
        raises (no_availability);
    set<AvailabilityClass> getAvailability (in string iDay)
        raises (not_this_day);
    set<AvailabilityClass> getAvailability (in string iDay, in Time iStart,
            in Time iEnd)
        raises (not_this_period);
    set<SkillClass> getSkills ()
        raises (no_skills);
};

class SkillClass
(extent AllSkills)
{
    attribute int skill_numb;
    attribute string skill_description;
    key skill_numb;
    relationship set<VolunteerClass> volunteers
        inverse VolunteerClass::skills_known;
    int getNumb();
    string getDescription();
    void setNumb (in int iNumb);
    void setDescription (in string iDescription);
    set<Volunteers> getVolunteers()
        raises (no_volunteers);
};

class AvailabilityClass
{
    attribute string day;
    attribute Time start_time;
    attribute Time end_time;
    relationship VolunteerClass volunteer
        inverse Volunteerclass::when_available;
    string getDay ();
    Time getStartTime ();
    Time getEndTime ();
    void setDay (in string iDay);
    void setStartTime (in Time iStart);
```

Listing 7-1: (Continued)   ODL schema for the volunteers database

```
        void setEndTime (in Time iEnd);
        Volunteer getVolunteer ();
};

Class JobClass
(extent AllJobs)
{
        attribute Date job_date;
        attribute Time start_time;
        attribute float estimated_duration;
        attribute string supervisor;
        attribute Time end_time;
        attribute boolean worked_flag;
        relationship VolunteerClass volunteer
            inverse VolunteerClass::jobs_scheduled;
        Date getDate();
        Time getStartTime();
        float getDuration();
        string getSupervisor();
        Time getEndTime();
        boolean getWorkedFlag();
        void setDate (in Date iDate);
        void setStartTime (in Time iStart);
        void setDuration (in float iDuration);
        void setSupervisor (in string iSupervisor);
        void setEndTime (in Time iEnd);
        void setWorkedFlag ();
        Volunteer getVolunteer();
};
```

Listing 7-1: (Continued)   ODL schema for the volunteers database

The Animal Tracking Database

The animal tracking database is considerably larger than the volunteers database. The application that will manipulate that database therefore is concomitantly larger, as demonstrated by the menu tree in Figure 7-20. (The File and Edit menus have been left off so that the diagram will fit across the width of the page. However, they are intended to be the first and second menus from the left, respectively. A Help menu can also be added along the right edge.)

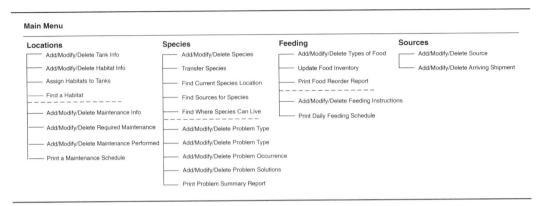

Figure 7-20:   Menu tree for the animal tracking database

The functionality requested by the animal handlers falls generally into four categories: the locations (the tanks) and their habitats, the species, the food, and the sources for animals. The organization of the application interface was therefore guided by those groupings.

Highlights of the Application Prototype

The screen and report layouts designed for the animal tracking application provide a good starting place for the database designers to identify the entities and attributes needed in the database. As with the volunteers application, there is not necessarily a one-to-one correspondence between an entity and an output.

> *Note: One of the common mistakes novices make when designing the interfaces of database application programs is to use one data entry form per table. Users do not look at their environment in the same way as a database designer, however, and often the organization imposed by tables does not make sense to the users. Another benefit of a prototype is therefore that it forces database and application designers to adapt to what the users really need, rather than the other way around.*

Food Management

One of the important functions mentioned by the aquarium's animal handlers was management of the animal feeding schedule and the food inventory. First, they wanted a daily feeding schedule, such as that in Figure 7-21. Knowing that each species can eat many types of food and that a type of food can be eaten by many species, a database designer realizes that there are at least four entities behind the sample output:

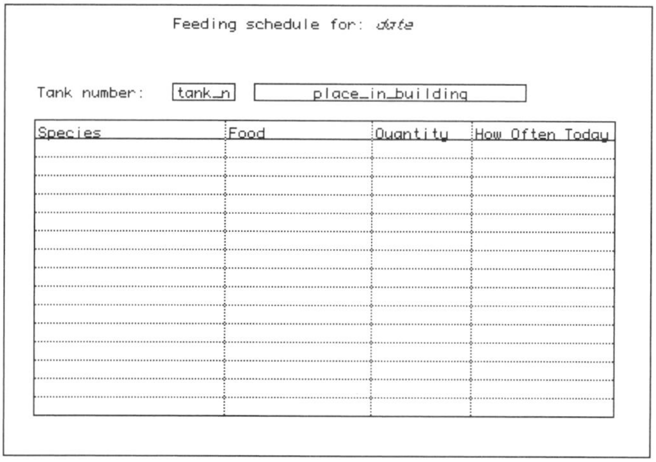

Figure 7-21:   Daily feeding schedule

◆ An entity that indicates which species lives in which tank (a composite entity between the tank and species entities)
◆ An entity describing a type of food
◆ An entity describing a species
◆ An entity that indicates which species eats which food and how often that food should be fed (a composite entity between the food and species entities)

Food inventory management—although it sounds like a separate function to the animal handlers—actually requires nothing more than the food entity. The food entity needs to store data about how much food is currently in stock and a reorder point. The application program can take care of decrementing how much has been fed when the animal handlers run the Update Food Inventory function.

Handling Arriving Animals

When a shipment arrives at the aquarium, animal handlers first check the contents of the shipment against the shipment's paperwork. They then take the animals and place them in the aquarium's quarantine area. The data entry form that the animal handlers will use to store data about arrivals therefore includes a place for entering an identifier for the tank in which the new animals have been placed (Figure 7-22). Given that the aquarium staff needs to be able to locate animals at any time, this suggests that the quarantine tanks should be handled no differently from the exhibit tanks and that there is only one entity for a tank.

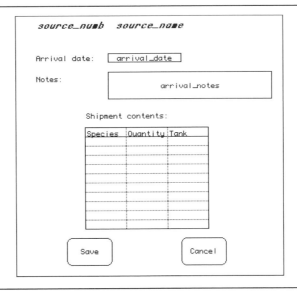

Figure 7-22:   Recording the arrival of a shipment of animals

After the quarantine period has expired and the animals are certified as healthy, they can be transferred to another location in the building. This means an application program must delete the species from their current tank (regardless of whether it is a quarantine tank or an exhibit tank) and insert data for the new tank. The screen form (Figure 7-23) therefore lets the user identify the species and its current location using popup menus. The user also uses a popup menu to indicate the new location. To a database designer, this translates into the deletion of one row from a table—a table representing a composite entity between tank and species entities—and the insertion of a new row. All the database design needs to do, however, is provide the table; the application program will take care of managing the data modification.

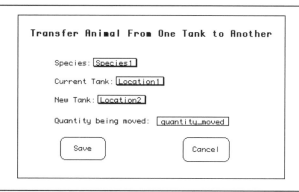

Figure 7-23:   Moving a species between tanks

Problem Analysis

The health of the animals in the aquarium is a primary concern of the animal handlers. They are therefore anxious to be able to analyze the problems that occur in the tanks for patterns. Perhaps a single species is experiencing more problems than any other; perhaps an animal handler is not paying as much attention to the condition of the tanks for which he or she is responsible.

The animal handlers want the information in Figure 7-24 included in the problem summary report. What cannot be seen from the sample screen created by the CASE tool is that the data will appear in a control-break layout. For example, each tank number will appear only once; each species will appear once for each tank in which it was the victim of a problem. By the same token, each type of problem will appear once for each tank and species it affected. Only the problem solutions will contain data for every row in the sample output table.

To a database designer, the form in Figure 7-24 suggests the need for five entities:

Problem Summary Report
starting_date   ending_date

Tank	Head Keepe	Date	Species	Problem Description	Problem Resolution

Figure 7-24: Problem summary report

- The species.
- The tank.
- The type of problem.
- A problem occurrence (a type of problem occurring in one tank and involving one species).
- A problem solution (a solution that has been tried for one problem occurrence). There may be many solutions to a single problem occurrence.

One of the best ways to handle problems is to avoid them. For this reason, the animal handlers also want to include maintenance data in their database. To make data entry simpler for the end users, the form for entering required maintenance (Figure 7-25) allows a user to select a tank and then enter as many maintenance activities as needed.

A database designer views such a form as requiring three entities: the tank, the maintenance activity, and the maintenance required for the tank (a composite entity between the tank and maintenance activity entities).

Figure 7-25:   Entering required maintenance

For Reference: The Relational Design

The relations in a pure relational database for the East Coast Aquarium are as follows:

```
species (species_numb, english_name, latin_name, quarantine_length)
location (tank_numb, place_in_building, fluid_capacity)
population (species_numb, tank_numb, number_of_animals)
habitat (habitat_numb, habitat_description)
can_live_in (species_numb, habitat_numb)
habitats_contained (tank_numb, habitat_numb)
problem (problem_type_numb, problem_description)
problem_occurrence (problem_numb, problem_date, tank_numb,
    species_numb, problem_type_numb)
problem_solution (problem_numb, solution_date, solution_applied)
source (source_numb, source_name, source_street, source_city,
    source_state, source_zip, source_phone, source_contact_person)
can_supply (source_numb, species_numb)
shipment (source_numb, shipment_date, arrival_notes)
shipment_animals (source_numb, arrival_date, species_numb,
    quantity_received)
food (food_type_numb, food_description, source_numb, units,
    amount_on_hand, reorder_point)
feeding (species_numb, food_type_numb, feeding_interval,
    feeding_amount)
maintenance_activity (activity_numb, activity_description)
maintenance_required (activity_numb, tank_numb, how_often)
maintenance_performed (activity_numb, tank_numb, activity_date)
```

Designing a Hybrid Database

Of all of the sample databases you have seen so far, the animals portion of the East Coast Aquarium database environment benefits the least from a hybrid design. The first portion of the ER diagram (Figure 7-26) is identical to the relational design. It does gain some clarity in the move from the Information Engineering model to UML in that it can use the n-ary association symbol to show the three-way relationship between location, species, and problem. This technique makes it very clear that the problem report is related to all three parent entities.

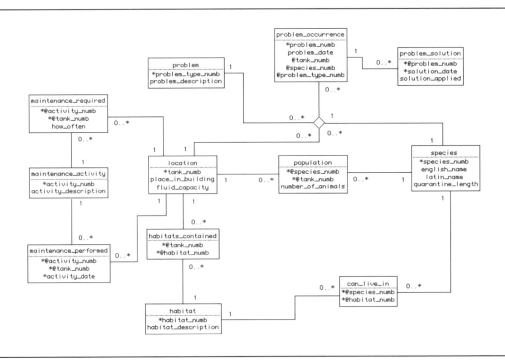

Figure 7-26:   A hybrid design for the animals database (part I)

The second portion of the ER diagram (Figure 7-27) incorporates the utility classes that you have seen already. Beyond those three classes, there is nothing that lends itself to grouping into a class rather than using individual columns.

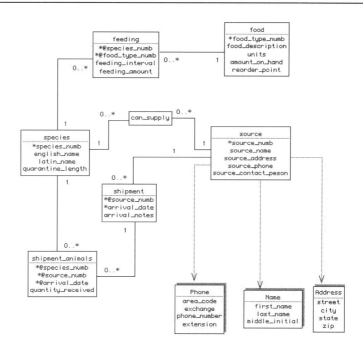

Figure 7-27: A hybrid design for the animals database (part II)

The hybrid schema therefore differs from the relational schema in only one relation:

```
source (source_numb, source_name, source_address, source_phone,
    source_contact_person)
```

The domain for the source_address attribute is the Address class, for the source_phone attribute the Phone class, and for the source_contact_person attribute the Name class.

Designing a Pure Object Database

A pure object database presents an opportunity for the animals database to store additional information about species yet still handle all species together. This can be done through inheritance. As you examine this design, keep in mind that when you declare several subclasses from the same superclass, you can typecast the subclasses back to their parent class. The typecast subclass objects can then be handled as if all were declared from the same class, even though some of their attributes and operations may be very different.

The ER Diagram

As with the ER diagram for the hybrid design, the pure object ER diagram has been split into two parts. Part I (Figure 7-28) deals with the species and their living quarters. Notice in particular that SpeciesClass is an abstract class, a class from which no objects will be created. It has five subclasses (Fish, Mammal, Amphibian, Crustacean, and Mollusc). All of the subclasses except Mollusc have attributes that are not part of SpeciesClass.

Doing this type of general to specific design is very clumsy with a relational database. You would, of course, start with a species table:

```
Species (species numb, english_name, latin_name, quarantine_length)
```

Now, what do you do about the attributes that are specific to a group of animals? One alternative is to add the extra attributes onto the species table and allow those that do not apply to a given animal remain NULL. To make this work, you will also need to add an attribute to indicate the group to which the animal belongs so that you will know which of the extra columns should contain data:

```
Species (species numb, english_name, latin_name, quarantine_length,
    animal_group, live_bearing, gestation_period, larval_period,
    egg_media, shedding_frequency)
```

The result is still a legal relation, but using it will be very cumbersome. You will need to query the animal_group column prior to processing data in any of the other columns.

An alternative is to mimic inheritance:

```
Species (species numb, english_name, latin_name, quarantine_length,
    animal_group)
Fish (species numb, live_bearing)
Mammal (species numb, gestation_period)
Amphibian (species numb. larval_period, egg_media)
Crustacean (species numb, shedding_frequency)
```

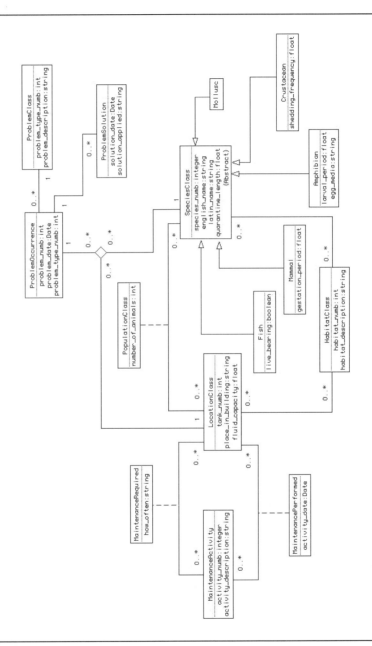

Figure 7-28:   A pure object design for the animals database (part I)

Although the first alternative wastes a bit of disk space with all the NULL values, this second solution is actually much worse. First, you must check the animal_group attribute in the special table to determine which of the secondary tables contains a row for a given animal. Then, you must perform a join between Species and the secondary table to obtain the information. Regardless of the number of rows involved, a retrieval using a join is certainly going to be slower than retrievals that involve only one table.

The bottom line is that there is no satisfactory way to handle a general–specific relationship (inheritance) in a relational database. This is therefore one situation in which an object-oriented database is a better solution.

If you look again at Figure 7-28, you'll notice that the subclasses of SpeciesClass do not participate in any relationships. Instead, all the relationships involve SpeciesClass. The idea here is that for the most part, all species are handled in the same way. (The subclasses are typecast to their superclass for processing.) Therefore, even though no objects are ever created from SpeciesClass, the object identifiers that are stored in related objects are identifiers of objects that have been typecast to SpeciesClass. A location, for example, can use a single relationship to hold identifiers for all species that live in that location, even if they are from different animal groups.

The remainder of the ER diagram can be found in Figure 7-29. Notice that the many-to-many relationship between SpeciesClass and SourceClass has no composite entity. There are no relationship data and therefore there is no need for an additional class. However, it does present one problem: There is no obvious way to document the meaning of the relationship. For that reason, a relationship name has been added to the diagram. (You can add names to any relationship, but in many cases the entities themselves contain enough information that names are not necessary.)

> *Note: The subclasses of SpeciesClass have not been repeated on this diagram for simplicity.*

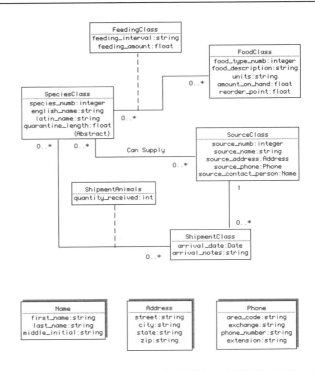

Figure 7-29: A pure object design for the animals database (part II)

The ODL Schema

The ODL syntax for the animals portion of the East Coast Aquarium database can be found in Listing 7-2 at the end of this chapter. As you might expect, the largest class is SpeciesClass, which forms the linchpin of the entire schema. There does not seem to be, however, any ODL syntax for designating an abstract class. Nonetheless, the intent here is that no objects are to be created from SpeciesClass. All animal objects are created from subclasses of SpeciesClass and then typecast back to the superclass when necessary.

To that end, all the relationships that involve animal objects are written using SpeciesClass rather than the subclasses. Each operation that manipulates these relationship sets will use the appropriate programming language syntax to perform the typecasting.

The Mollusc class currently has no attributes or methods added to those of its superclass. Theoretically, if SpeciesClass were not abstract, there would be no reason that objects for molluscs could not be created directly from SpeciesClass. Given the overall design of this schema, however, that would not be a good choice. First, it would be confusing: Some animal objects would be created from subclasses of SpeciesClass while others would be created directly from SpeciesClass. Second, if the time does arise that the aquarium wants to specialize data about molluscs, not only would the schema need to be modified to handle the additions but also the database itself would need to be changed. Creating the Mollusc class, even without added elements, solves both of these problems.

It may seem that some of the classes are missing operations to insert objects into relationships. This is because operations from a class on one side of the relationship take care of the entire process. For example, when maintenance is performed on a location, the add-MaintPerformed method in LocationClass creates an object of the MaintenancePerformed class and inserts its object identifier into both the LocationClass object and the appropriate Maintenance-Activity object. Therefore, when "insert" and "remove" operations do not exist in a class, the relationship is handled by the class at the other end of the relationship.

Most of these operations require the key of the object at the other end of the relationship as an input parameter. The method will then search for the related object so that the DBMS can correctly handle maintaining the necessary inverse relationships. However, there is always a chance that a program or user will supply an invalid key. You will therefore notice that the operations raise "no such" exceptions, indicating that an object with the supplied key could not be found.

As with any database environment, the operations that have been defined depend a great deal on the requirements of the specific environment. It is vital, for example, to know whether a type of food needs to be reordered (the NeedsReorder method). The program that prints an order list will call this method for each FoodClass object, using the AllFood extent to access the objects. It is also important to be able to retrieve feeding information for each species (the displayFeeding method in SpeciesClass).

The bottom line is that there is no "correct" way to write this schema. The version you have just seen is based on assumptions as to what the organization using the database will need to do with it.

Note: The Name, Address, and Phone utility classes are the same as those you have seen previously and therefore have not been repeated in this schema.

```
class SpeciesClass
(extent AllSpecies)
{
    attribute int species_numb;
    attribute string english_name;
    attribute string latin_name;
    attribute float quarantine_length;
    key species_numb;
    relationship set<PopulationClass> homes
        inverse PopulationClass::species;
    relationship set<HabitatClass> habitats
        inverse HabitatClass::species;
    relationship set<ProblemOccurrence> problems
        inverse ProblemOccurrence::species;
    relationship set<ShipmentAnimals> shipments
        inverse ShipmentAnimals::species;
    relationship set<SourceClass> sources
        inverse SourceClass::species;
    relationship set<FeedingClass> food
        inverse FeedingClass::species;
    int getNumb();
    string getEnglish ();
    string getLatin ();
    float getQuarantine();
    void setNumb (in int iNumb);
    void setEnglish (in string iEnglish);
    void setLatin (in string iLatin);
    void setQuarantine (in float iLength);
    void displayHabitats ()
        raises (no_habitats);
    void displayHomes
        raises (no_population);
    void displayProblems
        raises (no_problems);
```

Listing 7-2:   ODL schema for the animals database

```
    void displayShipments ()
        raises (no_shipments);
    void displaySources ()
        raises (no_sources);
    void displayFeeding ()
        raises (no_food);
    void addHabitat (in int iNumb);
    void deleteHabitat (in int iNumb)
        raises (no_such_habitat);
    void addPopulation (in int iNumb, in int iQuantity);
    void decreasePopulation (in int iNumb, in int iQuantity)
        raises (no_such_population);
    void deletePopulation (in int iNumb);
    void addSource (in int iNumb)
        raises (no_such_source);
    void deleteSource (in int iNumb)
        raises (no_such_source);
    void addFood (in int iFoodNumb, in string iInterval, in float iAmount);
    void modifyFood (in int iFoodNumb, in string iInterval)
        raises (not_fed);
    void modifyFood (in int iFoodNumb, in float iAmount)
        raises (not_fed);
    void deleteFood (in int iFoodNumb)
        raises (not_fed);
    void displayFeeding ()
        raises (no_food);
};

class Fish extends SpeciesClass
{
    attribute boolean live_bearing;
    boolean getLiveBearing();
    void setLiveBearing (in boolean iLive);
};

class Mammal extends SpeciesClass
{
    attribute float gestation_period;
    float getGestation();
    void setGestation (in float iGestation);
};

Class Mollusc extends SpeciesClass
{

};
```

Listing 7-2: (Continued)   ODL schema for the animals database

```
class Amphibian extends SpeciesClass
{
    attribute float larval_period;
    attribute string egg_media;
    float getPeriod();
    string getMedia();
    void setPeriod (in float iPeriod);
    void setMedia (in string iMedia);
};

class Crustacean extends SpeciesClass
{
    attribute float shedding_frequency;
    float getShedding();
    void setShedding (in float iShedding);
};

class LocationClass
{
    attribute int tank_numb;
    attribute string place_in_building;
    attribute float fluid_capacity;
    key tank_numb;
    relationship set<PopulationClass> population
        inverse PopulationClass::tank;
    relationship set<HabitatClass> habitats
        inverse HabitatClass::locations;
    relationship set<ProblemOccurence> problems
        inverse ProblemOccurrence::tank;
    relationship set<MaintenanceRequired> required_maintenance
        inverse MaintenanceRequired::tank;
    relationship set<MaintenancePerformed> performed_maintenance
        inverse MaintenancePerformed::tank;
    int getNumb();
    string getPlace();
    float getCapacity();
    void setNumb (in int iNumb);
    void setPlace (in string iPlace);
    void setCapacity (in float iCapacity);
    void addPopulation (in int iSpeciesNumb, in int iQuantity)
        raises (no_such_species);
    void decreasePopulation (in int iSpeciesNumb, in int iQuantity)
        raises (quantity_lt_zero);
    void displayInhabitants ()
        raises (no_inhabitants);
    void addHabitat (in int iHabitatNumb);
    void deleteHabitat (in int iHabitatNumb)
        raises (no_such_habitat);
```

Listing 7-2: (Continued)   ODL schema for the animals database

```
    void addMaintRequirement (in int iActivityNumb, in string iHowOften)
        raises (no_such_activity);
    void deleteMaintRequirement (in int iActivityNumb)
        raises (no_such_activity);
    void addMaintPerformed (in int iActivityNumb, in Date iDate);
    void displayMaintRequired()
        raises (none_required);
    void displayMaintPerformed()
        rasies (none_performed);
    void displayProblems ()
        raises (no_problems);
    void displayProblems (in Date iDate)
        raises (no_problems);
    void displayProblems (in Date iStart, in Date iEnd)
        rasies (no_problems);
};


class PopulationClass
{
    attribute int number_of_animals;
    relationship LocationClass tank
        inverse Locationclass::population;
    relationship SpeciesClass species
        inverse SpeciesClass::homes;
    int getHowMany();
    void setHowMany (in int iHowMany);
    void addAnimals (in int iHowMany);
    void subtractAnimals (in int iHowMany)
        raises (quantity_lt_zero);
};


class HabitatClass
(extent AllHabitats)
{
    attribute int habitat_numb;
    attribute string habitat_description;
    key habitat_numb;
    relationship set<LocationClass> locations
        inverse LocationClass::habitats;
    relationship set<SpeciesClass> species
        inverse SpeciesClass::habitats;
    int getNumb();
    string getDescription();
    void setNumb(in int iNumb);
    void setDescription (in string iDescription);
    set<SpeciesClass> getSpecies()
        raises (no_species);
```

Listing 7-2: (Continued)   ODL schema for the animals database

```
    set<LocationClass> getLocations()
        raises (no_tanks);
};

class FeedingClass
{
    attribute string feeding_interval;
    attribute float feeding_amount;
    relationship SpeciesClass species
        inverse SpeciesClass::food;
    relationship FoodClass food_type;
        inverse FoodClass species;
    string getInterval(0;
    float getAmount();
    void setInterval (in string iInterval);
    void setAmount (in float iAmount);
};

class FoodClass
(extend AllFood)
{
    attribute int food_type_numb;
    attribute string food_description;
    attribute string units;
    attribute float amount_on_hand;
    attribute float reorder_point;
    relationship set<FeedingClass> species
        inverse FeedingClass::food_type;
    key food_type_numb;
    int getNumb();
    string getDescription();
    string getUnits();
    float getAmount();
    float getReorder();
    void setNumb (in int iNumb);
    void setDescription (in string iDescription);
    void setUnits (in string iUnits);
    void setAmount (in float iAmount);
    void addAmount (in float iAmount);
    void subtractAmount (in float iAmount)
        raises (amount_lt_zero);
    void setReorder (in float iReorder);
    boolean needsReorder();
    void displaySpecies()
        raises (no_species);
    set<Speciesclass> getSpecies()
        raises (no_species);
};
```

Listing 7-2: (Continued)   ODL schema for the animals database

```
class ProblemSolution
{
    attribute Date solution_date;
    attribute string solution_applied;
    relationship ProblemOccurrence occurrence
        inverse ProblemOccurrence::solutions;
    Date getDate();
    string getSolution();
    void setDate (in Date iDate);
    void setSolution (in string iSolution);
};

class ProblemClass
(extent AllProblems)
{
    attribute int problem_type_numb;
    attribute string problem_description;
    key problem_type_numb;
    relationship set<ProblemOccurrence> occurrences
        inverse ProblemOccurrence::type;
    int getNumb();
    string getDescription();
    void setNumb (in int iNumb);
    string setDescription (in string iDescription);
    set<ProblemOccurrence> getOccurrences()
        raises (no_occurrences);
    set<ProblemOccurrence> getOccurrence (in Date iDate)
        raises (no_occurrences);
    set<ProblemOccurrence> getOccurrence (in Date iStart, in Date iEnd)
        raises (no_occurrences);
    void addOccurrence (in ProblemOccurrence iOccurrence)
        raises (no_such_occurrence);
    void deleteOccurrence (in ProblemOccurrence iOccurrence)
        riases (no_such_occurrence);
};

class MaintenanceRequired
{
    attribute string how_often;
    relationship MaintenanceActivity activity
        inverse MaintenanceAcvitivy::frequency;
    relationship LocationClass tank
        inverse LocationClass::required_maintenance;
    string getHowOften();
    void setHowOften (in string iHowOften);
};
```

Listing 7-2: (Continued)   ODL schema for the animals database

```
class MaintenancePerformed
{
    attribute Date activity_date;
    relationship MaintenanceActivity activity
        inverse MaintenanceActivity::performed;
    relationship LocationClass tank
        inverse LocationClass::performed_maintenance;
    Date getDate();
    void setDate (in Date iDate);
};

class ProblemOccurrence
(extent Occurrences)
{
    attribute int problem_numb;
    attribute Date problem_date;
    key problem_numb;
    relationship ProblemClass type
        inverse ProblemClass::occurrences;
    relationship set<ProblemSolution> solutions
        inverse ProblemSolution::occurrence;
    relationship SpeciesClass species
        inverse SpeciesClass::problems;
    relationship LocationClass tank
        inverse LocationClass::problems;
    int getNumb();
    Date getDate();
    void setNumb (in int iNumb());
    void setDate (in Date iDate);
    void addSolution (in ProblemSolution iSolution);
    void deleteSolution (in ProblemSolution iSolution);
    set<ProblemSolution> getSolutions()
        raises (no_solutions);
    void displaySolutions()
        raises (no_solutions);
    void setSpecies (in SpeciesClass iSpecies);
    void setLocation (in LocationClass iLocation);
};

class MaintenanceActivity
(extend AllMaintenance)
{
    attribute int activity_numb;
    attribute string activity_description;
    key activity_numb;
    relationship set<MaintenanceRequired> frequency
        inverse MaintenceRequired::activity;
```

Listing 7-2: (Continued) ODL schema for the animals database

```
    relationship set<MaintenancePerformed> performed
        inverse MaintenancePerformed::activity;
    int getNumb();
    string getDescription();
    void setNumb (in int iNumb);
    void setDescription (in string iDescription);
    set<LocationClass> getLocationsWhereNeeded()
        raises (no_tanks);
    void displayLocationsWhereNeeded()
        raises (no_tanks);
    void displayWhenPerformed()
        raises (never_performed);
};

class ShipmentAnimals
{
    attribute int quantity_received;
    relationship SpeciesClass species
        inverse SpeciesClass::shipments;
    relationship ShipmentClass shipment
        inverse ShipmentClass::contents;
    int getQuantity;
    void setQuantity (in int iHowMany);
};

class SourceClass
(extent AllSources)
{
    attribute int source_numb;
    attribute string source_name;
    attribute Address source_address;
    attribute Phone source_phone;
    attribute Name source_contact_person;
    key source_numb;
    relationship set<SpeciesClass> species
        inverse SpeciesClass::sources;
    relationship set<ShipmentClass> shipments
        inverse ShipmentClass::source;
    int getNumb();
    string getName();
    Address getAddress();
    Phone getPhone();
    Name getContact();
    void setNumb (in int iNumb);
    void setName (in string iName);
    void setAddress (in Address iAddress);
    void setPhone (in Phone iPhone);
    void setContact (in Name iContact);
```

Listing 7-2: (Continued)   ODL schema for the animals database

```
        void displaySpeciesAvail ()
            raises (no_species);
        set<SpeciesClass> getSpeciesAvail ()
            raises (no_species);
        void displayShipments()
            raises (no_shipments);
        void displaySpeciesShipped ()
            raises (no_shipments);
        set<SpeciesClass> getSpeciesShipped ()
            raises (no_shipments);
        void addShipment (in Date iDate, in string iNotes);
        void deleteShipment (in Date iDate)
            raises (no_such_shipment);
};

class ShipmentClass
{
        attribute Date arrival_date;
        attribute string arrival_notes;
        relationship SourceClass source
            inverse SourceClass::shipments;
        relationship set<ShipmentAnimals> contents
            inverse ShipmentAnimals::shipment;
        Date getDate();
        string getNotes();
        void setDate (in Date iDate);
        void setNotes (in string iNotes);
        void addAnimal (in int iQuantity, in int iSpeciesNumb)
            raises (no_such_species);
        void deleteAnimal (in int iSpeciesNumb)
            raises (no_such_species);
        void displayContents ()
            raises (no_contents);
        set<SpeciesClass> displaySpeciesOn ()
            raises (no_contents);
```

Listing 7-2: (Continued)   ODL schema for the animals database

8

Database Design Case Study #3: International Intelligence Agency

In the preceding two case studies, we have encountered several database design challenges, including the need to determine whether one or more databases are required, incomplete specifications, and a large number of many-to-many relationships. The final case study we are going to consider presents two different challenges: First, the specifications have been written by people who are more concerned with security than they are with helping database designers; second, the environment contains an enormous number of repeating groups. In addition, this is the largest database you have seen so far. Although at the outset it may appear that there are two or three separate databases, the parts of the database share just enough data that the only way to meet all the organization's requirements is to maintain a single schema.

Note: The cases in the two preceding chapters have to some extent been based on real organizations. However, this case is a pure flight of fancy. (The author had been watching too many spy movies when she wrote it!)

Organizational Overview

A group of database designers have been hired to provide updated information systems for the Independent Intelligence Agency (IIA). Given the nature of the agency's work, the designers realize that they will, in some cases, be working with limited information about the way in which the organization functions. In particular, the design team must accept specifications in whatever format they are provided; team members are not permitted to identify or question agency personnel other than the Vice President for Information Services, who has been their sole contact with the organization. In addition, they will be given few details about the application programs that will be interacting with the database they design.

The Independent Intelligence Agency, headquartered in Geneva, is a nonaligned, worldwide organization that specializes in the gathering and dissemination of covert intelligence. Established during the aftermath of World War II (1947), the IIA is quick to emphasize that while it employs undercover field agents and uses other methods common to intelligence agencies, it has not, is not, and will not be involved in manipulating or in any way influencing the affairs of any country; its sole purpose is to gather information and to sell it to whoever is willing to pay. The IIA will accept commissions to gather specific intelligence as long as doing so does not violate the restriction on becoming active in the affairs of governments. All of IIA's financial resources come from fees paid by clients for information and from investments made with those fees. All transactions are strictly confidential; unauthorized disclosure of information by any employee is cause for immediate dismissal.

The IIA's headquarters building in Geneva contains offices for the Executive Director, Internal Affairs (responsible for monitoring the conduct of field agents, readers, and administrative personnel), Human Resources, and Finance. Because space in the headquarters building is limited, Information Systems has been moved to a renovated warehouse behind the headquarters.

IIA's organization divides the planet into six bureaus, one for each continent except Antarctica. (Any intelligence that comes out of the research stations in Antarctica is handled through one of the northern Canadian stations.) Within the bureaus there are separate *stations* that conduct field operations. Each bureau has a Director, and each station has a Chief who reports to his or her bureau Director. (Note that the central offices for the European Bureau and the Geneva station are on the other side of the city. This arrangement was created to give the Director of the European Bureau and the Chief of the Geneva station the freedom to operate without the constant surveillance of top-level management.)

Stations have three types of people with whom they interact:

- *Field agents* are actively involved in the collection of intelligence. They are typically full-time employees of the IIA.
- *Readers* work inside station buildings reviewing print, audio, video, and electronic materials. Much of a reader's work involves intercepting and decoding international cable and satellite transmissions. Readers are typically full-time employees of the IIA.
- *Informants* are people who are contacted by field agents for information. Informants are usually paid based on the perceived value of the information they provide. They are not IIA employees. Some informants have become so valuable to the IIA, however, that they have been hired as field agents.

Occasionally field agents and readers will exchange roles. For example, a field agent who has spent too long in the field may become a reader and work at that job until retirement. By the same token, a promising reader may undergo field agent training and move into that role.

Stations also have administrative personnel. Although many administrative personnel have little contact with intelligence data or client lists, the security requirements for those employees are as rigorous as for field agents and readers.

Each station has its own budget and manages its own accounting. The Finance Department works at the top organizational level to determine the budget, but once funds are allocated, each station handles the ordering of its own supplies, pays its own expenses (including payments to informants), and cuts its own paychecks. Sales of information may be handled by any level in the organizational hierarchy. Payment is received by the agency making the sale, but all funds are deposited in a single, centralized account in Geneva. The Finance Department's auditors and Internal Affairs staff keep close watch to ensure that all funds collected end up in the bank.

Current Information Systems

IIA maintains a distributed file processing system using ISAM file organization that has been in place since 1974. Each station has its own minicomputer or server that is used to handle the station's accounting functions. These data are available to the Finance Department at the Geneva headquarters building, the station's bureau, and the station's area. Personnel files are kept on the Geneva headquarters' mainframe. The data are available to all stations.

The personnel files, however, contain data about IIA employees only. Each field agent keeps his or her own list of informants. In some cases, those lists have been placed on station computers, but the use is not consistent and, in many cases, agents have been reluctant to share their sources.

Data gathered by field agents are stored in the file processing system. The files containing these raw facts are then indexed to allow retrieval by major topics—countries, individuals, and events. An online query language is available, but attempts to retrieve by a characteristic on which there is no index are unacceptably slow.

The IIA does not sell raw facts but instead sells verified pieces of intelligence. To obtain a sellable piece of intelligence, the IIA must receive confirmation of the same raw fact from several sources. When a field agent or reader reports raw data, he or she also reports a confidence level (from 0 to 100) in the accuracy of that data. Printouts of sorted raw data along with their confidence levels are then examined by readers to find data that support each other with increasing confidence levels. When the confidence levels reach a specific point—IIA will not reveal exactly what that level is—a sellable piece of intelligence is entered into the data file containing sellable merchandise. The reader certifying the piece of intelligence affixes an approximate price, but the exact selling price will be negotiated when the intelligence is actually sold. Of all the tasks that the IIA undertakes, this is the most labor intensive and delays in certifying sellable intelligence can cost the IIA a significant amount in sales.

The IIA has informed the database designers working on a new information system that application programmers will be preparing an expert system to automate the verification of raw data into sellable pieces of intelligence. Although the database designers will not be given any details on how the expert system will work, they will be told exactly what data the expert system will need to function.

The file processing system has become difficult to maintain. The volume of data added to the files is so high that the station IS staff must reblock the files as often as once every two weeks. The reblocking is time consuming and results in unacceptable downtime during working hours.

Security Concerns

Many of IIA's clients are extremely sensitive to the exclusiveness of the data they are buying: They wish to be the *only* purchasers. Exclusive sales command much higher fees than those for pieces of intelligence that can be sold to more than one buyer.

Some data are also extremely sensitive. The IIA believes that the release of those data to the public would violate the IIA's policy against manipulating or influencing existing governments. Therefore, the security of the intelligence data is of primary concern to the IIA.

The ISAM file system they are currently using has no built-in security. Instead, each record of data added to the files contains a field with a security classification. Each user name that the computer recognizes has a security classification as well. Access to data is granted if the user has a classification equal to or above the classification of the data. The classification scheme is an all-or-nothing affair. Anyone who can supply a user name and password that the computer will recognize receives the classification level of the user name and can read all data at that level or below and can modify all data at that classification level. Because users can modify only data at their classification level, highly privileged users who need to modify data at lower classification levels will have more than one account on the system, once for each classification level below them.

The need for a single user to maintain more than one account has led to numerous security breaches. Users who could not remember all of the user names, passwords, and their associated classification levels have written the information down and either taped it to their monitors in full view of an entire office or placed it in the top center drawer of a desk that is never locked. IIA would therefore like a security system where access can be more tightly tailored to an individual's needs so that only a single account is needed for each user.

The IIA's VP for Information Services has told the design team that the IIA is willing to install retina scanners for user identification in all locations. Portable scanners are also available to be issued with laptop computers.

Equipment Development

To augment its intelligence collection activities, the IIA develops and manufactures about half of its own intelligence gathering equipment. Some of this equipment is then sold to intelligence agencies around the world. In keeping with its position of strict neutrality, the IIA sells equipment to any government that has the money to purchase it.

Currently, control over equipment inventory, usage, testing, and sales is very lax. The VP for Information Services, however, has informed the database design team that a new system must include equipment tracking. Although the equipment development is managed separately from the intelligence gathering, most field equipment tests are performed by field agents and most equipment sales are to clients who also purchase intelligence.

Subject Classifications

The current indexing of the existing data files by commonly used keywords has given the IIA's IS staff an idea that could potentially increase sales of pieces of intelligence. The staff would like to assign subject classifications to verified sellable merchandise, much in the same way a library assigns subject headings to books.

Classifications would then be matched with customers in three ways:

- Subject areas about which a customer wants to be notified whenever something is available.
- Subject areas from which the customer has previously made a purchase.
- Subject areas about which a customer has made a request but then subsequently declined to purchase.

Searches on these matchings of customers and subject classifications could potentially tailor sales calls to client purchasing habits, providing a better use of administrative personnel time.

Summary of IS Needs

The IIA is therefore faced with four major IS problems:

- The file processing system is slow and hard to maintain.
- The file processing system does not provide enough flexibility for current application program technologies. In

particular, it cannot support the expert system that will be created to verify sellable pieces of intelligence.
- The system is far less secure than IIA requires.
- The distributed file system has led to inconsistencies in the types of data that are stored on the organization's various computers.

To remedy these problems, the IIA has hired a number of IS teams that will be working independently on various parts of the organization's new system. (The isolation of the teams is for security purposes.) The database will still be distributed, but because it will be a true database rather than a file processing system, it will be possible to use a common schema throughout the entire organization.

Accounting functions, which are of interest only to each local station and its supervising bureau, will continue to use the file processing system, at least temporarily. Any upgrades to that system will take place as a separate project.

System Specifications

Prior to hiring the database design team, the bureau directors, continent directors, and local station chiefs came together to prepare a document that described the data they needed in a database. Input for the meeting came from discussions at the stations with field agents, readers, and administrative personnel.

The following outline of data dealing with intelligence gathering and sales that should be stored in the IIA's database was presented to the database design team:

- Personnel
  - Classification (field agent, reader, or administrative)
  - Real name
  - Birthdate
  - Local country identification number (for example, U.S. Social Security Number)

- Driver's license country (and state, if applicable) and number
- Photo
- Fingerprints
- Retina print
- Height in centimeters
- Weight in kilograms
- Eye color
- Vision
- Current address and phone number
- Aliases (all aliases used, currently or in the past)
  - § Name
  - § Photo
  - § Birthdate
  - § Local country identification number (for example, U.S. Social Security Number)
  - § Driver's license country (and state, if applicable) and number
  - § Height
  - § Weight
  - § Eye color
  - § Address and phone number (if any)
  - § Date last used
- All previous addresses including dates of residence
- Family members (parents; all spouses; biological, adopted, step, and foster children; biological, adopted, step, and foster siblings)
  - § Real name
  - § Birthdate
  - § Current address and phone number
  - § Highest level of education
  - § Current job
  - § Photo
- Education (all schools attended and degrees earned)
- Work history
- Criminal record
- Religion
- Organizations other than IIA to which person belongs

- ◆ Informants
  - Real name
  - Birthdate
  - Local country identification number (for example, U.S. Social Security Number)
  - Driver's license country (and state, if applicable) and number
  - Photo
  - Fingerprints
  - Height
  - Weight
  - Eye color
  - Vision
  - Current address and phone number
  - Aliases (all aliases used, currently or in the past)
    - § Name
    - § Photo
    - § Birthdate
    - § Local country identification number (for example, U.S. Social Security Number)
    - § Driver's license country (and state, if applicable) and number
    - § Height
    - § Weight
    - § Eye color
    - § Address and phone number (if any)
    - § Date last used
  - All previous addresses including dates of residence
  - Family members (parents; all spouses; biological, adopted, step, and foster children; biological, adopted, step, and foster siblings)
    - § Real name
    - § Birthdate
    - § Current address and phone number
    - § Highest level of education
    - § Current job
    - § Photo
  - Education (all schools attended and degrees earned)
  - Work history

- Criminal record
- Religion
- Organizations to which person belongs
- Field agent who recruited the informant
- Contacts made with agents
  - § Date of contact
  - § Outcome of contact
  - § Payment received at contact
  - § Data presented at contact
  - § Agent making the contact

♦ Intelligence data (raw facts)
- Date collected
- Source (for example, informant, printed document, agent observation)
- Location collected (country, city, or town)
- How gathered
- The data itself
- Confidence level
- Cost of the data

♦ Verified piece of intelligence
- The piece of intelligence itself
- Subject classifications
- Customers who purchased the piece of intelligence
- Price paid by each customer
- Date each purchase was made
- Whether sold exclusively

♦ Customers
- Name
- Contact person
- Address
- Phone number
- Fax number
- Subject classifications of previous purchases
- Subject classification of previous inquiries that did not lead to purchases

- Subject classifications for which the customer has requested notification
- Purchases made
- Whether customer requires exclusive sales

Internal Affairs, the department responsible, among other things, for monitoring security, wants additional data kept about access to the database:

- ♦ System logon data (kept about each attempt to log on to the system)
  - User ID
  - Date
  - Time on
  - Workstation ID (if access was not from an IIA workstation, but over a phone line, then the phone number from which the call was placed)
  - Time off (will be null if logon attempt is unsuccessful)

- ♦ Information request data
  - User ID
  - Date
  - Time
  - Workstation ID or phone number of remote call
  - Data item requested
    § Table name
    § Row identifier(s)
  - Result (access granted or denied)
  - Action performed (retrieve, insert, modify, delete)

The final portion of the database will handle the equipment inventory, testing, use, and sales:

- ♦ Current equipment inventory
  - Classification (for example, tape recorder, microphone, camera)
  - Description
  - Location (station at which equipment is stored when not in use)

- Current condition
- Restrictions on use

◆ Equipment use records
- Classification
- Date used
- Agent using equipment
- Where used
- How used
- Result of use

◆ Equipment sales
- Customer
- Date of purchase
- Items purchased
- Amount paid for each item
- Total amount of purchase

◆ Equipment under development
- Classification
- Description
- Intended use
- Station where development is taking place
- Employees involved in development
- Estimated date of completion
- Testing data
    § Date of test
    § Type of test
    § Test results
    § Location of test
    § Agent performing test

For Reference: The Relational Design

There are certainly several ways to prepare a relational schema for the IIA's database. The schema that this book will be using as a reference point is as follows:

```
person (person_ID, classification, first_name, last_name, birthdate,
    local_ID, driver_license_country, driver_license_state,
    driver_license_number, photo, retina_print, height, weight,
    eye_color, vision, religion, street_address, city, state,
    country, zip_post_code, phone, recruiting_agent)
person_types (classification, classification_description)
alias (person_ID, last_name, first_name, photo, birthdate, local_ID,
    driver_license_country, driver_license_state,
    driver_license_number, height, weight, eye_color,
    street_address, city, state, country, zip_post_code, phone,
    date_last_used)
former_address (person_ID, date_moved_in, date_moved_out,
    street_address, city, state, country, zip_post_code)
education (person_ID, school_ID, date_entered, date_left,
    degree_earned, major_subject, minor_subject)
relative (person_ID, first_name, last_name, birthdate, how_related,
    street_address, city, state, country, zip_post_code, phone,
    photo, current_employer, education, current_job)
school (school_ID, school_name, city, state, country)
job (person_ID, company_ID, date_started, date_left, job_title)
company (company_ID, company_name, street_address, city, state,
    zip_post_code, phone)
conviction (person_ID, conviction_date, crime, counts, sentence)
organization (organization_ID, organization_name,
    non_profit_status, street_address, city, state, zip_post_code,
    country, phone)
membership (person_ID, organization_ID, date_joined, date_quit)
fingerprints (person_ID, finger, print)
contact (informant_ID, agent_ID, contact_date, contact_time,
    fee_paid, outcome)
raw_data (data_ID, source_ID, source_type, country, city,
    how_gathered, data_value, confidence_level, data_content,
    fact_ID)
source (source_ID, source_description)
intelligence (fact_ID, fact_value, sold_exclusively, fact_content)
subject (subject_ID, subject_heading)
subjects_assigned (subjectID, fact_ID)
customer (customer_ID, customer_name, customer_contact_person,
    street_address, city, state, zip_post_code, country, phone, fax,
    exclusive_sales)
purchase (fact_ID, customer_ID, date_sold, amount_paid)
subjects_purchased (customer_ID, subject_ID)
subjects_not_purchased (customer_ID, subject_ID)
subjects_to_notify (customer_ID, subject_ID)
user_account (account_ID, person_ID, date_created)
logon (logon_ID, account_ID, logon_date, logon_time, logoff_time)
data_access (logon_ID, access_time, table_used, fact_or_data_ID,
    action_performed)
equipment_item (item_ID, storage_location, current_condition,
    type_ID)
usage_restriction (type_ID, restriction_description)
```

```
equipment_use (item_ID, use_date, use_time, person_ID, use_location,
    how_used, use_results)
equipment_type (type_ID, type_classification, type_description,
    quantity_owned)
equipment_sale (customer_ID, sale_date, sale_total)
sale_item (customer_ID, sale_date, type_ID, quantity_purchased,
    price_each, line_cost)
under_development_item (item_ID, intended_use,
    development_location, estimated_completion_date, type_ID)
item_developer (item_ID, person_ID)
equipment_test (item_ID, test_ID, test_date, person_ID,
    test_location, test_results)
test (test_ID, test_description)
```

Notice that agents, readers, and informants are handled as a single entity—Person. The extra attribute associated with an informant (the ID number of the agent who recruited the informant) is NULL for agent and reader rows. In addition, the relational schema contains a classification attribute that indicates the type of person a row describes.

Designing the Hybrid Database

The complexity of the IIA database allows it to take better advantage of classes as domains than the databases you have seen in the preceding two chapters. In Figure 8-1, the first of four parts, you will find the Person entity and the entities that are necessary to handle the many repeating groups in this database environment. Figure 8-1 also contains the utility classes that are used as domains throughout the database.

The utility classes, especially the Description class, significantly simplify the data that describe agents, informants, and their aliases. In addition, the Description class encapsulates a great deal of related data so that it can be handled as a whole. An application programmer or user working with SQL can therefore retrieve an entire description with a single attribute name, rather than needing to retrieve the individual pieces of the description.

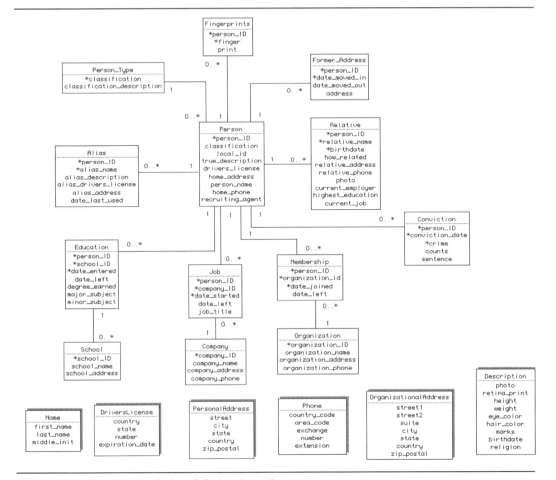

Figure 8-1:   The object–relational design (part I)

The Description class exemplifies the two major benefits of adding objects as domains to a relational schema: You simplify the overall logical design of the database and you simplify the task of retrieving logically grouped attributes that will always be accessed together. On the other hand, there would appear to be no drawbacks to adding the objects.

The second portion of the ER diagram appears in Figure 8-2. Notice that the Contact entity is actually a composite entity that handles the many-to-many relationship between two Person entities, one of which is an agent and one of which is an informant. The two relationships between Contact and Person have therefore been labeled to clarify the meaning of each relationship.

The Raw_Data entity participates in a mutually exclusive relationship with either a Contact or a Source. In other words, a piece of raw data can come from a contact with an informant or another source (for example, print or video material) but not both. UML represents such a relationship by connecting the two relationships with a dashed line that is labeled with the word OR.

The third portion of the design (Figure 8-3) deals with online access to data by IIA employees. A person can access either raw data or a verified piece of intelligence but only one item at a time. Therefore, there is a second mutually exclusive relationship between the Data_Access entity and either the Raw_Data or Intelligence entity. The remainder of the diagram is a standard relational design.

The final portion of the ER diagram (Figure 8-4) concerns the development and use of IIA's equipment. Because the attributes needed to describe equipment in use and equipment under development are so very different, it isn't practical to handle them in a single relation. Unlike the situation with people, where the informants have just one extra attribute, the two categories of equipment have only one attribute in common: the equipment ID. In a practical sense, this is rather awkward. When a piece of equipment is certified ready for use, a row must be removed from the Under_Development_Item table and a new row created for the Equipment_Item table. In addition, the integrity constraint that verifies the uniqueness of the item_ID attribute must apply to both tables rather than to each table individually. However, without the benefit of inheritance, it is impossible to generalize the two types of equipment into a single entity.

Given the issues that have just been discussed and the ER diagrams you have seen, an object–relational design for the IIA database could be written as follows:

```
person (person_ID, classification, local_ID, true_description,
    driver_license, home_address, person_name, home_phone,
    recruiting_agent)
```

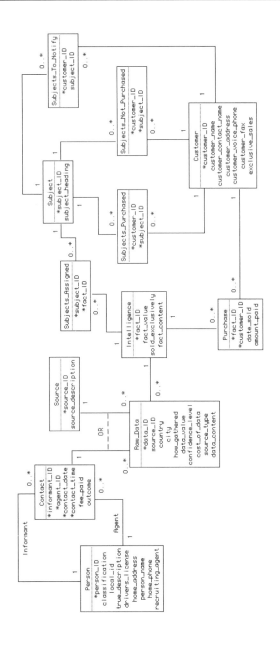

Figure 8-2:   The object–relational design (part II)

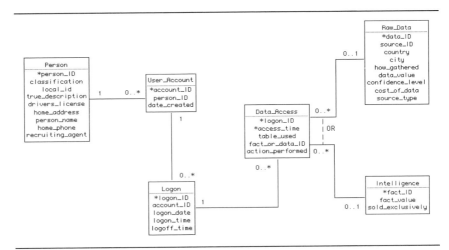

Figure 8-3:   The object–relational design (part III)

```
person_type (classification, classification_description)
alias (person_ID, alias_name, alias_description,
    alias_drivers_license, alias_address, date_last_used)
former_address (person_ID, date_moved_in, date_moved_out, address)
education (person_ID, school_ID, date_entered, date_left,
    degree_earned, major_subject, minor_subject)
relative (person_ID, relative_name, birthdate, how_related,
    relative_address, relative_phone, photo, current_employer,
    education, current_job)
school (school_ID, school_name, school_address)
job (person_ID, company_ID, date_started, date_left, job_title)
company (company_ID, company_name, coompany_address, company_phone)
conviction (person_ID, conviction_date, crime, counts, sentence)
organization (organization_ID, organization_name,
    organization_address, organization_phone)
membership (person_ID, organization_ID, date_joined, date_quit)
fingerprints (person_ID, finger, print)
contact (informant_ID, agent_ID, contact_date, contact_time,
    fee_paid, outcome)
raw_data (data_ID, source_ID, source_type, country, city,
    how_gathered, data_value, confidence_level, data_content,
    fact_ID)
source (source_ID, source_description)
intelligence (fact_ID, fact_value, sold_exclusively, fact_content)
subject (subject_ID, subject_heading)
subjects_assigned (subjectID, fact_ID)
customer (customer_ID, customer_name, customer_contact_person,
    customer_address, customer_phone, customer_fax, exclusive_sales)
purchase (fact_ID, customer_ID, date_sold, amount_paid)
subjects_purchased (customer_ID, subject_ID)
```

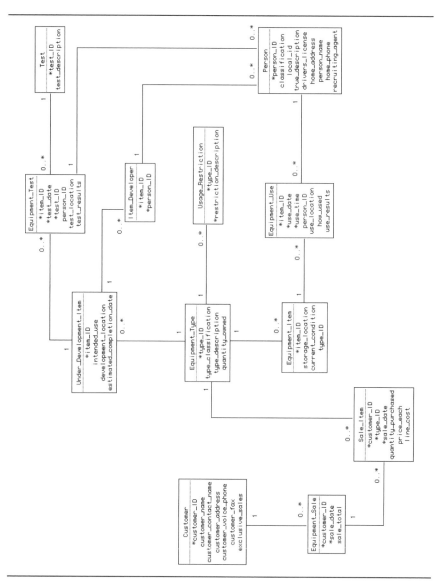

Figure 8-4:   The object–relational design (part IV)

```
subjects_not_purchased (customer_ID, subject_ID)
subjects_to_notify (customer_ID, subject_ID)
user_account (account_ID, person_ID, date_created)
logon (logon_ID, account_ID, logon_date, logon_time, logoff_time)
data_access (logon_ID, access_time, table_used, fact_or_data_ID,
    action_performed)
```

```
equipment_item (item_ID, storage_location, current_condition,
    type_ID)
usage_restriction (type_ID, restriction_description)
equipment_use (item_ID, use_date, use_time, person_ID, use_location,
    how_used, use_results)
equipment_type (type_ID, type_classification, type_description,
    quantity_owned)
equipment_sale (customer_ID, sale_date, sale_total)
sale_item (customer_ID, sale_date, type_ID, quantity_purchased,
    price_each, line_cost)
under_development_item (item_ID, intended_use,
    development_location, estimated_completion_date, type_ID)
item_developer (item_ID, person_ID)
equipment_test (item_ID, test_ID, test_date, person_ID,
    test_location, test_results)
test (test_ID, test_description)
```

Utility classes:

```
Name (first_name, last_name, middle_init)
Description (photo, retina_print, height, weight, eye_color,
    hair_color, marks, birthdate, religion)
DriversLicense (country, state, number, expiration_date)
PersonalAddress (street, city, state, country, zip_postal)
Phone (country_code, area_code, exchange, number, extension)
OrganizationalAddress (street1, street2, suite, city, state,
    country, zip_postal)
```

Like any relational schema, the object–relational schema for the IIA has difficulty representing a relationship between two entities whose primary keys are defined over the same domain. In particular, representing a contact—where two occurrences of the Person entity are related to one another—requires a concatenated key of which two parts are the person_ID attribute. The problem, of course, is that no two attributes in the same relation can have the same name. They must therefore be renamed, as they are in the Contact relation. Nonetheless, both agent_ID and informant_ID are defined over the person_ID domain.

The primary key constraint involving these two attributes is more complex than a standard primary key constraint. For example, the constraint for agent_ID is

```
agent_ID exists in Person and classification = "agent"
```

SQL does not allow expressions of this type as primary key constraints. Therefore, should the IIA choose to use an object–relational approach, it needs to look for a DBMS that not only supports the hybrid model, but also supports the SQL-92 CONSTRAINT syntax so that the additional primary key condition can be stored in the data dictionary.

The utility classes included in this design are classes, not relations. Although the preceding may seem like an obvious statement, its implications are significant. First, the classes may appear on paper here just like relations, but no attributes have been underlined to indicate primary keys: They do not require primary keys. In fact, keys are optional for classes. Second, the classes appear unconnected to any of the relations in the database. This is because they are really definitions of domains rather than entities. They are indeed unrelated to anything else in the database.

Designing the Pure Object Database

The IIA database works extremely well as an object-oriented design. Inheritance (both single and multiple) can be used to handle the problems of similar objects with rather different attributes that at times need to be handled as if they were created from the same class. This design therefore makes far greater use of object-oriented techniques than any schema you have seen so far.

The ER Diagram

The first portion of the ER diagram for the pure object design for the IIA database can be found in Figure 8-5. As you examine this illustration, there are several important things to consider.

> Note: As with the East Coast Aquarium design, the extents have been omitted from the diagram for clarity.

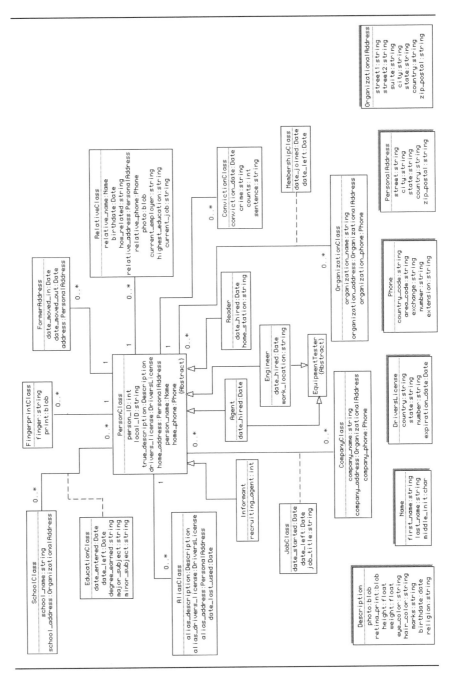

Figure 8-5: A pure object-oriented design (part I)

Handling People

At times we want to be able to handle all the people in the database (with the exception of the relatives) in the same way. However, there are also times where we need to deal with specific subsets of people. Therefore, this is a perfect situation for inheritance. The design includes PersonClass, an abstract base class from which specific types of people classes have been derived. The subclasses currently in the database include Informat, Agent, Reader, and Engineer (a person who develops equipment).

Agent and Engineer also inherit from an interface called EquipmentTester. This is a typical use of an interface to give classes additional identities. Agent and Engineer can be typecast to PersonClass (their superclass) so they can be aggregated with all the other people. However, by implementing the interface, they can also be typecast to the interface. EquipmentTester can then used as a single class that is related to equipment testing.

> Note: UML has no notation for differentiating an interface from a class. Therefore, the interfaces in this design appear as abstract classes with no attributes.

The use of the interface removes the need to support a mutually exclusive relationship. A test on a piece of equipment can be performed by an agent in the field or by an engineer in the lab but not both. However, a test is always performed by an equipment tester, any object with the interface's identity. You will see other examples of this technique throughout this design.

Including Graphics

If you look carefully at the data types in Description, RelativeClass, and PersonClass, you will see something called a *blob*. A blob is a Binary Large Object, the data format used by many DBMSs to store binary data such as images. The assumption here is that the images actually become a part of the database.

However, other DBMSs do not include graphic images in the database files. They instead store the location of a separate graphic file.

In that case, the data type for images will probably be string, because the attribute will contain a path name.

Using the Derived Classes

In the second part of the ER diagram (Figure 8-6) you will find the first use of the classes derived from PersonClass. There is a many-to-many relationship between Agent and Informant. ContactClass contains the intersection data for that relationship.

This situation is one in which the object-oriented approach does very well. Agent and Informant are two distinct classes, regardless of the fact that they have the same superclass. There is no need to implement complex integrity rules to verify that a contact is related to exactly one agent and one informant. The inverse relationship that you will see defined in the ODL schema will take care of that.

Additional Interfaces

Figure 8-6 contains two more interfaces. SourceClass eliminates the need for a mutually exclusive relationship involving RawData. Raw data can come from either a contact, a print source, or an audio/video source but not more than one. Therefore, if ContactClass, PrintSource, and VideoAudioSource implement the SourceClass interface, they can be handled as a single class in the relationship to RawData but yet retain their own, very different, attributes.

The AccessibleItem interface is used in the third portion of the ER diagram (Figure 8-7) to indicate an item that has been retrieved by an agent, reader, or engineer. Because both RawData and IntelligenceClass objects can be retrieved, implementation of the AccessibleItem interface gives the two distinct classes a common identity.

Direct Many-to-Many Relationships

There are three many-to-many relationships between Customer-Class and SubjectClass in Figure 8-6. None of them have any relationship data, but all have different meanings. It is therefore vital that there be labels on the relationships in the diagram so that someone looking at the diagram recognizes why there are three identical relationships.

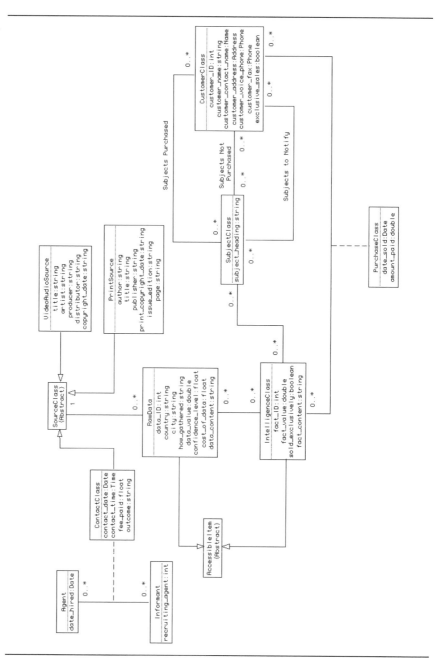

Figure 8-6: A pure object-oriented design (part II)

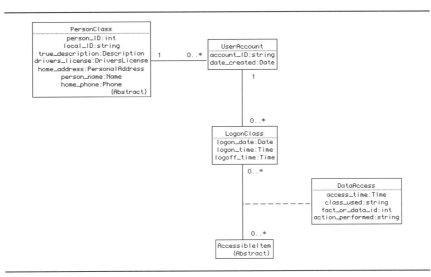

Figure 8-7:   A pure object-oriented design (part III)

Using an Aggregate Class

The fourth portion of the ER diagram (Figure 8-8) contains an aggregate class, EquipmentType. Each object of Equipment Type contains data values that describe a group of Equipment objects.

Equipment is an abstract class that provides a common superclass for the two types of equipment (equipment in use and equipment under development). It allows equipment objects to be aggregated by EquipmentType, regardless of the equipment item's status.

When a new piece of equipment is entered into the database, the user must specify a type classification for the item so that its object can be related to the correct EquipmentType object. In addition, the operation that creates a new piece of equipment must modify the quantity_owned attribute in the appropriate Equipment Type object.

Notice that using the Equipment class as a superclass for both types of equipment items does not eliminate the problem that arises when a piece of equipment under development is certified to be ready for regular use. The UnderDevelopmentItem object must be deleted

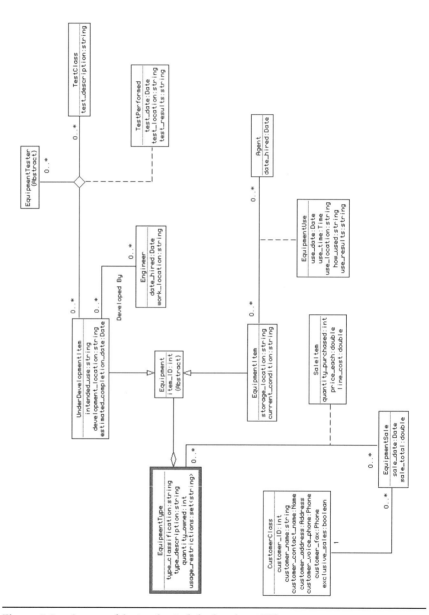

Figure 8-8:   A pure object-oriented design (part IV)

and EquipmentItem object created, just as a row must be deleted from Under_Development_Item and added to Equipment_Item in both relational and object–relational implementations. Nonetheless, the Equipment class does allow all equipment to be treated in the same way when necessary.

Handling an N-ary Relationship

A test that is performed on a piece of equipment under development in Figure 8-8 is a relationship between an item under development (UnderDevelopmentItem), an equipment tester (EquipmentTester), and a type of test (TestClass). As you may remember, UML uses a small diamond to indicate an n-ary relationship between more than two entities or classes. Because the TestPerformed class contains relationship data for this three-way relationship, it is connected to the diamond with a dashed line.

The ODL Schema

The ODL schema for the IIA database can be found at the end of this chapter in Listing 8-1. Because of its complexity and the need to include relationships and operations, it is quite long. Even the Person-Class, which takes up nearly three pages in this book, is nonetheless probably missing some operations.

One of the major drawbacks to a pure object-oriented database is that the schema is difficult to change. It usually cannot be modified while the database is running, as can a relational schema. Database designers therefore attempt to anticipate all methods that might be required before installing the schema. However, even if an object-oriented schema includes every method needed when the database is first put into production use, needs will still change over time. At some point in the future, the database will have to be taken off line and the schema modified.

On the other hand, this schema shifts the application development effort away from the application programmers and places it under the umbrella of the database designers. Once the schema has been installed and the bodies for all the operations have been defined, the task of the application developer is considerably simpler than it would be in a pure relational or hybrid object–relational environment: The majority of the methods that traverse the schema have already been written.

In a pure object-oriented environment, writing the methods once may not be enough. A set of methods must exist for every programming language that will be used to write application programs. If, for example, you are going to let application programmers work in either C++ or Java, every method for every class must be written and tested twice, once in each language.

Inheritance versus Interfaces

When you look at PersonClass, Agent, Engineer, and Equipment-Tester, it is easy to see why EquipmentTester is an interface: Agent and Engineer already inherit from PersonClass. The only way to provide the multiple inheritance is to use an interface.

However, what about SourceClass and AccessibleItem? Source-Class is a class and AccessibleItem is an interface. Neither of these is involved in multiple inheritance. Why would you choose to make one a class and the other an interface?

There is no straightforward answer. Given that neither SourceClass nor AccessibleItem has attributes of its own, they can be either. As a result, the choice must be based on the meaning of the entities involved. SourceClass is logically a more general form of its subclasses—the subclasses are all a type of source—and Source-Class therefore meets the logical criteria for being a superclass.

In contrast, the idea of something being accessible via computer does not necessarily imply a generalization-specialization relationship. Rather, it is a type of behavior that could theoretically be added to any class in the database. Therefore, AccessibleItem is more logically an interface rather than a superclass.

Should a database designer disagree with this reasoning, the database design will not necessarily suffer. As with all database schemas, there is more than one "correct" way to design it.

```
class PersonClass // abstract - could be an interface
(extent people)
{
    attribute int person_ID;
    attribute string local_ID;
    attribute Description true_description;
    attribute PersonalAddress home_address;
    attribute Name person_name;
    attribute Phone home_phone;
    key person_ID;
    relationship set<FingerprintClass> prints
        inverse FingerPrintClass::person;
    relationship set<FormerAddress> addresses
        inverse FormerAddress::person;
    relationship set<RelativeClass> relatives
        inverse RelativeClass::person;
    relationship set<ConvictionClass> convictions
        inverse ConvictionClass::person;
    relationship set<MembershipClass> memberships
        inverse MembershipClass::person;
    relationship set<JobClass> jobs
        inverse JobClass::person;
    relationship set<AliasClass> aliases
        inverse AliasClass::person;
    relationship set<EducationClass> education
        inverse EducationClass::person;
    relationship set<UserAccount> accounts
        inverse UserAccount::owner;
    int getPersonID ();
    string getLocalID ();
    Description getDesc ();
    PersonalAddress getAddress ();
    Name getName ();
    Phone getPhone ();
    void setPersonID (in int iID);
    void setLocalID (in string iID);
    void setDesc (in Description iDesc);
    void setAddress (in PersonalAddress iAddress);
    void setName (in Name iName);
    void setPhone (in Phone iPhone);
    set<FingerprintClass> getPrints ()
        raises (no_prints);
    set<PersonalAddress> getAddress ()
        raises (no_addresses);
```

Listing 8-1:   ODL schema for the object-oriented IIA database

```
set<PersonalAddress> findAddress (in Date iDate)
    raises (no_addresses);
set<PersonalAddress> findAddress (in Date iStart, in Date iEnd)
    raises (no_addresses);
set<RelativeClass> getRelatives ()
    raises (no_relatives);
set<RelativeClass> findRelative (in Name iName)
    raises (no_relatives);
set<RelativeClass> findRelative (in Date iBirthdate)
    raises (no_relative);
void addRelative (in RelativeClass iRelative);
void modifyRelative (in RelativeClass iRelative)
    raises (no_such_relative);
void deleteRelative (in Name iName, in Date iDate)
    raises (no_such_relative);
set<ConvictionClass> getConvictions ()
    raises (no_convictions);
set<ConvictionClass> findConvictions (in string iCrime)
    raises (no_convictions);
set<ConvictionClass> findConvictions (in Date iStart, in Date iEnd)
    raises (no_convictions);
void addConviction (in ConvictionClass iConviction);
void modifyConviction (in ConvictionClass iConviction)
    raises (no_such_conviction);
void deleteConviction (in Date iDate, in string iCrime)
    raises (no_such_conviction);
set<MembershipClass> getMemberships ()
    raises (no_memberships);
set<MembershipClass> findMemberships (in string iOrgName)
    raises (no_memberships);
void addMembership (in MemberShipClass iMembership,
    in string iOrganization);
void modifyMembership (in string iOrganization, in Date iJoined,
    in Date iLeft)
    raises (no_such_membership);
void deleteMembership (in string iOrganization, in Date iJoined)
    raises (no_such_membership);
set<JobClass> getJobs ()
    raises (no_jobs);
set<JobClass> findJobs (in Date iStart, in Date iEnd)
    raises (no_jobs);
set<JobClass> findJobs (in string iCompanyName)
    raises (no_jobs);
void addJob (in JobClass iJob, in string iCompany);
void modifyJob (in string iCompany, in Date iStart, in Date iEnd)
    raises (no_such_job);
void deleteJob (in string iCompany, in Date iStart)
    raises (no_such_job);
set<AliasClass> getAliases ()
    raises (no_aliases);
```

Listing 8-1: (Continued)   ODL schema for the object-oriented IIA database

```
    AliasClass findAlias (in string iName)
        raises (no_such_alias);
    set<Aliases> findAliases (in Date iStart, in Date iEnd)
        raises (no_aliases);
    void addAlias (in AliasClass iAlias);
    void modifyAlias (in AliasClass iAlias)
        raises (no_such_alias);
    void deleteAlias (in Name iName)
        raises (no_such_alias);
    set<EducationClass> getEducation ()
        raises (no_education);
    set<EducationClass> getEducation (in Date iStart, in Date iEnd)
        raises (no_education);
    EducationClass findEducation (in string iSchool, in Date iStart)
        raiaes (no_such_education);
    void addEducation (in EducationClass iEducation);
    void modifyEducation (in EducationClass iEducation)
        raises (no_such_education);
    void deleteEducation (in string iSchool, in Date iStart)
        raises (no_such_education);
    set<UserAccount> getAccounts();
    set<AccessibleItem> getItemsAccessed ()
        raises (no_access);
    set<AccessibleItem> getItemsAccessed (in Date iStart, in Date iEnd)
        raises (no_access);
    void addAccount (in UserAccount iAccount);
    void deleteAccount (in string account_ID)
        raises (no_such_account);
    void getActions (out set<DataAccess> accesses,
        out set<AccessibleItem> items)
        raises (no_access);
    void getActions (out set<DataAccess> accesses,
        out set<AccessibleItem> items, in Date iStart, in Date iEnd)
        raises (no_access);
    set<LogonClass> getLogons ()
        raises (no_logons);
    set<LogonClass< getLogons (in Date iStart, in Date iEnd)
        raises (no_logons);
};

class Informant extends PersonClass
(extent informants)
{
    attribute int recruiting_agent;
    relationship set<ContactClass> contacts
        inverse ContactClass::informant;
    int getRecruiter ();
```

Listing 8-1: (Continued)   ODL schema for the object-oriented IIA database

```
        void setRecruiter (in int iAgent);
        void getContactDetails (inout set<ContactClass> contacts,
            inout set<Agent> agents)
            raises (no_contacts);
        void findContacts (inout set<ContactClass> contacts,
            inout set<Agent> agents, in Date iStart, in Date iEnd)
            raises (no_contacts);
};

class Reader extends PersonClass
(extent readers)
{
    attribute Date date_hired;
    attribute string home_station;
    Date getHireDate ();
    string getStation();
    void setHireDate (in Date iDate);
    void setStation (in string iStation);
};

Class Engineer extends PersonClass : EquipmentTester
(extent engineers)
{
    attribute Date date_hired;
    attribute string work_location;
    relationship set<UnderDevelopmentItem> items
        inverse UnderDevelopmentItem::engineers;
    Date getHireDate ();
    string getLocation();
    void setHireDate (in Date iDate);
    void setLocation (in string iLocation);
    set<UnderDevelopmentItem> getItems();
};

Class Agent extends PersonClass : EquipmentTester
(extent agents)
{
    attribute Date date_hired;
    relationship set<ContactClass> contacts
        inverse ContactClass::agent;
    relationship set<EquipmentUse> items_used
        inverse EquipmentUse::agent;
    Date getHireDate();
    void setHireDate (in Date iDate);
    void getContactDetails (inout set<ContactClass> contacts,
        inout set<Informant> informants)
        raises (no_informants);
```

Listing 8-1: (Continued)   ODL schema for the object-oriented IIA database

```
      void findContacts (inout set<ContactClass> contacts,
          inout set<Informant> informants, in Date iStart, in Date iEnd)
          raises (no_contacts);
      void getEquipmentUsed (out set<EquipmentUse> uses,
          out set<EquipmentItem> items)
          raises (no_use);
      void getEquipmentUsed (out set<EquipmentUse> uses,
          out set<EquipmentItem> items, in Date iStart, in Date iEnd)
          raises (no_use);
};

interface EquipmentTester
{
    relationship set<TestPerformed> tests
        inverse TestPerformed::tester;
    set<TestPerformed> getTests ()
        raises (no_tests);
    set<TestPerformed> getTests (in Date iStart, in Date iEnd)
        raises (no_tests);
};

class FingerPrintClass
(extent prints)
{
    attribute string finger;
    attribute blob print;
    relationship PersonClass person
        inverse PersonClass::prints;
    string getFinger();
    blob getPrint();
    void setFinger (in string iFinger);
    void setPrint (in blob iPrint);
    PersonClass getPerson();
};

class RelativeClass
(extent relatives)
{
    attribute Name relative_name;
    attribute Date birth_date;
    attribute string how_related;
    attribute PersonalAddress relative_address;
    attribute Phone relative_phone;
    attribute blob photo;
    attribute string current_employer;
    attribute string highest_education;
    attribute string current_job;
    key relative_name, birth_date;
```

Listing 8-1: (Continued)   ODL schema for the object-oriented IIA database

```
    relationship PersonClass person
        inverse PersonClass::relatives;
    Name getName ();
    Date getBirthdate ();
    String getHowRelated();
    PersonalAddress getAddress ();
    Phone getPhone ();
    blob getPhoto ();
    string getEmployer ();
    string getEducation ();
    string getJob ();
    void setName (in Name iName);
    void setBirthdate (in Date iDate);
    void setHowRelated (in string iHow);
    void setAddress (in PersonalAddress iAddress);
    void setPhone (in Phone iPhone);
    void setPhoto (in blob iPhoto);
    void setEmployer (in string iEmployer);
    void setEducation (in string iEducation);
    void setJob (in string iJob);
    PersonClass getPerson ();
};

class FormerAddress
(extent addresses)
{
    attribute Date date_moved_in;
    attribute Date date_moved_out;
    attribute PersonalAddress address;
    relationship PersonClass person
        inverse PersonClass::addresses;
    Date getMovedIn ();
    Date getMovedOut ();
    PersonalAddress getAddress();
    void setMovedIn (in Date iDate);
    void setMovedOut (in Date iDate);
    void setAddress (in PersonalAddress iAddress);
    PersonClass getPerson ();
};

class ConvictionClass
(extent convictions)
{
    attribute Date conviction_date;
    attribute string crime;
    attribute int counts;
    attribute string sentence;
```

Listing 8-1: (Continued)   ODL schema for the object-oriented IIA database

```
     relationship PersonClass person
         inverse PersonClass::convictions;
     Date getDate();
     string getCrime();
     int getCounts ();
     string getSentence ();
     void setDate (in Date iDate);
     void setCrime (in string iCrime);
     void setCounts (in int iCounts);
     void setSentence (in string iSentence);
     PersonClass getPerson ();
{;

Class OrganizationClass
(extent organizations}
{
     attribute string organization_name;
     attribute OrganizationalAddress organization_address;
     attribute Phone organization_phone;
     relationship set<MembershipClass> members
         inverse MembershipClass::organization;
     string getName ();
     OrganizationalAddress getAddress ();
     Phone getPhone();
     void setName (in string iName);
     void setAddress (in OrganizationalAddress iAddress);
     void setPhone (in Phone iPhone);
     set<PersonClass> getMembers ()
         raises (no_members);
     set<PersonClass> getCurrentMembers ()
         raises (no_members);
     void addMembership (in MembershipClass iMember, in int person_ID);
     void mmodifyMembership (in MembershipClass iMember, in int person_ID)
         raises (no_such_member);
     void deleteMembership (in person_ID, in Date iStart)
         raises (no_such_member);
};

class MembershipClass
{
     attribute Date date_joined;
     attribute Date date_left;
     relationship PersonClass person
         inverse PersonClass::memberships;
     relationship OrganizationClass organization
         inverse OrganizationClass::members;
     Date getJoined();
     Date getLeft();
```

Listing 8-1: (Continued)   ODL schema for the object-oriented IIA database

```
      void setJoined (in Date iDate);
      void setLeft (in Date iDate);
      PersonClass getPerson();
      OrganizationClass getOrganization();
};

class CompanyClass
(extent companies)
{
      attribute string company_name;
      attribute OrganizationalAddress company_address;
      attribute Phone company_phone;
      key company_name;
      relationship set<JobClass> employees
          inverse JobClass::company;
      string getName ();
      OrganizationalAddress getAddress();
      Phone getPhone ();
      void setName (in Name iName);
      void setAddress (in OrganizationalAddress iAddress);
      void setPhone (in Phone iPhone);
      set<PersonClass> getCurrentEmployees ()
          raises (no_employees);
      boolean personEmployed (in int person_ID);
      void getJobProfile (in int person_ID, inout JobClass)
          raises (not_employed);
      void addEmployee (in JobClass iJob, in int person_ID);
      void modifyEmployee (in JobClass iJob, in int person_ID)
          raises (no_such_employee);
      void deleteEmployee (in int person_ID, in Date iStart)
          raises (no_such_employee);
};

class JobClass
{
      attribute Date date_started;
      attribute Date date_left;
      attribute string job_title;
      relationship PersonClass person
          inverse PersonClass::jobs;
      relationship CompanyClass company
          inverse CompanyClass::employees;
      Date getStartDate ();
      Date getLeftDate ();
      string getJobTitle();
      void setStartDate (in Date iDate);
      void setLeftDate (in Date iDate);
      void setJobTitle (in string iTitle);
```

Listing 8-1: (Continued)   ODL schema for the object-oriented IIA database

```
    PersonClass getPerson ();
    CompanyClass getCompany ();
};

class AliasClass
(extent aliases)
{
    attribute Description alias_description;
    attribute DriversLicense alias_drivers_license;
    attribute PersonalAddress alias_address;
    attribute Date date_last_used;
    relationship PersonClass person
        inverse PersonClass::aliases;
    Description getDescription();
    DriversLicense getLicense();
    PersonalAddress getAddress();
    Date getLastUsed ();
    void setDescription (in Description iDescription);
    void setDriversLicense (in DriversLicense iLicense);
    void setAddress (in PersonalAddress iAddress);
    void setLastUsed (in Date iDate);
    PersonClass getPerson ();
};

class SchoolClass
(extent schools)
{
    attribute string school_name;
    attribute OrganizationalAddress school_address;
    key school_name;
    relationship set<EducationClass> students
        inverse EducationClass::school;
    string getName ();
    OrganizationalAddress getAddress ();
    void setName (in string iName);
    void setAddress (in OrganizationalAddress iAddress);
    set<PersonClass> getCurrentStudents ()
        raises (no_students);
    EducationClass getStudentProfile (in int person_ID, in Date iDate);
    boolean verifyAttendance (in int person_ID);
    void addStudent (in int person_ID, in EducationClass iEducation);
    void modifyStudent (in int person_ID, in EducationClass iEducation)
        raises (no_such_student);
    void deleteStudent (in int person_ID, in Date iDate)
        raises (no_such_student);
};
```

Listing 8-1: (Continued)   ODL schema for the object-oriented IIA database

```
class EducationClass
{
    attribute Date date_entered;
    attribute Date date_left;
    attribute string degree_earned;
    attribute string major_subject;
    attribute string minor_subject;
    relationship PersonClass person
        inverse PersonClass::education;
    relationship SchoolClass school
        inverse SchoolClass::students;
    Date getEntered();
    Date getleft ();
    string getDegree();
    string getMajor ();
    string getMinor ();
    void setEntered (in Date iDate);
    void setLeft (in Date iDate);
    void setDegree (in string iDegree);
    void setMajor (in string iMajor);
    void setMinor (in string iMinor);
    PersonClass getPerson();
    SchoolClass getSchool();
};

class SourceClass // abstract
{extent sources}
{
    relationship set<RawData> data
        inverse RawData::source;
    set<RawData> getData ();
    void addData (in RawData iData);
    void deleteData (in int iDataID)
        raises (no_such_data);
};

class ContactClass extends SourceClass
(extent contacts)
{
    attribute Date contact_date;
    attribute Time contact_time;
    attribute float fee_paid;
    attribute string outcome;
    relationship Agent agent
        inverse Agent::contacts;
    relationship Informant informant
        inverse Informant::contacts;
```

Listing 8-1: (Continued) ODL schema for the object-oriented IIA database

```
    Date getDate();
    Time getTime();
    float getFee();
    string getOutcome();
    void setDate (in Date iDate);
    void setTime (in Time iTime);
    void setFee (in float iFee);
    void setOutcome (in string iOutcome);
    Agent getAgent();
    Informant getInformant();
};

class VideoAudoSource extends SourceClass
{
    attribute string title;
    attribute string artist;
    attribute string producer;
    attribute string distributor;
    attribute string copyright_date;
    string getTitle();
    string getArtist();
    string getProducer();
    string getDistributor();
    string getCopyright();
    void setTitle (in string iTitle);
    void setArtist (in string iArtist);
    void setProducer (in string iProducer);
    void setDistributor (in string iDistributor);
    void setCopyright (in string iCopyright);
};

class PrintSource extends SourceClass
{
    attribute string author;
    attribute string title;
    attribute string publisher;
    attribute string print_copyright_date;
    attribute string issue_edition;
    attribute string page;
    string getAuthor();
    string getTitle();
    string getPublisher();
    string getCopyright();
    string getIssue();
    string getPage();
    void setAuthor (in string iAuthor);
    void setTitle (in string iTitle);
    void setPublisher (in string iPublisher);
```

Listing 8-1: (Continued)   ODL schema for the object-oriented IIA database

```
      void setCopyright (in string iCopyright);
      void setIssue (in string iIssue);
      void setpage (in string iPage);
};

interface AccessibleItem
(extent dataItems)
{
    relationship set<DataAccess> accesses
        inverse DataAccess::item;
    set<PersonClass>set< getAccessors ()
        raises (no_access);
    PersonClass> getAccessors (in Date iStart, in Date iEnd)
        raises (no_access);
    void getWhenAccessed (out set<DataAccess> accesses,
        out set<LogonClass> logons)
        raises (no_access;
    void getWhenAccessed (in Date iStart, in Date iEnd,
        out set<DataAccess> accesses, out set<LogonClass> logons)
        raises (no_access);
};

class RawData : Accessibleitem
(extent data)
{
    attribute int data_ID;
    attribute string country;
    attribute string city;
    attribute string how_gathered;
    attribute double data_value;
    attribute float confidence_level;
    attribute float cost_of_data;
    attribute string data_content;
    key data_ID;
    relationship SourceClass source
        inverse SourceClass::data;
    relationship set<IntelligenceClass> facts
        inverse Intelligence::data;
    int getID();
    string getCountry();
    string getCity();
    string getHowGathered();
    double getValue();
    float getConfidence();
    float getCost();
    string getContent();
    void setID (in int iID);
    void setCountry (in string iCountry);
```

Listing 8-1: (Continued)   ODL schema for the object-oriented IIA database

```
    void setCity (in string iCity);
    void setHowGathered (in string iHow);
    void setValue (in double iValue);
    void setConfidence (in float iConfidence);
    void setCost (in float iCost);
    void setContent (in string iContent);
    SourceClass getSource();
    set<IntelligenceClass> getIntelligence();
};

class IntelligenceClass : AccessibleItem
(extent intelligence)
{
    attribute int fact_ID;
    attribute double fact_value;
    attribute boolean sold_exclusively;
    attribute string fact_content;
    key fact_ID;
    relationship set<RawData> data
        inverse RawData::facts;
    relationship set<SubjectClass> subjects_assigned
        inverse SubjectClass::facts;
    relationship set<PurchaseClass> sales
        inverse PurchaseClass::fact;
    int getID();
    double getValue();
    boolean checkExclusiveSale();
    string getContent();
    void setID (in int iID);
    void setValue (in double iValue);
    void setSale (in boolean iSale);
    void string setContent (in string iContent);
    void addSubject (in string subject_heading)
        raises (no_such_subject);
    void deleteSubject (in string subject_heading)
        raises (no_such_subject);
    set<SubjectClass> getSubjects();
    void addRawData (in int iID)
        raises (no_such_data);
    void deleteRawData (in int iID)
        raises (no_such_data);
    set<RawData> getData();
    void addPurchase (in PurchaseClass iPurchase);
    void deletePurchase (in int Customer_ID, in Date iDate)
        raises (no_such_purchase);
    void getPurchases (out set<PurchaseClass> iPurchases,
        inout set<CustomerClassset> iCustomers);
};
```

Listing 8-1: (Continued)   ODL schema for the object-oriented IIA database

```
class PurchaseClass
{
    attribute Date date_sold;
    attribute double amount_paid;
    relationship IntelligenceClass fact
        inverse IntelligenceClass::purchases;
    relationship CustomerClass customer
        inverse CustomerClass::purchases;
    Date getDate();
    double getAmount();
    void setDate (in Date iDate);
    void setAmount (in double iAmount);
    IntelligenceClass getFact ();
    CustomerClass getCustomer ();
};

class SubjectClass
{extent subjects)
{
    attribute string subject_heading;
    relationship set<IntelligenceClass> facts
        inverse IntelligenceClass::subjects;
    relationship set<CustomerClass> purchased
        inverse CustomerClass::purchased;
    relationship set<CustomerClass> not_purchased
        inverse CustomerClass::not_purchased;
    relationship set<CustomerClass> notify
        inverse Customerclass::notify;
    string getHeading();
    void setHeading (in string iHeading);
    set<IntelligenceClass> getIntelligence();
    set<CustomerClass> getPurchased ();
    set<CustomerClass> getNotPurchased ();
    set<CustomerClass> getNotify ();
};

class CustomerClass
(extent customers)
{
    attribute int customer_ID;
    attribute string customer_name;
    attribute Name customer_contact_name;
    attribute OrganizationalAddress customer_address;
    attribute Phone customer_voice_phone;
    attribute Phone customer_fax;
    attribute boolen exclusive_sales;
    key customer_ID;
```

Listing 8-1: (Continued)   ODL schema for the object-oriented IIA database

```
    relationship set<PurchaseClass> purchases
        inverse PurchaseClass::customer;
    relationship set<SubjectClass> purchased
        inverse SubjectClass::purchased;
    relationship set<SubjectClass> not_purchased
        inverse SubjectClass::not_purchased;
    relationship set<SubjectClass> notify
        inverse SubjectClass::notify;
    relationship set<EquipmentSale> equipment_purchased
        inverse EquipmentSale::customer;
    int getID();
    string getName();
    Name getContact();
    OrganizationalAddress getAddress();
    Phone getVoicePhone();
    Phone getFax();
    boolean checkExclusiveSales();
    void setID (in int iID);
    void setName (in string iName);
    void setAddress (in OrganizationalAddress iAddress);
    void setVoicePhone (in Phone iPhone);
    void setFax (in Phone iFax);
    void setExSales (in boolean iEx);
    set<IntelligenceClass> getPurchases ();
    void addPurchase (in int fact_ID, in PurchaseClass iPurchase);
    void deletePurchase (in int fact_ID, in Date iDate)
        raises (no_such_purchase);
    set<SubjectClass> getSubjectsPurchased ()
        raises (no_subjects);
    // Subjects purchased are addded by the addPurchase operation
    set<SubjectClass> getSubjectsNotPurchased ()
        raises (no_subjects);
    void addNotPurchased (in string subject_heading)
        raises (no_such_subject);
    void deleteNotPurchased (In string subject_reading)
        raises (no_such_subject);
    set<SubjectClass> getSubjectsToNotify()
        raises (no_subjects);
    void addSubjectToNotify (in string subject_heading)
        raises (no_such_subject);
    void deleteSubjectToNotify (in string subject_heading)
        raises (no_such_subject);
    void addEquipmentPurchase (in EquipmentSale iSale);
    void deleteEquipmentPurchase (in Date iDate)
        raises (no_such_purchase);
    set<EquipmentType> getEquipmentTypesPurchased ();
    void getEquipmentPurchases (out set<EquipmentSale> Purchases,
        out set<SaleItem> items)
        raises (no_purchases);
};
```

Listing 8-1: (Continued)   ODL schema for the object-oriented IIA database

```
class UserAccount
(extents accounts)
{
    attribute string account_ID;
    attribute Date date_created;
    relationship PersonClass owner
        inverse personClass::accounts;
    relationship set<LogonClass> logons
        inverse LogonClass::account;
    string getID ();
    Date getDate();
    void setID (in string iID);
    void setDate (in Date iDate);
    PersonClass getPerson();
    set<LogonClass> getLogons();
    set<LogonClass> getLogons (in Date iStart, in Date iEnd);
    void addLogon (in LogonClass iLogon);
};

class LogonClass
{
    attribute Date logon_date;
    attribute Time logon_time;
    attribute Time logoff_time;
    relationship UserAccount account
        inverse UserAccount::logons;
    relationship set<DataAccess> uses
        inverse DataAccess::logon
    Date getDate();
    Time getTimeOn();
    time getTimeOff();
    void setDate (in Date iDate);
    void setTimeOn (in Time iTime);
    void setTimeOff (in Time iTime);
    PersonClass getPerson ();
    UserAccount getAccount ();
    set<AccessibleItem> getItemsAccessed ()
        raises (no_items);
    void getItemsAccessed (out set<AccessibleItem> items,
        out set<DataAccess> actions)
        raises (no_items);
};
```

Listing 8-1: (Continued)   ODL schema for the object-oriented IIA database

```
class DataAccess
{
    attribute Time access_Time;
    attribute string class_used;
    attribute int fact_or_data_ID;
    attribute string action_performed;
    relationship LogonClass logon
        inverse LogonClass::uses;
    relationship AccessibleItem item
        inverse AccessibleItem::accesses;
    Time getTime();
    string getClass();
    int getID();
    string getAction();
    void setTime (in Time iTime);
    void setClass (in string iClass);
    void setID (in int ID);
    void setAction (in string iAction);
    PersonClass getPerson ();
    UserAccount getAccount ();
    LogonClass getLogon ();
    AccessibleItem getItem ();
};

class EquipmentType // This is the aggregate class for the Equipment class
{extent equipmentTypes)
{
    attribute string type_classification;
    attribute string type_description;
    attribute int quantity_owned;
    attribute set<string> usage_restrictions;
    relationship set<Equipment> gadgets
        inverse Equipment::type;
    relationship set<SaleItem> sales
        inverse SaleItem::type;
    string getClass ();
    string getType ();
    int getQuantity ();
    set<string> getRestrictions ();
    void setClass (in string iClass);
    void setType (in string iType);
    void setQuantity(in int iQuantity);
    void modifyQuantity (in int iQuantity);
    void setRestrictions (in set<string> iRules);
    void addRestriction (in string iRule);
```

Listing 8-1: (Continued)   ODL schema for the object-oriented IIA database

```
    void deleteRestriction (in string iRule)
        raises (no_such_restriction);
    void addGadget (in Equipment iGadget);
    void deleteGadget (in Equipment iGadget)
        raises (no_such_gadget);
    void addSaleItem (in SaleItem iItem);
    void deleteSaleItem (in SaleItem iItem)
        raises (no_such_item);
};


class Equipment // abstract
(extent equipment)
{
    attribute int item_ID;
    key item_ID;
    relationship EquipmentType type
        inverse EquipmentType::gadgets;
    void addToTypes (in string type_classification)
        raises (no_such_type);
    void deleteFromTypes (in string type_classification)
        raises (no_such_type);
    Equipmenttype getType();
    int getID();
    void setID (in int iID);
};

class EquipmentSale
{
    attribute Date sale_date;
    attribute double sale_total;
    relationship CustomerClass customer
        inverse CustomerClass::equipment_purchased;
    relationship set<SaleItem> items_on
        inverse SaleItem::sale;
    Date getDate();
    double getTotal();
    void setDate (in Date iDate);
    void setTotal (in double iTotal);
    void getItemsSold (out set<EquipmentType> types, out set<SaleItem> items)
        raises (no_items);
    CustomerClass getCustomer ();
};
```

Listing 8-1: (Continued)   ODL schema for the object-oriented IIA database

```
class SaleItem
{
    attribute int quantity_purchased;
    attribute double price_each;
    attribute double line_cost;
    relationship EquipmentType type
        inverse EquipmentType::sales;
    relationship EquipmentSale items_on
        inverse EquipmentSale::sale;
    int getQuantity();
    double getPrice();
    double getLine();
    void setQuantity (in int iQuantity);
    void setPrice (in double iPrice);
    void computeLine ();
    EquipmentType getType();
    EquipmentSale getSale ();
};

class EquipmentItem extends Equipment
(extent useItems)
{
    attribute string storage_location;
    attribute string current_condition;
    relationship set<EquipmentUse> uses
        inverse EquipmentUse::item;
    string getStorage();
    string getLocation();
    void setStorage (in string iStorage);
    void setLocation (in String iLocation);
    set<EquipmentUse> getUses()
        raises (not_used);
    set<EquipmentUse> getUses (in Date iStart, in Date iEnd)
        raises (not_used);
};

class EquipmentUse
{
    attribute Date use_date;
    attribute Time use_time;
    attribute string use_location;
    attribute string how_used;
    attribute string use_results;
    relationship EquipmentItem item
        inverse EquipmentItem::uses;
    relationship Agent agent
        inverse Agent::items_used;
```

Listing 8-1: (Continued)   ODL schema for the object-oriented IIA database

```
    Date getDate();
    Time getTime();
    string getLocation();
    string getHowUsed();
    string getResults();
    void setDate (in Date iDate);
    void setTime (in Time iTime);
    void setLocation (in string iLocation);
    void setHowUsed (in string iHow);
    void setResults (in string iResults);
    EquipmentItem getItem();
    Agent getAgent();
};

class UnderDevelopmentItem extends Equipment
(extent developmentItems)
{
    attribute string intended_use;
    attribute string development_location;
    attribute Date estimated_completion_date;
    relationship set<Engineers> engineers
        inverse Engineers::items;
    relationship set<TestPerformed> tests
        inverse TestPerformed::item;
    string getUse();
    string getLocation();
    Date getDate();
    void setUse (in string iUse);
    void setLocation (in string iLocation);
    void setDate (in Date iDate);
    void addEngineer (in Engineer iEngineer);
    void deleteEngineer (in Engineer iEngineer)
        raises (no_developers);
    set<Engineer> getDevelopers ()
        raises (no_developers);
};
class TestClass
(extent tests)
{
    attribute string test_description;
    relationship set<TestPerformed> tests
        inverse TestPerformed::type;
    string getDescription();
    void setDescription (in string iDescription);
```

Listing 8-1: (Continued)   ODL schema for the object-oriented IIA database

```
        void getTests(out set<Textperformed> tests,
            out set<EquipmentTester testers,
            out set<UnderDevelopmentItem> items)
            raises (no_tests);
        void getTests(out set<Textperformed> tests,
            out set<EquipmentTester testers,
            out set<UnderDevelopmentItem> items, in Date iStart, in Date iEnd)
            raises (no_tests);
};


class TestPerformed
{
    attribute Date test_date;
    attribute string test_location;
    attribute string test_results;
    relationship UnderDevelopmentItem item
        inverse UnderDevelopmentItem::tests;
    relationship TestClass type
        inverse TestClass::tests;
    relationship EquipmentTester tester
        inverse EquipmentTester::tests;
    Date getDate();
    string getLocation();
    string getResults();
    void setDate (in Date iDate);
    void setLocation (in string iLocation);
    void setResults (in string Results);
    UnderDevelopmentItem getItem();
    TestClass getType();
    EquipmentTester getTester();
};

class Description
{
    attribute blob photo;
    attribute blob retina_print;
    attribute float height;
    attribute float weight;
    attribute string eye_color;
    attribute string hair_color;
    attribute string marks;
    attribute Date birthdate;
    attribute string religion;
    blob getPhoto();
    blob getRetina();
    float getHeight();
    float getWeight();
```

Listing 8-1: (Continued) ODL schema for the object-oriented IIA database

```
    string getEyes ();
    string getHair();
    string getMarks ();
    Date getBirthdate();
    string getReligion();
    void setPhoto (in blob iPhoto);
    void setRetina (in blob iRetina);
    void setHeight (in float iHeight);
    void setWeight (in float iWeight);
    void setEyes (in string iEyes);
    void setHair (in string iHair);
    void setMarks (in string iMarks);
    void setBirthdate (in Date iDate);
    void setReligion (in string iReligion);
};

class Name
{
    attribute string first_name;
    attribute string last_name;
    attribute char middle_init;
    string getFirstName();
    string getLastName();
    string getMiddleInit();
    string getLastFirst();
    string getFirstLast();
    void setName (in string iFirst, in string iLast, in char iMiddle)
        raises (data_missing);
};

class DriversLicense
{
    attribute string country;
    attribute string state;
    attribute string number;
    attribute Date expiration_date;
    string getCountry();
    string getState();
    string getNumber ();
    Date getExpDate ();
    void setCountry (in string iCountry);
    void setState (in string iState);
    void setNumber (in string iNumber);
    void setExpDate (in Date iDate);
};
```

Listing 8-1: (Continued)   ODL schema for the object-oriented IIA database

```
class Phone
{
    attribute string country_code;
    attribute string area_code;
    attribute string exchange;
    attribute string number;
    attribute string extension;
    string getCountry();
    string getPhone();
    string getAreaCode();
    string getExchange();
    void setCountry (in string iCountry);
    void setAreaCode (in string iCode)
    void setExchange (in string iExchange);
    void setNumber (in string iNumber);
    void setExtension (in string iExt);
};

class PersonalAddress
{
    attribute string street;
    attribute string city;
    attribute string state;
    attribute string zip;
    string getStreet();
    string getCity();
    string getState();
    string getZip();
    void setStreet (in string iStreet);
    void setCity (in string iCity);
    void setState (in string iState);
    void inZip (in string iZip);
    string getLabel ();
};
```

Listing 8-1: (Continued)   ODL schema for the object-oriented IIA database

```
class OrganizationalAddress
{
    attribute string street1;
    attribute string street2;
    attribute string suite;
    attribute string city;
    attribute string state;
    attribute string country;
    attribute string zip_postal;
    string getStreet1();
    string getStreet2();
    string getSuite();
    string getCity();
    string getState();
    string getCountry();
    string getZipPostal();
    void setStreet1 (in string iStreet);
    void setStreet2 (in string iStreet);
    void setSuite (in string iSuite);
    void setCity (in string iCity);
    void setState (in string iState);
    void setCountry (in string iCountry);
    void setZipPostal (in string iZip);
};
```

Listing 8-1: (Continued)   ODL schema for the object-oriented IIA database

9

Implementation Example #1: Oracle

Oracle is the most widely used DBMS in the world. It was the first DBMS to implement SQL and the first DBMS to support retrieval from distributed databases. Oracle also runs on nearly every combination of hardware and operating system imaginable. The most current version at the time this book was written—Oracle 8i— provides true support for hybrid object–relational databases, where classes are declared as data types that can then be used as column domains.

In this chapter you will see an example of Oracle's extensions to SQL to support the incorporation of objects. Oracle is certainly not the only DBMS to provide this capability, but its position as a market leader and its adherence to the theoretically standard method of handling objects make it a good choice as an example.

Because the IIA database presented in Chapter 8 takes the best advantage of the object–relational model, that database will be used as the sample schema for the Oracle implementation.

Note: If you are not a programmer, than some of what you read in this chapter may not make sense. Unfortunately, complete implementation of objects, even in a hybrid database, does require programming skill.

Classes as Data Types

Oracle classes are defined as data types, using a CREATE TYPE statement with the following general syntax:

```
CREATE TYPE type_name {IS | AS} OBJECT (
attribute_name datatype[, attribute_name datatype]...
[{MAP | ORDER} MEMBER function_specification,]
[ MEMBER {procedure_specification | function_specification}
| restrict_references_pragma
[, MEMBER {procedure_specification | function_specification}
| restrict_references_pragma]]...);
```

In the preceding syntax, a MEMBER is an operation, what Oracle calls a "method." If it returns a value through the traditional programming return mechanism, it is declared as a function; it if does not return a value, it is declared as a procedure, although output and input–output parameters are supported.

Once the data type for a class has been declared, you can then provide the implementation, written in a combination of extended SQL and PL/SQL (Oracle's Pascal-like language):

```
[CREATE TYPE BODY type_name {IS | AS}
{ {MAP | ORDER} MEMBER function_body;
| MEMBER {procedure_body | function_body};}
[MEMBER {procedure_body | function_body};]... END;]
```

Both the declaration of the class and its implementation are therefore stored in the database's data dictionary.

You will find the declarations and implementation of the utility classes for the IIA database beginning below this paragraph in Listing 9-1. The most important thing to notice is that these classes do not have the "get" and "set" methods that you might expect to see. This is because Oracle's SQL has been extended to include syntax for manipulating the objects, including inserting, modifying, deleting, and retrieving values. Therefore, other than the initialize method that sets attributes to NULL, you need to include only operations that manipulate the contents of the class in some other way.

```
CREATE TYPE Name AS OBJECT (
    first_name CHAR (15),
    last_name CHAR (15),
    middle_init CHAR (1);
    MEMBER PROCEDURE initialize,,;

CREATE TYPE BODY Name AS
    MEMBER PROCEDURE initialize IS
    BEGIN
        first_name := NULL;
        last_name := NULL;
        middle_init := NULL;
    END initialize;
END;

CREATE TYPE DriversLicense AS OBJECT (
    country CHAR (20),
    state CHAR (2),
    number CHAR (20),
    expiration_date DATE,
    MEMBER PROCEDURE initialize );

CREATE TYPE BODY DriversLicense AS
    MEMBER PROCEDURE initialize IS
    BEGIN
        country := NULL;
        state := NULL;
        number := NULL;
        expiration_date := '1/1/1000'
    END initialize;
END;
```

Listing 9-1: PL/SQL declarations and implementations for IIA utility classes

```
CREATE TYPE PersonalAddress AS OBJECT (
    street CHAR (25),
    city CHAR (20),
    state CHAR (2),
    country CHAR (15),
    zip_postal CHAR (10),
    MEMBER PROCEDURE initialize );

CREATE TYPE BODY PersonalAddress AS
    MEMBER PROCEDURE initialize IS
    BEGIN
        street := NULL;
        city := NULL;
        state := NULL;
        country := NULL;
        zip_postal := NULL;
    END initialize;
END;

CREATE TYPE OrganizationalAddress AS OBJECT
    street1 CHAR (25),
    street2 CHAR (25),
    suite CHAR (10),
    city CHAR (20),
    state CHAR (2),
    country CHAR (15),
    zip_postal CHAR (10),
    MEMBER PROCEDURE initialize );

CREATE TYPE BODY PersonalAddress AS
    MEMBER PROCEDURE initialize IS
    BEGIN
        street1 := NULL;
        street2 := NULL;
        suite := NULL:
        city := NULL;
        state := NULL;
        country := NULL;
        zip_postal := NULL;
    END initialize;
END;

CREATE TYPE Phone AS OBJECT (
    country_code CHAR (6),
    area_code CHAR (6),
    exchange CHAR (6),
    number CHAR (6),
    extension CHAR (5),
    MEMBER PROCEDURE initialize );
```

Listing 9-1: (Continued)   PL/SQL declarations and implementations for IIA utility classes

```
CREATE TYPE BODY Phone AS
    MEMBER PROCEDURE initialize IS
    BEGIN
        country_code := NULL;
        area_code := NULL;
        exchange := NULL;
        number := NULL;
        extension := NULL;
    END initialize;
END;

CREATE TYPE Description AS OBJECT (
    photo BLOB,
    retina_print BLOB,
    height REAL (5,2),
    weight INTEGER,
    eye_color CHAR (10),
    hair_color CHAR (10),
    marks VARCHAR (100),
    birthdate DATE,
    religion CHAR (15),
    MEMBER PROCEDURE initialize );

CREATE TYPE BODY Description AS
    MEMBER PROCEDURE initialize IS
    BEGIN
        photo = NULL;
        retina_print = NULL;
        height := 0.0;
        weight := 0;
        eye_color := NULL;
        hair_color := NULL;
        marks := NULL;
        birthdate := '1/1/1000';
        religion := NULL;
    END initialize;
END;
```

Listing 9-1: (Continued)   PL/SQL declarations and implementations for IIA utility classes

A Sample Schema

Once the classes have been declared and implemented, they can be used as data types in table declarations, using standard SQL syntax (see the CREATE TABLE statements in Listing 9-2). As you look through this schema, you will notice that it is only marginally different from a pure relational schema: Some of the user-defined data types may be classes, but they are used in the same way as any other user-defined data type (UDT).

```
CREATE TABLE person
(
    person_ID INT,
    classification INT,
    birthdate DATE,
    local_ID CHAR (15),
    driver_license DriversLicense,
    true_description Description,
    home_address PersonalAddress,
    phone Phone,
    person_name Name,
    recruiting_agent INT,
    PRIMARY KEY (person_ID),
    FOREIGN KEY (classification) REFERENCES person_types
);

CREATE TABLE person_types
(
    classification INT,
    classification_description CHAR (15),
    PRIMARY KEY (classification)
);

CREATE TABLE former_address
(
    person_ID INT,
    date_moved_in DATE,
    date_moved_out DATE,
    previous_address PersonalAddress,
    PRIMARY KEY (person_ID, date_moved_in),
    FOREIGN KEY (person_ID) REFERENCES person
);
```

Listing 9-2:   Oracle schema for the object–relational version of the IIA database

```
CREATE TABLE alias
(
    person_ID INT,
    alias_name Name,
    alias_description Description
    local_id CHAR (15),
    alias_drivers_license DriversLicense,
    alias_address PersonalAddress,
    alias_phone Phone,
    date_last_used DATE,
    PRIMARY KEY (person_ID, last_name, first_name),
    FOREIGN KEY (person_ID) REFERENCES person
);

CREATE TABLE relative
(
    person_ID INT,
    relative_name Name,
    birthdate DATE,
    how_related CHAR (30),
    relative_address PersonalAddress,
    relative_phone Phone,
    photo BLOB,
    current_employer CHAR (30),
    education CHAR (30),
    current_job CHAR (30),
    PRIMARY KEY (person_ID, first_name, last_name, birthdate),
    FOREIGN KEY (person_ID) REFERENCES person
);

CREATE TABLE education
(
    person_ID INT,
    school_ID INT,
    date_entered DATE,
    date_left DATE,
    degree_earned CHAR (10),
    major_subject CHAR (15),
    minor_subject CHAR (15),
    PRIMARY KEY (person_ID, school_ID, date_entered) );

CREATE TABLE school
(
    school_ID INT,
    school_name CHAR (50),
    school_address OrganizationAddress,
    PRIMARY KEY (school_ID) );
```

Listing 9-2: (Continued)   Oracle schema for the object–relational version of the IIA database

```
CREATE TABLE job
(
    company_ID INT,
    date_started DATE,
    date_left DATE,
    job_title CHAR (50),
    person_ID INT,
    PRIMARY KEY (company_ID, date_started),
    FOREIGN KEY (company_ID) REFERENCES company,
    FOREIGN KEY (person_ID) REFERENCES person );

CREATE TABLE company
(
    company_ID INT,
    company_name CHAR (50),
    company_address OrganizationalAddress,
    company_phone Phone,
    PRIMARY KEY (company_ID) );

CREATE TABLE fingerprints
(
    person_ID INT,
    finger CHAR (15),
    print BLOB,
    PRIMARY KEY (person_ID, finger),
    FOREIGN KEY (person_ID) REFERENCES person );

CREATE TABLE conviction
(
    person_ID INT,
    conviction_date DATE,
    crime CHAR (50),
    counts INT,
    sentence CHAR (50),
    PRIMARY KEY (person_ID, conviction_date, crime) );

CREATE TABLE organization
(
    organization_ID INT,
    organization_name CHAR (50),
    non_profit_status CHAR (1),
    organization_address OrganizationalAddress,
    organization_phone Phone,
    PRIMARY KEY (organization_ID) );
```

Listing 9-2: (Continued)   Oracle schema for the object–relational version of the IIA database

```
CREATE TABLE membership
(
    person_ID INT,
    organization_ID INT,
    date_joined DATE,
    date_quit DATE,
    PRIMARY KEY (person_ID, organization_ID, date_joined),
    FOREIGN KEY (person_ID) REFERENCES person,
    FOREIGN KEY (organization_ID) REFERENCES organization );

CREATE TABLE contact
(
    informant_ID INT
        CHECK (EXISTS (SELECT * FROM person
            WHERE VALUE = person_ID and classification = 4)),
    agent_ID INT
        CHECK (EXISTS (SELECT * FROM person
            WHERE VALUE = person_ID and classification = 1)),
    contact_date DATE,
    contact_time TIME,
    fee_paid DECIMAL (8,2),
    outcome CHAR (50),
    PRIMARY KEY (informant_ID, agent_ID, contact_date,
        contact_time));

CREATE TABLE raw_data
(
    data_ID INT,
    source_ID INT,
    source_type CHAR (!5),
    country CHAR (30),
    city CHAR (30),
    how_gathered CHAR (50),
    data_value CHAR (255),
    confidence_level INT,
    cost_of_data DECIMAL (8,2),
    fact_ID INT,
    PRIMARY KEY (data_ID),
    FOREIGN KEY (fact_ID) REFERENCES intelligence
    CHECK (source_type = 'informant' AND
        EXISTS (SELECT * FROM person
        WHERE source_ID = person_ID AND classification = 4)
        OR
        source_type = 'document' AND
        EXISTS (SELECT * FROM source
        WHERE source_ID = source.source_ID)));
```

Listing 9-2: (Continued)   Oracle schema for the object–relational version of the IIA database

```
CREATE TABLE source
(
    source_ID INT,
    source_description CHAR (255),
    PRIMARY KEY (source_ID) );

CREATE TABLE intelligence
(
    fact_ID INT,
    fact_value CHAR (255),
    sold_exclusively CHAR (1),
    PRIMARY KEY (fact_ID) );

CREATE TABLE subject
(
    subject_ID INT,
    subject_heading CHAR (50),
    PRIMARY KEY (subject_ID) );

CREATE TABLE subjects_assigned
(
    subject_ID INT,
    fact_ID INT,
    PRIMARY KEY (subject_ID, fact_ID),
    FOREIGN KEY (subject_ID) REFERENCES subject,
    FOREIGN KEY (fact_ID) REFERENCES intelligence );

CREATE TABLE customer
(
    customer_ID INT,
    customer_name CHAR (50),
    customer_contact_person Name,
    customer_address OrganizationalAddress,
    phone Phone,
    fax Phone,
    exclusive_sales CHAR (1),
    PRIMARY KEY (customer_ID) );

CREATE TABLE purchase
(
    fact_ID INT,
    customer_ID INT,
    date_sold DATE,
    amount_paid DECIMAL (8,2),
    PRIMARY KEY (fact_ID, customer_ID),
    FOREIGN KEY (fact_ID) REFERENCES intelligence,
    FOREIGN KEY (customer_ID) REFERENCES customer );
```

Listing 9-2: (Continued)   Oracle schema for the object–relational version of the IIA database

```
CREATE TABLE subjects_purchased
(
    customer_ID INT,
    subject_ID INT,
    PRIMARY KEY (customer_ID, subject_ID),
    FOREIGN KEY (customer_ID) REFERENCES customer,
    FOREIGN KEY (subject_ID) REFERENCES subject );

CREATE TABLE subjects_not_purchased
(
    customer_ID INT,
    subject_ID INT,
    PRIMARY KEY (customer_ID, subject_ID),
    FOREIGN KEY (customer_ID) REFERENCES customer,
    FOREIGN KEY (subject_ID) REFERENCES subject );

CREATE TABLE subjects_to_notify
(
    customer_ID INT,
    subject_ID INT,
    PRIMARY KEY (customer_ID, subject_ID),
    FOREIGN KEY (customer_ID) REFERENCES customer,
    FOREIGN KEY (subject_ID) REFERENCES subject );

CREATE TABLE user_account
(
    account_ID INTCHAR (10),
    person_ID INT,
    date_created DATE,
    PRIMARY KEY (account_ID),
    FOREIGN KEY (person_ID) REFERENCES person);

CREATE TABLE logon
(
    account_ID INTCHAR (10),
    logon_date DATE,
    logon_time TIME,
    logoff_time TIME,
    logon_ID INT,
    PRIMARY KEY (logon_ID),
    FOREIGN KEY (account_ID) REFERENCES user_account
);
```

Listing 9-2: (Continued)   Oracle schema for the object–relational version of the IIA database

```
CREATE TABLE data_access
(
    logon_ID INT,
    table_used CHAR (30),
    fact_or_data_ID INT,
    access_time TIME,
    action_performed CHAR (30),
    PRIMARY KEY (logon_ID, access_time),
    FOREIGN KEY (logon_ID) REFERENCES logon
    CHECK (table_used = 'raw_data' AND
        EXISTS (SELECT * FROM raw_date
        WHERE fact_or_data_ID = data_ID)
        OR
        (table_used = 'intelligence' AND
        EXISTS (SELECT * FROM intelligence
        WHERE fact_or_data_ID = fact_ID)));

CREATE TABLE equipment_item
(
    item_ID INT,
    storage_location CHAR (30),
    current_condition CHAR (10),
    type_ID INT,
    PRIMARY KEY (item_ID),
    FOREIGN KEY (type_ID) REFERENCES equipment_type);

CREATE TABLE usage_restriction
(
    type_ID INT,
    restriction_description CHAR (50),
    PRIMARY KEY (type_ID, restriction_description),
    FOREIGN KEY (type_ID) REFERENCES equipment_type );

CREATE TABLE equipment_use
(
    item_ID INT,
    use_date DATE,
    use_time TIME,
    person_ID INT,
    use_location CHAR (50),
    how_used CHAR (255),
    use_results CHAR (255),
    PRIMARY KEY (item_ID, use_date, use_time),
    FOREIGN KEY (item_ID) REFERENCES equipment_item,
    FOREIGN KEY (person_ID) REFERENCES person );
```

Listing 9-2: (Continued)   Oracle schema for the object–relational version of the IIA database

```
CREATE TABLE equipment_type
(
    type_ID INT,
    type_classification CHAR (15),
    type_description CHAR (50),
    quantity_owned INT,
    PRIMARY KEY (type_ID) );

CREATE TABLE equipment_sale
(
    customer_ID INT,
    sale_date DATE,
    sale_total DECIMAL (8,2),
    PRIMARY KEY (customer_ID, sale_date),
    FOREIGN KEY (customer_ID) REFERENCES customer );

CREATE TABLE sale_item
(
    customer_ID INT,
    sale_date DATE,
    type_ID INT,
    quantity_purchased INT,
    price_each DECIMAL (8,2),
    line_cost DECIMAL (8,2),
    PRIMARY KEY (customer_ID, sale_date, type_ID),
    FOREIGN KEY (customer_ID) REFERENCES equipment_sale,
    FOREIGN KEY (sale_date) REFERENCES equipment_sale,
    FOREIGN KEY (type_ID) REFERENCES equipment_type );

CREATE TABLE under_development_item
(
    item_ID INT,
    intended_use CHAR (50),
    development_location CHAR (50),
    estimated_completion_date DATE,
    type_ID INT,
    PRIMARY KEY (item_ID),
    FOREIGN KEY (type_ID) REFERENCES equipment_type );

CREATE TABLE item_developer
(
    item_ID INT,
    person_ID INT,
    PRIMARY KEY (item_ID, person_ID),
    FOREIGN KEY (person_ID) REFERENCES person );
```

Listing 9-2: (Continued)   Oracle schema for the object–relational version of the IIA database

```
CREATE TABLE equipment_test
(
    item_ID INT,
    test_ID INT,
    test_date DATE,
    person_ID INT,
    test_location CHAR (50),
    test_results CHAR (255),
    PRIMARY KEY (item_ID, test_ID, test_date),
    FOREIGN KEY (item_ID) REFERENCES under_development_item,
    FOREIGN KEY (test_ID) REFERENCES test,
    FOREIGN KEY (person_ID) REFERENCES person );

CREATE TABLE test
(
    test_ID INT,
    test_description CHAR (255),
    PRIMARY KEY (test_ID)
);
```

Listing 9-2: (Continued)   **Oracle schema for the object–relational version of the IIA database**

10

Implementation Example #2: Jasmine

Unlike the hybrid object–relational DBMSs that can use the SQL standard as a starting point, pure object DBMSs have no accepted standard. They therefore tend to differ more than object–relational DBMSs in terms of their data definition language. With that in mind, this chapter examines Jasmine, a product of Computer Associates, a company that is a member of the team that is working on the object–database standards.

As you will see, Jasmine differs from the proposed ODL standard in several major areas. This is typical of object-oriented DBMSs today. Regardless of how well you understand the proposed standard, you will need to modify your schema to match the requirements of the specific product you are using.

Jasmine's Implementation of the Object-Oriented Data Model

Jasmine's implementation of the object-oriented data model has the following features:

◆ A schema is defined using Jasmine's Object Database Query Language (ODQL). Like SQL, ODQL is not just a query language: It can also be used to define database structure.

◆ A class has a name and characteristics. Characteristics include both attributes (called "properties") and operations (called "methods").

◆ All data types, even primitive data types, such as integers, are represented as classes. You will therefore find that all data type names begin with capital letters (the convention for naming classes). Dates and times are both represented by the Chrono class.

◆ Jasmine supports multiple inheritance. There are therefore no interfaces.

◆ There is no way to define an abstract class.

◆ Relationships are defined simply as properties whose data types are other classes. Properties can be single valued or multivalued (in other words, collections such as sets).

◆ There are no extents. However, classes have two types of properties. Instance properties apply to each object created from the class. Class properties apply to all objects as a whole, as if the objects were gathered into an extent.

◆ ODQL provides "add" and "delete" methods for collection objects. There is therefore no need to include those methods in class definitions.

◆ There is no support for inverse relationships. It is therefore up to the programs that insert data into and remove data from relationship properties to maintain integrity.

◆ The is no syntax for indicating key properties of classes. A developer can, however, define indexes separate from class definitions to speed access on the values of one or more properties. In addition, attributes can be designated as unique or mandatory. Attributes can also be given default values.

♦ There is no way to concatenate unique attributes to make a composite key. If a class requires a unique key made up of multiple attributes, the class will need to include an additional attribute to hold the value of that concatenation.

♦ Method signatures do not include exceptions.

ODQL has the following general syntax for defining a class

```
defineClass class-identifier
[ super : class-identifier [ (class-identifier ) ...] ]
[ description : string-constant ]
{ [ maxInstanceSize : size ; ]
characteristics } ;
```

The only required elements in the definition are the class name and the characteristics. Superclasses, the class description, and a maximum size for each object created from the class are optional.

A Sample Jasmine Schema

As an example, you will find a rewrite of the IIA object-oriented database using Jasmine's ODQL (see Listing 10-1 at the end of this chapter). Jasmine syntax uses colons as separators between keywords and the values assigned to the keywords. Even if a keyword has no value, the colon is still required. For example, to require unique values for an attribute, you add

```
unique :
```

A semicolon terminates each property definition.

> *Note: The boldface type used for the keywords in the class declarations are simply to make the classes easier to read. They are not part of ODQL.*

Although Jasmine has no relationship integrity, it is possible to maintain some integrity by making relationship attributes mandatory. For example, in FingerprintClass the attribute whose data type is PersonClass forms the relationship between a fingerprint and a person. To ensure integrity of that relationship—to ensure that no fingerprint object is ever left without being related to a person—a value in the PersonClass attribute is mandatory This technique can be used to require any child object to be related to its parent but will not work in reverse—when a parent object can have zero related objects.

```
defineClass PersonClass
description : "Superclass for the person class hierarchy"
{
    class:
    Integer last_ID default : 0;
    Integer getNextID();
    PersonClass createObject (String iLocal, Description iDescription,
    PersonalAddress iAddress, Name iName, Phone iPhone);
    PersonClass findPerson (Integer iID);

    instance:
    Integer person_ID unique :;
    String local_ID;
    Description true_description;
    PersonalAddress home_address mandatory :;
    Name person_name mandatory :;
    Phone home_phone mandatory :;
    set<FingerprintClass> prints;
    set<FormerAddress> addresses;
    set<RelativeClass> relatives;
    set<ConvictionClass> convictions;
    set<MembershipClass> memberships;
    set<JobClass> jobs;
    set<AliasClass> aliases;
    set<EducationClass> education;
    set<UserAccount> accounts;

    Integer getPersonID ();
    String getLocalID ();
    Description getDesc ();
    PersonalAddress getAddress ();
    Name getName ();
    Phone getPhone ();
    void setPersonID (,in Integer iID);
    void setLocalID (,in String iID);
```

Listing 10-1:   Jasmine's ODQL statements for declaring the IIA schema

```
    void setDesc (,in Description iDesc);
    void setAddress (,in PersonalAddress iAddress);
    void setName (in Name iName);
    void setPhone (. in Phone iPhone);
    set<FingerprintClass> getPrints ();
    set<PersonalAddress> getAddress ();
    set<PersonalAddress> findAddress (Chrono iDate);
    set<PersonalAddress> findAddress (Chrono iStart, Chrono iEnd);
    set<RelativeClass> getRelatives ();
    set<RelativeClass> findRelative (Name iName);
    set<RelativeClass> findRelative (Chrono iBirthdate);
    set<ConvictionClass> getConvictions ();
    set<ConvictionClass> findConvictions (String iCrime);
    set<ConvictionClass> findConvictions Chrono iStart, Chrono iEnd);
    set<MembershipClass> getMemberships ();
    set<MembershipClass> findMemberships (String iOrgName);
    set<JobClass> getJobs ();
    set<JobClass> findJobs (Chrono iStart, Chrono iEnd);
    set<JobClass> findJobs (String iCompanyName);
    set<AliasClass> getAliases ();
    AliasClass findAlias (String iName);
    set<Aliases> findAliases (Chrono iStart, Chrono iEnd);
    set<EducationClass> getEducation ();
    set<EducationClass> getEducation (Chrono iStart,
        Chrono iEnd);
    EducationClass findEducation (String iSchool,
        Chrono iStart);
    set<UserAccount> getAccounts();
    set<AccessibleItem> getItemsAccessed ();
    set<AccessibleItem> getItemsAccessed (Chrono iStart,
        Chrono iEnd);
    void getActions (set<DataAccess> accesses,
        set<AccessibleItem> items);
    void getActions (set<DataAccess> accesses,
        set<AccessibleItem> items, Chrono iStart, Chrono iEnd);
    set<LogonClass> getLogons ();
    set<LogonClass< getLogons (Chrono iStart, Chrono iEnd);
};


defineClass Informant
super : PersonClass
description : "People who gather information for agents"
{
    class:
    Informant createObject (Integer iAgent);
    set<Informant> getInformants ();
    set<Informant) findRecruitedBy (Integer iID);
```

Listing 10-1: (Continued)   Jasmine's ODQL statements for declaring the IIA schema

```
    instance:
    Integer recruiting_agent;
    set<ContactClass> contacts;
    Integer getRecruiter ();
    void setRecruiter (Integer iAgent);
    void getContactDetails (set<ContactClass> contacts,
        set<Agent> agents);
    void findContacts (set<ContactClass> contacts,
        set<Agent> agents, Chrono iStart, Chrono iEnd);
};


defineClass Reader
super : PersonClass
description : "People who examine print and non-print media for info"
{
    class:
    Reader createObject (Chrono iDate, String iStation, Chrono iHireDate);
    set<Readers> getReaders ();
    set<Readers> getReadersAtStation (String iStation);
    instance:
    Chrono date_hired;
    String home_station;
    Chrono getHireDate ();
    String getStation();
    void setHireDate (Chrono iDate);
    void setStation (String iStation);
};


defineClass Engineer
super : PersonClass, EquipmentTester
description : "People who develop and test equipment"
{
    class:
    Engineer createObject (Chrono iDate, String iLocation);
    set<Engineers> getEngineers ();
    set<Engineers> getEngineersAtLocation (String iLocation);
    instance:
    Chrono date_hired;
    String work_location;
    set<UnderDevelopmentItem> items;
    Chrono getHireDate ();
    String getLocation();
    void setHireDate (Chrono iDate);
    void setLocation (String iLocation);
    set<UnderDevelopmentItem> getItems();
};
```

Listing 10-1: (Continued)   Jasmine's ODQL statements for declaring the IIA schema

```
defineClass Agent
super : PersonClass, EquipmentTester
description: "People who work in the field to collect info"
{
    class:
    Agent createObject (Chrono iDate);
    set<Agent> getAgents ();
    instance:
    Chrono date_hired;
    set<ContactClass> contacts;
    set<EquipmentUse> items_used;
    Chrono getHireDate();
    void setHireDate (Chrono iDate);
    void getContactDetails (set<ContactClass> contacts,set<Informant> informants);
    void findContacts (set<ContactClass> contacts,
        set<Informant> informants, Chrono iStart, Chrono iEnd);
    void getEquipmentUsed (set<EquipmentUse> uses, set<EquipmentItem> items);
    void getEquipmentUsed (,set<EquipmentUse> uses,
        set<EquipmentItem> items, Chrono iStart, Chrono iEnd);
};


defineClass EquipmentTester
description : "People who test equipment"
{
    class:
    set<EquipmentTester> getTesters ();
    instance:
    set<TestPerformed> tests;
    set<TestPerformed> getTests ();
    set<TestPerformed> getTests (Chrono iStart, Chrono iEnd);
};


defineClass FingerprintClass
description : "Images of fingerprints"
{
    class:
    FingerprintClass createObject(String iFinger,BLOB iPrint,PersonClass iPerson);
    PersonClass matchPrint (BLOB iPrint);
    instance:
    String finger;
    BLOB print;
    PersonClass person mandatory :;
    String getFinger();
    BLOB getPrint();
    void setFinger (String iFinger);
    void setPrint (BLOB iPrint);
    PersonClass getPerson();
};
```

Listing 10-1: (Continued) Jasmine's ODQL statements for declaring the IIA schema

```
defineClass RelativeClass
description : "Relatives of employees and informants"
{
    class:
    RelativeClass createObject (Name iName, Chrono iDate,
        String iHowRelated, PersonalAddress iAddress, Phone iPhone,
        BLOB iPhoto, String iEmployer, String iEducation, String iJob,
        PersonClass iPerson);
    set<RelativeClass> findRelatives (PersonClass iPerson);
    instance:
    Name relative_name  mandatory :;
    Chrono birth_date  mandatory :;
    String how_related;
    PersonalAddress relative_address;
    Phone relative_phone;
    BLOB photo;
    String current_employer;
    String highest_education;
    String current_job;
    PersonClass person mandatory :;
    Name getName ();
    Chrono getBirthdate ();
    String getHowRelated();
    PersonalAddress getAddress ();
    Phone getPhone ();
    BLOB getPhoto ();
    String getEmployer ();
    String getEducation ();
    String getJob ();
    void setName (Name iName);
    void setBirthate (Chrono iDate);
    void setHowRelated (String iHow);
    void setAddress (PersonalAddress iAddress);
    void setPhone (Phone iPhone);
    void setPhoto (BLOB iPhoto);
    void setEmployer (String iEmployer);
    void setEducation (String iEducation);
    void setJob (String iJob);
    PersonClass getPerson ();
};

defineClass FormerAddress
description : "Previous places where people have lived"
{
    class:
    FormerAddress createObject (Chrono iDateIn,
        Chrono iDateOut, PersonalAddress iAddress, PersonClass iPerson);
    set<FormerAddress> getAddresses (PersonClass iPerson);
```

Listing 10-1: (Continued)   Jasmine's ODQL statements for declaring the IIA schema

```
    instance:
    Chrono date_moved_in;
    Chrono date_moved_out;
    PersonalAddress address mandatory :;
    PersonClass person mandatory :;
    Chrono getMoved();
    Chrono getMoved();
    PersonalAddress getAddress();
    void setMoved(Chrono iDate);
    void setMoved(Chrono iDate);
    void setAddress (PersonalAddress iAddress);
    PersonClass getPerson ();
};

defineClass ConvictionClass
description : "Criminal convictions"
{
    class:
    ConvictionClass createObject (Chrono iDate,
        String iCrime, Integer iCounts, String iSentence,
        PersonClass iPerson);
    set<ConvictionClass> getConvictions (,PersonClass iPerson);
    instance:
    Chrono conviction_date;
    String crime mandatory :;
    Integer counts;
    String sentence;
    PersonClass person mandatory :;

    Chrono getDate();
    String getCrime();
    Integer getCounts ();
    String getSentence ();
    void setDate (Chrono iDate);
    void setCrime (String iCrime);
    void setCounts (Integer iCounts);
    void setSentence (String iSentence);
    PersonClass getPerson ();
};

defineClass OrganizationClass
description : "Organizations to which people belong"
{
    class:
    OrganizationClass createObject (String iName,
        OrganizationalAddress iAddress, Phone iPhone);
    set<OrganizationClass> getOrganizations ();
    OrganizationClass findOrganization (String iName);
```

Listing 10-1: (Continued) Jasmine's ODQL statements for declaring the IIA schema

```
    instance:
    String organization_name  mandatory : unique :;
    OrganizationalAddress organization_address;
    Phone organization_phone;
    set<MembershipClass> members;
    String getName ();
    OrganizationalAddress getAddress ();
    Phone getPhone();
    void setName (String iName);
    void setAddress (OrganizationalAddress iAddress);
    void setPhone (Phone iPhone);
    set<PersonClass> getMembers ();
    set<PersonClass> getCurrentMembers ();
};


defineClass MembershipClass
description : "Memberships in organizations"
{
    class:
    MembershipClass createObject (Chrono iJoined,
        Chrono iLeft, PersonClass iPerson);
    instance:
    Chrono date_joined;
    Chrono date_left;
    PersonClass person  mandatory :;
    OrganizationClass organization_address  mandatory :;
;
    Chrono getJoined();
    Chrono getLeft();
    void setJoined (Chrono iDate);
    void setLeft (Chrono iDate);
    PersonClass getPerson();
    OrganizationClass getOrganization();
};


defineClass CompanyClass
description : "Companies that people work for"
{
    class:
    CompanyClass createObject (String iName, OrganizationalAddress iAddress,
        Phone iPhone);
    set<CompanyClass> getCompanies ();
    CompanyClass findCompany (String iName);
    instance:
    String company_name  mandatory : unique :;
    OrganizationalAddress company_address;
    Phone company_phone;
    set<JobClass> employees;
```

Listing 10-1: (Continued) Jasmine's ODQL statements for declaring the IIA schema

```
    String getName ();
    OrganizationalAddress getAddress();
    Phone getPhone ();
    void setName (Name iName);
    void setAddress (OrganizationalAddress iAddress);
    void setPhone (Phone iPhone);
    set<PersonClass> getCurrentEmployees ();
    Boolean personEmployed (Integer person_ID);
    void getJobProfile (Integer person_ID, inJobClass);
};

defineClass JobClass
description : "Jobs people have held"
{
    class:
    JobClass createObject (Chrono iStart, Chrono iLeft,
        String iTitle, PersonClass iPerson, CompanyClass iCompany);
    instance:
    Chrono date_started;
    Chrono date_left;
    String job_title;
    PersonClass person  mandatory :;
    CompanyClass company  mandatory :;
    Chrono getStartDate ();
    Chrono getLeftDate ();
    String getJobTitle();
    void setStartDate (Chrono iDate);
    void setLeftDate (Chrono iDate);
    void setJobTitle (String iTitle);
    PersonClass getPerson ();
    CompanyClass getCompany ();
};

defineClass AliasClass
description : "Aliases used by agents and informants"
{
    class:
    AliasClass createObject (Description iDescription,
        DriversLicense iLicense, PersonalAddress iAddress, Chrono iDate,
        PersonClass iPerson);
    PersonClass findPerson (Description iDescription);
    AliasClass findAlias (String iDescription);
    instance:
    Description alias_description;
    DriversLicense alias_drivers_license;
    PersonalAddress alias_address;
    Chrono date_last_used;
    PersonClass person  mandatory :;
```

Listing 10-1: (Continued)   Jasmine's ODQL statements for declaring the IIA schema

```
    Description getDescription();
    DriversLicense getLicense();
    PersonalAddress getAddress();
    Chrono getLastUsed ();
    void setDescription (Description iDescription);
    void setDriversLicense (DriversLicense iLicense);
    void setAddress (PersonalAddress iAddress);
    void setLastUsed (Chrono iDate);
    PersonClass getPerson ();
};

defineClass SchoolClass
description : "Schools that people have attended"
{
    class:
    SchoolClass createObject (String iName,
        OrganizationalAddress iAddress);
    set<SchoolClass> getSchools ();
    SchoolClass findSchool (String iName);
    instance:
    String school_name mandatory : unique :;
    OrganizationalAddress school_address;
    set<EducationClass> students;

    String getName ();
    OrganizationalAddress getAddress ();
    void setName (. String iName);
    void setAddress (OrganizationalAddress iAddress);
    set<PersonClass> getCurrentStudents ();
    set<PersonClass> getAllStudents ();
    EducationClass getStudentProfile (Integer person_ID,
        Chrono iDate);
    Boolean verifyAttendance (Integer person_ID);
};

defineClass EducationClass
description : "Education records"
{
    class:
    EducationClass createObject (Chrono iEntered,
        Chrono iLeft, String iDegree, String iMajor, String iMinor,
        PersonClass iPerson, SchoolClass iSchool);
    set<EducationClass> findEducation (Integer iPersonID);
    instance:
    Chrono date_entered;
    Chrono date_left;
    String degree_earned;
    String major_subject;
```

Listing 10-1: (Continued)   Jasmine's ODQL statements for declaring the IIA schema

```
        String minor_subject;
        PersonClass person  mandatory :;
        SchoolClass school  mandatory :;
        Chrono getEntered();
        Chrono getleft ();
        String getDegree();
        String getMajor ();
        String getMinor ();
        void setEntered (Chrono iDate);
        void setLeft (Chrono iDate);
        void setDegree (String iDegree);
        void setMajor (String iMajor);
        void setMinor (String iMinor);
        PersonClass getPerson();
        SchoolClass getSchool();
};


defineClass SourceClass
description : "Base class for data sources"
{
    class:
    SourceClass createObject (String iName);
    SourceClass findSource (String iName);

    instance:
    String source_name  mandatory :  unique :;
    set<RawData> data;

    set<RawData> getData ();
    void addData (RawData iData);
    void deleteData (Integer iDataID);
};


defineClass ContactClass
super: SourceClass
description : "Contact between an agent and an informant"
{
    class:
    ContactClass createObject (Chrono iDate, Chrono iTime,
        Real iFee, String iOutcome, Agent iAgent, Informant iInformant);
    set<ContactClass> findContacts (Agent iAgent);
    set<ContactClass> findContacts (Informant iInformant);
    set<ContactClass> findContacts (Agent iAgent,
        Informant iInformant);
    set<ContactClass> findContacts (Chrono iDate);
    set<ContactClass> findContacts (Chrono iDate,
        Agent iAgent);
```

Listing 10-1: (Continued)   Jasmine's ODQL statements for declaring the IIA schema

```
    set<ContactClass> findContacts (Chrono iDate,
        Informant iInformant);
    set<ContactClass> findContacts (Chrono iDate,
        Agent iAgent, Informant iInformant);
    set<ContactClass> findContacts (Chrono iStart,
        Chrono iEnd);
    set<ContactClass> findContacts (Chrono iStart,
        Chrono iEnd, Agent iAgent);
    set <ContactClass> findContacts (Chrono iStart,
        Chrono iEnd, Informant iInformant);
    set <ContactClass>. findContacts (Chrono iStart,
        Chrono iEnd, Agent iAgent, Informant iInformant);
    instance:
    Chrono contact_date mandatory :;
    Chrono contact_time;
    Real fee_paid;
    String outcome;
    Agent agent mandatory :;
    Informant informant mandatory :;
    Chrono getDate();
    Chrono getTime();
    Real getFee();
    String getOutcome();
    void setDate (Chrono iDate);
    void setTime (Chrono iTime);
    void setFee (Real iFee);
    void setOutcome (String iOutcome);
    Agent getAgent();
    Informant getInformant();
};


defineClass VideoAudioSource
super : SourceClass
description : "Video or audio data source"
{
    class:
    VideoAudioSource createObject (String iTitle, String
        iArtist, String iProducer, String iDistributor, String iCopyright);
    VideoAudioSource findSource (String iTitle, iArtist);
    set<VideoAudioSource> findSource (iProducer);
    set<VideoAudioSource> findSource (iDistributor);
    set<VideoAudioSource> findSource (iCopyright);
    instance:
    String title mandatory :;
    String artist mandatory :;
    String producer;
    String distributor;
    String copyright_date;
```

Listing 10-1: (Continued)   Jasmine's ODQL statements for declaring the IIA schema

```
    String getTitle();
    String getArtist();
    String getProducer();
    String getDistributor();
    String getCopyright();
    void setTitle (String iTitle);
    void setArtist (String iArtist);
    void setProducer (String iProducer);
    void setDistributor (String iDistributor);
    void setCopyright (String iCopyright);
};

defineClass PrintSource
super : SourceClass
description : "Print data sources"
{
    class:
    PrintSource createObject (String iAuthor,
        String iTitle, String iPublisher, String iCopyright,
        String iIssue, String iPage);
    PrintSource findSource (String iAuthor,
        String iTitle);
    set<PrintSource> findSource (String iPublisher);
    set<PrintSource> findSource (String iCopyright);

    instance:
    String author mandatory :;
    String title mandatory :;
    String publisher;
    String print_copyright_date;
    String issue_edition;
    String page;
    String getAuthor();
    String getTitle();
    String getPublisher();
    String getCopyright();
    String getIssue();
    String getPage();
    void setAuthor (String iAuthor);
    void setTitle (String iTitle);
    void setPublisher (String iPublisher);
    void setCopyright (String iCopyright);
    void setIssue (String iIssue);
    void setpage (String iPage);
};
```

Listing 10-1: (Continued) Jasmine's ODQL statements for declaring the IIA schema

```
defineClass AccessibleItem
description : "Base class for items that can be accessed via computer"
{
    class:
    AccessibleItem createObject ();

    instance:
    set<DataAccess> accesses;

    set<PersonClass>set< getAccessors ()
    PersonClass> getAccessors (Chrono iStart, Chrono iEnd);
    void getWhenAccessed (set<DataAccess> accesses,
        set<LogonClass> logons);
    void getWhenAccessed (Chrono iStart, Chrono iEnd,
        set<DataAccess> accesses, set<LogonClass> logons);
};

defineClass RawData
super: Accessibleitem
description : "Raw data collected from a source"
{
    class:
    Integer last_ID default :0;
    Integer getNextID ();
    RawData createObject (String iCountry, String iCity, String iHowGathered,
        Real iValue, Real iConfidence, Real iCost, String iContent,
        SourceClass iSource);
    set<RawData> findData (String iContent);

    instance:
    Integer data_ID mandatory : unique :;
    String country;
    String city;
    String how_gathered;
    Real data_value;
    Real confidence_level;
    Real cost_of_data;
    String data_content mandatory :;
    SourceClass source mandatory :;
    set<IntelligenceClass> facts;

    Integer getID();
    String getCountry();
    String getCity();
    String getHowGathered();
    Real getValue();
    Real getConfidence();
```

Listing 10-1: **(Continued)**   **Jasmine's ODQL statements for declaring the IIA schema**

```
    Real getCost();
    String getContent();
    void setID (Integer iID);
    void setCountry (String iCountry);
    void setCity (String iCity);
    void setHowGathered (String iHow);
    void setValue (Real iValue);
    void setConfidence (Real iConfidence);
    void setCost (Real iCost);
    void setContent (String iContent);
    SourceClass getSource();
    set<IntelligenceClass> getIntelligence();
};

defineClass IntelligenceClass
super : AccessibleItem
description : "Verified intelligence facts that can be sold"
{
    class:
    Integer last_ID default :0;
    Integer getNextID ();
    IntelligenceClass createObject (Real iValue, Boolean iSold, String iContent);
    set<IntelligenceClass> findFact (String iContent);
    set<IntelligenceClass> findFact (String iSubject);

    instance:
    Integer fact_ID mandatory : unique :;
    Real fact_value;
    Boolean sold_exclusively;
    String fact_content mandatory :;
    set<RawData> data;
    set<SubjectClass> subjects_assigned;
    set<PurchaseClass> sales;

    Integer getID();
    Real getValue();
    Boolean checkExclusiveSale();
    String getContent();
    void setID (Integer iID);
    void setValue (Real iValue);
    void setSale (Boolean iSale);
    void String setContent (String iContent);
    set<SubjectClass> getSubjects();
};
```

Listing 10-1: (Continued)   Jasmine's ODQL statements for declaring the IIA schema

```
defineClass PurchaseClass
description : "The purchase of a single intelligence fact"
{
    class:
    PurchaseClass createObject (Chrono iDate, Real iAmount,
        IntelligenceClass iFact, CustomerClass iCustomer);
    set<PurchaseClass> findPurchases (CustomerClass iCustomer);
    set<PurchaseClass> findPurchases (
        IntelligenceClass iFact);
    instance:
    Chrono date_sold;
    Real amount_paid;
    IntelligenceClass fact  mandatory :;
    CustomerClass customer  mandatory :;

    Chrono getDate();
    Real getAmount();
    void setDate (Chrono iDate);
    void setAmount (Real iAmount);
    IntelligenceClass getFact ();
    CustomerClass getCustomer ();
};

defineClass SubjectClass
description : "Subject headings"
{
    class:
    SubjectClass createObject (String iHeading);
    SubjectClass findSubject (String iHeading);
    set<CustomerClass> findPurchased (String iHeading);
    set<CustomerClass> findNotPurchased (String iHeading);
    set<CustomerClass> findToNotify (String iHeading);
    set<IntelligenceClass> findFact (String iHeading);

    instance:
    String subject_heading  mandatory :;
    set<IntelligenceClass> facts;
    set<CustomerClass> purchased;
    set<CustomerClass> not_purchased;
    set<CustomerClass> notify;

    String getHeading();
    void setHeading (String iHeading);
    set<IntelligenceClass> getIntelligence();
    set<CustomerClass> getPurchased ();
    set<CustomerClass> getNotPurchased ();
    set<CustomerClass> getNotify; ()
};
```

Listing 10-1: (Continued)   Jasmine's ODQL statements for declaring the IIA schema

```
defineClass CustomerClass
description : "Customers who purchase intelligence facts"
{
    class:
    Integer last_ID default :0;
    Integer getNextID ();
    CustomerClass createObject (String iName, Name iContact,
        OrganizationalAddress iAddress, Phone iVoice, Phone, iFax,
        Boolean iExclusive);
    set<CustomerClass> getCustomers ();
    CustomerClass findCustomer (Integer iID);
    CustomerClass findCustomer (String iName);

    instance:
    Integer customer_ID mandatory : unique :;
    String customer_name mandatory :;
    Name customer_contact_name;
    OrganizationalAddress customer_address mandatory :;
    Phone customer_voice_phone mandatory :;
    Phone customer_fax;
    Boolean exclusive_sales;
    set<PurchaseClass> purchases;
    set<SubjectClass> purchased;
    set<SubjectClass> not_purchased;
    set<SubjectClass> notify;
    set<EquipmentSale> equipment_purchased;

    Integer getID();
    String getName();
    Name getContact();
    OrganizationalAddress getAddress();
    Phone getVoicePhone();
    Phone getFax();
    Boolean checkExclusiveSales();
    void setID (Integer iID);
    void setName (String iName);
    void setAddress (OrganizationalAddress iAddress);
    void setVoicePhone (. Phone iPhone);
    void setFax (. Phone iFax);
    void setExSales (Boolean iEx);
    set<IntelligenceClass> getPurchases ();
    set<SubjectClass> getSubjectsPurchased ();
    set<SubjectClass> getSubjectsNotPurchased ()
    set<SubjectClass> getSubjectsToNotify();
    set<EquipmentType> getEquipmentTypesPurchased ();
    void getEquipmentPurchases (set<EquipmentSale> Purchases,
        set<SaleItem> items);
};
```

Listing 10-1: (Continued)   Jasmine's ODQL statements for declaring the IIA schema

```
defineClass UserAccount
description : "Computer accounts"
{
    class:
    UserAccount createObject (String iID, Chrono iDate,
        PersonClass iOwner);
    UserAccount findAccount (String iID);
    set<UserAccount> findAccounts (PersonClass iPerson);
    instance:
    String account_ID mandatory : unique :;
    Chrono date_created;
    PersonClass owner mandatory :;
    set<LogonClass> logons;
    String getID ();
    Chrono getDate();
    void setID (String iID);
    void setDate (Chrono iDate);
    PersonClass getPerson();
    set<LogonClass> getLogons();
    set<LogonClass> getLogons (Chrono iStart, Chrono iEnd);
};

defineClass LogonClass
description : "Computer logons"
{
    class:
    LogonClass createObject (Chrono iDate, Chrono iOn,
        Chrono iOff, UserAccount iUser);
    set<LogonClass> findLogons (UserAccount iUser);
    set<LogonClass> findLogons (UserAccount iUser,
        Chrono iDate);
    set<LogonClass> findLogons (Chrono iDate);

    instance:
    Chrono logon_date mandatory :;
    Chrono logon_time;
    Chrono logoff_time;
    UserAccount account mandatory :;
    set<DataAccess> uses;
    Chrono getDate();
    Chrono getTimeOn();
    time getTimeOff();
    void setDate (Chrono iDate);
    void setTimeOn (,Chrono iTime);
    void setTimeOff (Chrono iTime);
    PersonClass getPerson ();
    UserAccount getAccount ();
```

Listing 10-1: (Continued)   Jasmine's ODQL statements for declaring the IIA schema

```
      set<AccessibleItem> getItemsAccessed ();
      void getItemsAccessed (set<AccessibleItem> items,
          set<DataAccess> actions);
};

defineClass DataAccess
description : "Computer access of raw data or intelligence fact"
{
    class:
    DataAccess createObject (Chrono iTime, String iClass,
        Integer iID, String iAction, LogonClass iLogon, AccessibleItem iItem);
    set<DataAccess> findAccesses (Integer iID);

    instance:
    Chrono access_Time;
    String class_used;
    Integer item_ID;
    String action_performed;
    LogonClass logon  mandatory :;
    AccessibleItem item  mandatory :;
    Chrono getTime();
    String getClass();
    Integer getID();
    String getAction();
    void setTime (Chrono iTime);
    void setClass (String iClass);
    void setID (Integer ID);
    void setAction (String iAction);
    PersonClass getPerson ();
    UserAccount getAccount ();
    LogonClass getLogon ();
    AccessibleItem getItem ();
};

defineClass EquipmentType
description : "Aggregate for the Equipment class"
{
    class:
    EquipmentType createObject (String iClass, String iDescript,
        Integer iQuantity, set<String> iRestrict);
    set<EquipmentType> getTypes ();
    set<EquipmentType> findType (String iClass);

    instance:
    String type_classification;
    String type_description;
    Integer quantity_owned;
```

Listing 10-1: (Continued)   Jasmine's ODQL statements for declaring the IIA schema

```
    set<String> usage_restrictions;
    set<Equipment> gadgets;
    set<SaleItem> sales;

    String getClass ();
    String getType ();
    Integer getQuantity ();
    set<String> getRestrictions ();
    void setClass (String iClass);
    void setType (String iType);
    void setQuantity(Integer iQuantity);
    void modifyQuantity (Integer iQuantity);
    void setRestrictions (set<String> iRules);
};


defineClass Equipment
description : "Base class for equipment"
{
    class:
    Integer last_ID default :0;
    Integer getNextID ();
    Equipment createObject (EquipmentType iType);
    set<Equipment> findEquipment (EquipmentType iType);
    Equipment findItem (Integer iID);

    instance:
    Integer item_ID mandatory : unique :;
    EquipmentType type mandatory :;
    Equipmenttype getType();
    Integer getID();
    void setID (Integer iID);
};


defineClass EquipmentSale
description : "Sale of equipment to a customer"
{
    class:
    EquipmentSale createObject (Chrono iDate, Real iTotal,
        CustomerClass iCustomer);
    set<EquipmentSale> findSales (Customer iCustomer);
    set<EquipmentSale> findSales (Chrono iDate);
    set<EquipmentSale> findSales (Chrono iStart, Chrono iEnd);

    instance:
    Chrono sale_date;
    Real sale_total;
    CustomerClass customer mandatory :;
    set<SaleItem> items_on;
```

Listing 10-1: (Continued)   Jasmine's ODQL statements for declaring the IIA schema

```
    Chrono getDate();
    Real getTotal();
    void setDate (Chrono iDate);
    void setTotal (Real iTotal);
    void getItemsSold (set<EquipmentType> types,
        set<SaleItem> items);
    CustomerClass getCustomer ();
};

defineClass SaleItem
description : "Type of equipment sold"
{
    class:
    SaleItem createObject (Integer iQuantity, Real iPrice,
        Real iLine, EquipmentType iType, EquipmentSale iSale);
    set<SaleItem> findItem (EquipmentType iType);
    instance:
    Integer quantity_purchased;
    Real price_each;
    Real line_cost;
    EquipmentType type  mandatory :;
    EquipmentSale items_on  mandatory :;

    Integer getQuantity();
    Real getPrice();
    Real getLine();
    void setQuantity (Integer iQuantity);
    void setPrice (Real iPrice);
    void computeLine ();
    EquipmentType getType();
    EquipmentSale getSale ();
};

defineClass EquipmentItem
super : Equipment
description : "Equipment in daily use"
{
    class:
    EquipmentItem createObject (String iLocation,
        String iCondition);

    instance:
    String storage_location;
    String current_condition;
    set<EquipmentUse> uses;
    String getStorage();
    String getLocation();
```

Listing 10-1: (Continued)   Jasmine's ODQL statements for declaring the IIA schema

```
    void setStorage (String iStorage);
    void setLocation (String iLocation);
    set<EquipmentUse> getUses();
    set<EquipmentUse> getUses (Chrono iStart, Chrono iEnd);
};


defineClass EquipmentUse
description : "Uses of equipment in the field"
{
    class:
    EquipmentUse createobject (Chrono iDate, Chrono iTime,
        String iLocation, String iHowUsed, String iResults, EquipmentItem iItem,
        Agent iAgent);
    set<EquipmentUse> findUses (Agent iAgent);
    set<EquipmentUse> findUses (EquipmentItem iItem);
    set<EquipmentUse> findUses (Chrono iDate);

    instance:
    Chrono use_date  mandatory :;
    Chrono use_time;
    String use_location;
    String how_used;
    String use_results;
    EquipmentItem item  mandatory :;
    Agent agent  mandatory :;
    Chrono getDate();
    Chrono getTime();
    String getLocation();
    String getHowUsed();
    String getResults();
    void setDate (Chrono iDate);
    void setTime (. Chrono iTime);
    void setLocation (String iLocation);
    void setHowUsed (String iHow);
    void setResults (String iResults);
    EquipmentItem getItem();
    Agent getAgent();
};


defineClass UnderDevelopmentItem
super : Equipment
description : "Equipment being developed in the lab"
{
    class:
    UnderDevelopmentItem createObject (String iUse,
        String iLocation, Chrono iDate);
    set<UnderDevelopmentItem> findItems (Engineer iEngineer);
```

Listing 10-1: (Continued)   Jasmine's ODQL statements for declaring the IIA schema

```
    instance:
    String intended_use;
    String development_location;
    Chrono estimated_completion_date;
    set<Engineere> engineers;
    set<TestPerformed> tests;
    String getUse();
    String getLocation();
    Chrono getDate();
    void setUse (String iUse);
    void setLocation (String iLocation);
    void setDate (Chrono iDate);
    set<Engineer> getDevelopers ();
    set<TestPerformed> getTests ();
    set<TestPerformed> findTests (Chrono iStart, Chrono iEnd);
};


defineClass TestClass
description : "Type of test performed on equipment"
{
    class:
    TestClass createObject (String iDescript);
    TestClass findTest (String iDescript);
    set<TestClass> getTests ();
    instance:
    String test_description mandatory :;
    set<TestPerformed> tests;
    String getDescription();
    void setDescription (String iDescription);
    void getTests(set<Textperformed> tests,
        set<EquipmentTester testers, set<UnderDevelopmentItem> items);
    void getTests(set<Textperformed> tests,
        set<EquipmentTester testers, set<UnderDevelopmentItem> items,
        Chrono iStart, Chrono iEnd);
};


defineClass TestPerformed
description : "Test performed on equipment"
{
    class:
    TestPerformed createObject (Chrono iDate, String iLocation,
        String iResults, UnderDevelopmentItem iItem, TestClass iType,
        EquipmentTest iTester);
    set<TestPerformed> findTests (Chrono iStart,
        Chrono iEnd);
    set<TestPerformed> findTests (EquipmentTester iTester);
    set<TestPerformed> findTests (UnderDevelopmentItem iItem);
    set<TestPerformed> findTests (TestClass iType);
```

Listing 10-1: (Continued)   Jasmine's ODQL statements for declaring the IIA schema

```
    instance:
    Chrono test_date  mandatory  :;
    String test_location;
    String test_results;
    UnderDevelopmentItem item;
    TestClass type  mandatory  :;
    EquipmentTester tester  mandatory  :;
    Chrono getDate();
    String getLocation();
    String getResults();
    void setDate (Chrono iDate);
    void setLocation (String iLocation);
    void setResults (String Results);
    UnderDevelopmentItem getItem();
    TestClass getType();
    EquipmentTester getTester();
};

defineClass Description
description : "Utility class for description of a person"
{
    class:
    Description createObject (BLOB iPhoto, BLOB iRetina,
        Real iHeight, Real iWeight, String iEye, String iHair, String iMarks,
        Chrono iBirthdate, String iReligion);

    instance:
    BLOB photo;
    BLOB retina_print;
    Real height;
    Real weight;
    String eye_color;
    String hair_color;
    String marks;
    Chrono birthdate;
    String religion;

    BLOB getPhoto();
    BLOB getRetina();
    Real getHeight();
    Real getWeight();
    String getEyes ();
    String getHair();
    String getMarks ();
    Chrono getBirthdate();
    String getReligion();
    void setPhoto (BLOB iPhoto);
    void setRetina (. BLOB iRetina);
```

Listing 10-1: (Continued)   Jasmine's ODQL statements for declaring the IIA schema

```
        void setHeight (Real iHeight);
        void setWeight (Real iWeight);
        void setEyes (String iEyes);
        void setHair (String iHair);
        void setMarks (String iMarks);
        void setBirthdate (Chrono iDate);
        void setReligion (String iReligion);
};

defineClass Name
description : "Utility class for peson names"
{
    class:
    Name createObject (String iFirst, String iLast,
        String iMiddle);
    instance:
    String first_name;
    String last_name;
    char middle_init;
    String getFirstName();
    String getLastName();
    String getMiddleInit();
    String getLastFirst();
    String getFirstLast();
    void setName (String iFirst, String iLast, char iMiddle);
};

defineClass DriversLicense
description: "Utility class for drivers licenses"
{
    class:
    DriversLicense createObject (String iCountry, String iState,
        String iNumber, Chrono iExpDate);

    instance:
    attibute String country;
    String state;
    String number;
    Chrono expiration_date;
    String getCountry();
    String getState();
    String getNumber ();
    Chrono getExpDate ();
    void setCountry (String iCountry);
    void setState (String iState);
    void setNumber (String iNumber);
    void setExpDate (Chrono iDate);
};
```

Listing 10-1: (Continued)   Jasmine's ODQL statements for declaring the IIA schema

```
defineClass Phone
description : "Utility class for phone numbers"
{
    class:
    Phone createObject (String iCountry, String iAreaCode,
        String iExchange, String iNumber, String iExtension);
    instance:
    String country_code;
    String area_code;
    String exchange;
    String number;
    String extension;

    String getCountry();
    String getPhone();
    String getAreaCode();
    String getExchange();
    void setCountry (String iCountry);
    void setAreaCode (String iCode)
    void setExchange (String iExchange);
    void setNumber (String iNumber);
    void setExtension (String iExt);
};

defineClass PersonalAddress
description : "Utility class for personal addresses"
{
    class:
    PersonalAddress createObject (String iStreet, String iCity,
        String iState, String iZip);

    instance:
    String street;
    String city;
    String state;
    String zip;

    String getStreet();
    String getCity();
    String getState();
    String getZip();
    void setStreet (String iStreet);
    void setCity (String iCity);
    void setState (String iState);
    void inZip (String iZip);
    String getLabel ();
};
```

Listing 10-1: (Continued) Jasmine's ODQL statements for declaring the IIA schema

```
defineClass OrganizationalAddress
description : "Utility class for organizational addresses"
{
    class:
    OrganizationalAddress createObject (String iStreet1,
        String iStreet2, String iSuite, String iCity, String iState,
        String iCountry, String iZip);
    instance:
    String street1;
    String street2;
    String suite;
    String city;
    String state;
    String country;
    String zip_postal;

    String getStreet1();
    String getStreet2();
    String getSuite();
    String getCity();
    String getState();
    String getCountry();
    String getZipPostal();
    void setStreet1 (,String iStreet);
    void setStreet2 (String iStreet);
    void setSuite (String iSuite);
    void setCity (String iCity);
    void setState (String iState);
    void setCountry (String iCountry);
    void setZipPostal (String iZip);
};
```

Listing 10-1: (Continued)   Jasmine's ODQL statements for declaring the IIA schema

Glossary

Abstract class: A class from which no objects can be created.

Abstract data type: Another term for a class, arising from the idea that a class can be viewed as a user-defined data type that can be assigned to attributes.

Abstract description: The external specification of a type, which has no implementation.

Accessor: A method that retrieves the value stored in an object's hidden attribute.

Aggregation: A class designed to collect or gather objects created from another class.

Application class: A class that represents a program.

Array: An ordered group of objects of the same type that can be accessed by position. It is similar to an array in a programming language. However, its size is dynamic rather than fixed. Elements can be inserted and removed from any position

Association: The object-oriented term for a logical database relationship between two or more classes.

Association class: The object-oriented term for a composite entity.

Attribute: A property of an object that contains a data value describing the object.

Bag: A multivalued attribute containing an unordered group of objects created from a single class. Duplicates are allowed.

Base class: A general class that has been specialized by classes below it in an inheritance hierarchy.

Blob (Binary Large Object): An undifferentiated block of binary data stored within a database, containing text, graphics, video, or audio.

Class: A specification from which objects are created; a template for objects. All objects created from the same class have values for the same attributes and share the same operations.

Collection object: The object-oriented database model's term for a container class.

Complex network data model: A navigational data model dating from the 1960s that supports direct many-to-many relationships.

Compound key: A key made up of multiple attributes.

Concrete class: A class from which objects can be created.

Constructor: A method that has the same name as its class and that is executed automatically whenever an object is created from the class.

Container class: A class whose objects contain other objects or references to other objects.

Context diagram: The top level of a data-flow diagram that shows major data sources.

Control class: A class whose purpose is to control the operation of an object-oriented program.

Copy constructor: A constructor that initializes a new object by copying data from an existing object.

Database: A collection of objects that are managed so that they can be accessed by multiple users.

Data encapsulation: A characteristic of the object-oriented paradigm in which the data values that describe an object and the details of how an object performs its operations are hidden from other objects.

Data modeling: The art of identifying the entities that must be represented in a database and the relationships among those entities.

Derived class: A class that is a more specific example of classes above it in an inheritance hierarchy.

Destructor: A method whose name is ~ followed by the name of its class and that is called whenever an object created from the class is destroyed.

Dictionary: A multivalued attribute made up of ordered keys, each of which is paired with a single value.

Entity class: A class that represents data. Object-oriented databases are created by defining relationships between entity classes.

Exception: A predictable error that can occur during the execution of an operation.

Extend: The relationship between superclasses and subclasses in an inheritance hierarchy where subclasses expand the definition of their superclasses rather than specializing them.

Extent: A container object used by an object-oriented database that holds all objects created from one specific class.

External specifications: The operations and properties of a type (including a class) that form the type's interface to the outside world. External specifications also include exceptions that can be raised by the type's operations.

Factory interface: The method provided by a language binding (always called "new") for creating new objects from a type.

Friend: One or more classes that have access to the private parts of another class.

Function: The specification of a single behavior of an object.

Generalization–specialization (gen-spec): A relationship between superclasses and subclasses in an inheritance hierarchy where subclasses are more specialized versions of their superclass.

Get method: A method that retrieves the value stored in an object's hidden attribute.

Hierarchical data model: The first logical data model used by database systems, which allows only one-to-many relationships between entities. Entities at the "many" end of a relationship can be related to only one other entity at the "one" end.

Hybrid DBMS: A relational DBMS that allows classes to be used as domains.

Implementation: The details of a type's attributes and operations written in a specific programming language.

Information hiding: A characteristic of the object-oriented paradigm in which the data values that describe an object and the details of how an object performs its operations are hidden from other objects.

Inheritance: The relating of classes in a general to specific hierarchy.

Instance: A real-world representation of a class or a type, described by values for the class or type's properties.

Interface: The declaration of a class from which objects cannot be created. In an object-oriented database, this is the equivalent of an abstract class.

Interface class: A class that manages one aspect of the user interface of an object-oriented program.

Inverse relationship: An integrity constraint placed on an object-oriented database ensuring that object identifiers are placed correctly in the two objects participating in a relationship.

Key: A unique identifier for a type.

Language binding: Programming language–specific implementation of a type's operations.

List: A multivalued attribute containing an ordered group of objects created from a single class.

Literal: A specific value, such as "female" or 3.1.

Message: The means of communication between objects.

Method: The specification of a single behavior of an object.

Most specific type: In the object-oriented database model, the type at the lowest level of an inheritance hierarchy.

Multiple inheritance: Inheriting from more than one base class (superclass).

Multiple parentage: A situation in which an entity is at the "many" end of more than one one-to-many relationship.

Mutator: A method that stores a value in an object's hidden attribute.

Navigational: A property of the hierarchical, network, and object-oriented data models where data access is limited to the traversal of predefined logical relationships.

Object: A collection of data and associated operations on those data that represent an occurrence of an entity.

Object identifier: A unique identifier assigned by an object-oriented DBMS to each object as it is created.

Operation: The specification of a single behavior of an object.

Overload: Include two methods with the same name but different signatures in the same class.

Parameter: A data value that is sent into or sent out of an operation and that is declared as part of the operation's signature.

Persistence: A property of objects such that the objects remain in existence after the program that created them has stopped running.

Polymorphism: Having operations with the same signature but different implementations in different classes in the same inheritance hierarchy.

Post-relational DBMS: A relational DBMS that allows classes to be used as domains.

Procedure: The specification of a single behavior of an object.

Property: A data value describing an object.

Prototype: The specification of an operation consisting of its signature but no implementation.

Prototyping: A process for developing a database system in which the designers prepare the user interface of an application program and let the users evaluate it. The feedback from the evaluation helps the database designers identify more rigorous specifications for the database.

Pure object-oriented DBMS: A DBMS whose data model is based totally on the object-oriented data model.

Raise (an exception): Trigger an error because an operation has encountered an undesirable situation.

Representation: A programming language–dependent data structure containing the type's attributes.

Root: In a hierarchical database, the entity that is at the top of a logical hierarchy of entities.

Service: The specification of a single behavior of an object.

Set: A multivalued attribute containing an unordered group of objects created from a single class. No duplicates are allowed.

Set method: A method that stores a value in an object's hidden attribute.

Signature: The public interface of an operation, consisting of its return data type, name, and parameter list.

Simple key: A key made up of a single attribute.

Simple network data model: A navigational data model dating from the 1960s in which one-to-many relationships and multiple parentage are allowed.

State (of an object): The collection of the current values of an object's properties.

Static: A term describing an attribute that is available to all objects created from a class and that contains a single value for all objects created from the class.

Structured objects: Classes for date, intervals, times, and time-stamps supplied as part of object-oriented DBMSs.

Subclass: A class that is a more specific example of classes above it in an inheritance hierarchy.

Subtype: The object-oriented database model's term for a subclass.

Superclass: A general class that has been specialized by classes below it in an inheritance hierarchy.

Supertype: The object-oriented database model's term for a super-class.

Transience: A property of an object such that the object is destroyed when the program that created it stops running.

Traversal path: All the objects and relationships that must be accessed to retrieve a desired object.

Type: A specification of the domain shared by objects and literals of that type. A class is a type.

Variable: A property of an object that contains a data value describing the object.

Virtual class: A class from which no objects can be created.

Virtual method: An operation that appears only as its signature without any implementation. The implementation must be provided by subclasses of the operation's owner.

Whole part: A relationship between classes such that subclasses are parts of a whole (the superclass).

Index

Related Titles from Morgan Kaufmann

Morgan Kaufmann

http://www.mkp.com

- **RELATIONAL DATABASE DESIGN CLEARLY EXPLAINED**
  Jan L. Harrington
  1998   ISBN: 0-12-326425-1

- **SQL CLEARLY EXPLAINED**
  Jan L. Harrington
  1998   ISBN: 0-12-326426-X

- **DATABASE-DRIVEN WEB SITES**
  Jesse Feiler
  1999   ISBN: 0-12-251336-3

- **UNIVERSAL DATABASE MANAGEMENT: A GUIDE TO OBJECT-RELATIONAL TECHNOLOGY**
  Cynthia Maro Saracco
  1998   ISBN: 1-555860-519-3